The Treasure of Grace

Sermons on the Grace of God
By

Charles Haddon Spurgeon

Contents:

1. THE TREASURE OF GRACE – 5

2. A GOSPEL WORTH DYING FOR – 23

3. THE WATER OF LIFE – 41

4. SALVATION ALL OF GRACE – 59

5. LESSONS ON DIVINE GRACE – 77

6. LAW AND GRACE – 91

7. SOVEREIGN GRACE AND MAN'S RESPONSIBILITY – 107

8. THE FULNESS AND THE FILLING – 123

9. THE GLORIES OF FORGIVING GRACE – 139

10. THE GREATEST WONDER OF GRACE – 157

11. THE SHANK-BONE SERMON; OR, TRUE BELIEVERS AND THEIR HELPERS – 171

12. GRACE FOR GRACE – 189

13. REAL GRACE FOR REAL NEED – 207

14. GRACE ABOUNDING OVER ABOUNDING SIN – 223

15. GROWTH IN GRACE – 241

16. GRACE EXALTED—BOASTING EXCLUDED – 257

17. EARLY AND LATE, OR HORÆ GRATIÆ – 275

THE TREASURE OF GRACE

A Sermon

Delivered on Sabbath Morning, January 22nd, 1860, by the

REV. C. H. SPURGEON,

at Exeter Hall, Strand

"The forgiveness of sins, according to the riches of his grace."—Ephesians 1:7.

As is Isaiah among the prophets, so is Paul among the apostles; each stands forth with singular prominence, raised up by God for a conspicuous purpose, and shining as a star of extraordinary brilliance. Isaiah spake more of Christ, and described more minutely his passion and his death than all the other prophets put together Paul proclaimed the grace of God—free, full, sovereign, eternal grace—beyond all the glorious company of the apostles. Sometimes he soared to such amazing heights, or dived into such unsearchable depths, that even Peter could not follow him. He was ready to confess that "our beloved brother Paul, according to the wisdom given unto him," had written "some things hard to be understood." Jude could write of the judgments of God, and reprove with terrible words, "ungodly men, who turned the grace of God into lasciviousness." But he could not tell out the purpose of grace as it was planned in the eternal mind, or the experience of grace as it is felt and realized in the human heart, like Paul. There is James again: he, as a faithful minister, could deal very closely with the practical evidences of Christian character. And yet he seems to keep very much on the surface; he does not bore down deep into the substratum on which must rest the visible soil of all spiritual graces. Even John, most favoured of all those apostles who were companions of our Lord on earth—sweetly as the beloved disciple writes of fellowship with the Father and his Son Jesus Christ—even John doth not speak of grace so richly as Paul, "in whom God first showed forth all long-suffering as a pattern to them which should hereafter believe on him to life everlasting." Not, indeed, that we are at any liberty to prefer one apostle above another. We may not divide the Church, saying, I am of Paul, I of Peter, I of Apollos; but we may acknowledge the instrument which God was pleased to use; we may admire the way in which the Holy Ghost fitted him for his work; we may, with the churches of Judea, "glorify God in Paul." Among the early fathers Augustine was singled out as the "Doctor of Grace;" so much did he delight in those doctrines that exhibit the freeness of divine favour. And surely we might affirm the like of Paul. Among his compeers he outstripped them all in declaring the grace that bringeth salvation. The sense of grace pervaded all his thoughts as the life blood circulates through all the veins of one's body. Does he speak of conversion, "he *was called by grace.*" Nay, he sees grace going before his conversion, and "separating him from his mother's womb." He attributes all his ministry to grace. "To me, who am less than the least of all saints, is this grace given, that I should preach among the Gentiles the unsearchable riches of Christ." See him at any time, and under any circumstances, whether bowed down with infirmity, or lifted to the third heavens with revelation, he has but one account to give of himself, "By the grace of God I am what I am."

There are no ministers who contend so fully and so unflinchingly for free, sovereign, unconditional grace, as those who before their conversion have revelled in gross and outrageous sin. Your gentleman preachers who have been piously brought up, and sent from their cradle to school, from school to college, and from college to the pulpit, without encountering much temptation, or being rescued from the haunts of profanity—they know comparatively little, and speak with little emphasis of *free grace*. It is a Bunyan who breathed curses, a Newton who was a very monster in sin; it is the like of these, who cannot forget for one hour of their lives afterwards, the grace that snatched them from the pit, and plucked them as brands from the burning. Strange indeed that God should have it so. The providence is inscrutable that permits some of the Lord's chosen people to wander and rove as far as sheep can stray. Such men, however, make the most valiant champions for that grace which only can rescue any sinner from eternal woe.

This morning we propose to expound to you "*the riches of God's grace*; this is the *Treasure;* then, secondly, we shall speak of the "*Forgiveness of Sins,*" which is to he judged of by that *Measure*; the forgiveness is *according* to the riches of his grace; and we shall afterwards wind up by considering some of the *privileges, connected therewith.*

I. First, consider the RICHES OF HIS GRACE. In attempting to search out that which is unsearchable, we must, I suppose, use some of those comparisons by which we are wont to estimate the wealth of the monarchs, and mighty ones of this world. It happened once that the Spanish ambassador, in the halcyon days of Spain, went on a visit to the French ambassador, and was invited by him to see the treasures of his master. With feelings of pride he showed the repositories, profusely stored with earth's most precious and most costly wealth. "Could you show gems so rich," said he, "or aught the like of this for magnificence of posessions in all your sovereign's kingdom?" "Call your master rich?" replied the ambassador of Spain, "why, my master's treasures have no bottom"—alluding, of course, to the mines of Peru and Petrosa. So truly in the riches of grace there are mines too deep for man's finite understanding ever to fathom. However profound your investigation, there is still a deep couching beneath that baffles all research. Who can ever discover the attributes of God? Who can find out the Almighty to perfection? We are at a loss to estimate the very quality and properties of grace as it dwells in the mind of Deity. Love in the human breast is a passion. With God it is not so. Love is an attribute of the divine essence. God is love. In men, grace and bounty may grow into a habit, but grace with God is an intrinsic attribute of his nature. He cannot but be gracious. As by necessity of his Godhead he is omnipotent, and omniprescent, so by absolute necessity of his divinity is he gracious.

Come then, my brethren, into this glittering mine of the attributes of the grace of God. Every one of God's attributes is infinite, and therefore this attribute of grace is without bounds. You cannot conceive the infinity of God, why, therefore, should I attempt to describe it. Recollect however, that as the attributes of God are of the like extent, the guage of one attribute must be the guage of another. Or, further, if one attribute is without limit, so is another attribute. Now, you cannot conceive any boundary to the omnipotence of God. What cannot he do? He can create, he can destroy; he can speak a myriad universes into existence; or he can quench the light of myriads of stars as readily as we tread out a spark. He hath but to will it, and creatures without number sing his praise; yet another volition, and those creatures subside into their naked nothingness, as a moment's foam subsides into the wave that bears it, and is lost for ever. The astronomer turns his tube to the remotest space, he cannot find a boundary to God's creating power; but could he seem to find a limit, we would then inform him that all the worlds on worlds that cluster in space, thick as the drops of morning dew upon the meadows, are but the shreds of God's power. He can make more than all these, can dash those into nothingness, and can begin again. Now as boundless as is his power, so infinite is his grace. As he hath power to do anything, so hath he grace enough to give anything—to give everything to the very chief of sinners.

Take another attribute if you please—God's omniscience, there is no boundary to that. We know that his eye is upon every individual of our race—he sees him as minutely as if he were the only creature that existed. It is boasted of the eagle that though he can outstare the sun, yet when at his greatest height, he can detect the movement of the smallest fish in the depths of the sea. But what is this compared with the omniscience of God? His eye tracks the sun in his marvellous course, his eye marks the winged comet as it flies through space, his eye discerns the utmost bound of creation inhabited or uninhabited. There is nothing hid from the light thereof, with him there is no darkness at all. If I mount to heaven he is there; if I dive to hell he is there; if I fly mounted on the morning ray beyond the western sea,

> "His swifter hand shall first arrive,
> And there arrest the fugitive."

There is no limit to his understanding, nor is there to his grace. As his knowledge comprehendeth all things, so doth his grace comprehend all the sins, all the trials all the infirmities of the people upon whom his heart is set. Now, my dear brethren, the next time we fear that God's grace will be exhausted, let us look into this mine, and then let us reflect that all that has ever been taken out of it has never diminished it a single particle. All the clouds that have been taken from the sea have never diminished its depth, and all the love, and all the mercy that God has given to all but infinite numbers of the race of man, has not diminished by a single grain the mountain of his grace. But to proceed further; we sometimes judge of the wealth of men, not only by their real estate in mines and the like, but by what they have on hand stored up in the treasury. I must take you now, my brethren, to the glittering treasury of divine grace. Ye know its name, it is called the Covenant, have you not heard the marvellous story of what was done in the olden time before the world was made. God foreknew that man would fall, but he determined of his own infinite purpose and will that he would raise out of this fall a multitude which no man can number. The Eternal Father held a solemn council with the Son and Holy Spirit. Thus spoke the Father:—"I will that those whom I have chosen be saved!" Thus said the Son:—"My Father, I am ready to bleed and die that thy justice may not suffer and that thy purpose may be executed." "I will," said the Holy Spirit, "that those whom the Son redeems with blood shall be called by grace, shall be quickened, shall be preserved, shall be sanctified and perfected, and brought safely home." Then was the Covenant written, signed, and sealed, and ratified between the Sacred Three. The Father gave his Son, the Son gave himself, and the Spirit promises all his influence, all his presence, to all the chosen. Then did the Father give to the Son the persons of his elect, then did the Son give himself to the elect, and take them into union with him; and then did the Spirit in covenant vow that these chosen ones should surely be brought safe home at last. Whenever I think of the old covenant of grace, I am perfectly amazed and staggered with the grace of it. I could not be an Arminian on any inducement; the very poetry of our holy religion lies in these ancient things of the everlasting hills, that glorious covenant signed and sealed, and ratified, in all things ordered well from old eternity.

Pause here, my hearer, awhile, and think before this world was made, ere God had settled the deep foundations of the mountains, or poured the seas from the laver of the bottom of his hand, he had chosen his people, and set his heart on them. To them he had given himself, his Son, his heaven, his all. For them did Christ determine to resign his bliss, his home, his life; for them did the Spirit promise all his attributes, that they might be blessed. O grace divine, how glorious thou art, without beginning, without end. How shall I praise thee? Take up the strain ye angels; sing these noble themes, the love of the Father, the love of the Son, and the love of the Spirit.

This, my brethren, if ye think it over, may well make you estimate aright the riches of God's grace. If you read the roll of the covenant from beginning to end, containing as it does, election, redemption, calling, justification, pardon, adoption, heaven, immortality—if you read all this, you will say, "This is riches of grace—God, great and infinite! Who is a God like unto thee for the riches of thy love!"

The riches of great kings again, may often be estimated by the munificence of the monuments which they reared to record their feats. We have been amazed in these modern times at the marvelous riches of the kings of Nineveh and Babylon. Modern monarchs with all their appliances, would fail to erect such monstrous piles of palaces as those in which old Nebuchadnezzar walked in times of yore. We turn to the pyramids, we see there what the wealth of nations can accomplish; we look across the sea to Mexico and Peru, and we see the relics of a semi-barbarous people but we are staggered and amazed to think what wealth and what mines of riches they must have possessed ere such works could have been accomplished. Solomon's riches are perhaps best judged of by us when we think of those great cities which he built in the wilderness, Tadmore and Palmyra. When we go and visit those ruins and see the massive columns and magnificent sculpture, we say, Solomon indeed was rich. We feel as we walk amid the ruins somewhat like the queen of Sheba, even in Scripture the half has not been told us of the riches of Solomon. My brethren, God has led us to inspect mightier trophies than Solomon, or Nebuchadnezzar, or Montezuma, or all the Pharaohs. Turn your eyes yonder, see that blood-bought host arrayed in white, surrounding the throne—hark, how they sing, with voice triumphant, with melodies seraphic, "Unto him that loved us, and washed us from our sins in his own blood, to him be glory and dominion for ever and ever." And who are these?

Who are these trophies of his grace? Some of them have come from the stews of harlotry; many of them have come from the taverns of drunkeness. Nay, more, the hands of some of those so white and fair, were once red with the blood of saints. I see yonder the men that nailed the Saviour to the tree; men who cursed God, and invoked on themselves death and damnation. I see there Manasseh, who shed innocent blood so much, and the thief who in the last moment looked to Christ, and said, "Lord, remember me." But I need not turn your gaze so far aloft; look, my brethren, around, you do not know your next neighbour by whom you are sitting this morning, it may be. But there are stories of grace that might be told by some here this morning, that would make the very angels sing more loudly than they have done before. Well, I know these cheeks have well nigh been scarlet with tears when I have heard the stories of free grace wrought in this congregation. Then are those known to me, but of course not so to you, who were among the vilest of men, the scum of society. We have here those to whom cursing was as their breath, and drunkenness had grown to be a habit; and yet here they are servants of God, and of his church; and it is their delight to testify to others what a Saviour they have found. Ah, but my hearer, perhaps thou art one of those trophies, and if so, the best proof of the riches of his grace is that which thou findest in thy own soul. I think God to be gracious when I see others saved, I know he is because he has saved me; that wayward, wilful boy, who scoffed a mother's love, and would not be melted by all her prayers, who only wished to know a sin in order to perpetrate it? Is he standing here to preach the gospel of the grace of God to you to-day? Yes. Then there is no sinner out of hell that has sinned too much for grace to save. That love which can reach to me, can reach to you. Now I know the riches of his grace, because I hope I prove it, and feel it in my own inmost heart, my dear hearer, and may you know it too, and then you will join with our poet, who says—

> "Then loudest of the crowd I'll sing,
> While heavens resounding mansions ring
> With shouts of sovereign grace."

Go a little further now. We have thus looked at the wine and treasures, and at the monuments. But more. One thing which amazed the queen of Sheba, with regard to the riches of Solomon, was the sumptuousness of his table. Such multitudes sat down to it to eat and drink, and though they were many, yet they all had enough and to spare. She lost all heart when she saw the provisions of a single day brought in. I forget just now, although I meant to refer to the passage, how many fat beast, how many bullocks of the pasture, how many bucks and fallow deer and game of all sorts, and how many measures of flour and how many gallons of oil were brought to Solomon's table every day, but it was something marvellous; and the multitudes that had to feast were marvellous also, yet had they all enough. And now think my brethren of the hospitalities of the God of grace each day. Ten thousand thousand of his people are this day sitting down to feast; hungry and thirsty they bring large appetites with them to the banquet, but not one of them returns unsatisfied; there is enough for each, enough for all, enough for evermore. Though the host that feed there is countless as the stars of heaven, yet I find that not one lacks his portion. He openeth his hand and supplies the want of every living saint upon the face of the earth. Think how much grace one saint requires, so much that nothing but the Infinite could supply him for one day. We burn so much fuel each day to maintain the fire of love in our hearts, that we might drain the mines of England of all their wealth of coal. Surely were it not that we have infinite treasures of grace, the daily consumption of a single saint might out-demand everything that is to be found upon the face of the earth. And yet it is not one but many saints, and many hundreds, not for one day, but for many years; not for many years only, but generation after generation, century after century, race after race of men, living on the fulness of God in Christ. Yet are none of them starved; they all drink to the full; they eat and are satisfied. What riches of grace then may we see in the sumptuousness of his hospitality.

Sometimes, my brethren, I have thought if I might but get the broken meat at God's back door of grace I should be satisfied; like the woman who said, "The dogs eat of the crumbs that fall from the master's table;" or like the prodigal who said, "Make me as one of thy hired servants." But you will remember that no child of God is ever made to live on husks; God does not give the parings of his grace to the meanest of them, but they are all fed like Mephibosheth; they eat from the kings own table the daintiest dishes. And if one may speak for the rest, I think in matters of grace we all have Benjamin's mess—we all have ten times as we could have expected, and though not more than our necessities, yet are we often amazed at the marvelous plenty of grace which God gives us in the covenant and the promise.

Now we turn to another point to illustrate the greatness of the riches of God's grace. A man's riches may often be judged of by the equipage of his children, the manner in which he dresses his servants and those of his household. It is not to be expected that the child of the poor man, though he is comfortably clothed, should be arrayed in like garments to those which are worn by the sons of princes. Let us see, then, what are the robes in which God's people are appareled, and how they are attended. Here again I speak upon a subject where a large imagination is needed, and my own utterly fails me. God's children are wrapped about with a robe, a seamless robe, which earth and heaven could not buy the like of if it were once lost. For texture it excels the fine linen of the merchants; for whiteness it it is purer than the driven snow; no looms on earth could make it, but Jesus spent his life to work my robe of righteousness. There was a drop of blood in every throw of the shuttle, and every thread was made of his own heart's agonies. 'Tis a robe that is divine, complete; a better one than Adam wore in the perfection of Eden. He had but a human righteousness though a perfect one, but we have a divinely perfect righteousness. Strangely, my soul, art thou arrayed, for thy Saviour's garment is on thee; the royal robe of David is wrapped about his Jonathan. Look at God's people as they are clothed too in the garments of sanctification. Was there ever such a robe as that? it is literally stiff with jewels. He arrays the meanest of his people every day as though it were a wedding day; he arrays them as a bride adorneth herself with jewels; he has given Ethiopia and Sheba for them, and he will have them dressed in gold of Ophir. What riches of grace then must there be in God who thus clothes his children!

But to conclude this point upon which I have not as yet begun. If you would know the full riches of divine grace, read the Father's heart when he sent his Son upon earth to die; read the lines upon the Father's countenance when he pours his wrath upon his only begotten and his well-beloved Son. Read too the mysterious handwriting on the Saviour's flesh and soul, when on the cross quivering in agony the waves of swelling grief do o'er his bosom roll. If ye would know love ye must repair to Christ, and ye shall see a man so full of pain, that his head, his hair, his garments bloody be. 'Twas love that made him sweat as it were great drops of blood. If ye would know love, you must see the Omnipotent mocked by his creatures, you must hear the Immaculate slandered by sinners, you must hear the Eternal One groaning out his life, and crying in the agonies of death, "My God, my God, why hast thou forsaken me?" In fine, to sum up all in one, the riches of the grace of God are infinite, beyond all limit; they are inexhaustible, they can never be drained; they are all-sufficient, they are enough for every soul that ere shall come to take of them; there shall be enough for ever while earth endureth, until the last vessel of mercy shall be brought home safely.

So much, then, concerning the riches of his grace.

II. For a minute or two, let me now dwell upon THE FORGIVENESS OF SINS. The *treasure* of God's grace is the *measure* of our forgiveness; this forgiveness of sins is according to the riches of his grace. We may infer, then, that the pardon which God gives to the penitent is no niggard pardon. Have not you asked a man's pardon sometimes, and he has said, "Yes, I forgive you," and you have thought, "Well, I would not even have asked for pardon if I thought you would have given it in such a surly style as that; I might as well have continued as I was, as to be so ungraciously forgiven." But when God forgives a man, though he be the chief of sinners, he puts out his hand and freely forgives; in fact, there is as much joy in the heart of God when he forgives, as there is in the heart of the sinner when he is forgiven; God is as blessed in giving as we are in receiving. It is his very nature to forgive; he must be gracious, he must be loving, and when he lets his heart of love out to free us from our sins it is with no stinted stream; he doth it willingly, he upbraideth it not. Again: if pardon be in proportion to the riches of his grace, we may rest assured it is not a limited pardon, it is not the forgiving of some sins and the leaving of others upon the back. No, this were not Godlike, it were not consistent with the riches of his grace. When God forgives he draws the mark through every sin which the believer ever has committed, or ever will commit. That last point may stagger you, but I do believe with John Kent, that in the blood of Christ

> "There's pardon for transgressions past,
> It matters not how black their cast;
> And, oh! my soul, with wonder view,
> For sins to come there's pardon too."

However many, however heinous, however innumerable your sins may have been, the moment you believe they are every one of them blotted out. In the Book of God there is not a single sin against any man in this place whose trust is in Christ, not a single one, not even the shadow of one, not a spot, or the remnant of a sin remaining, all is gone. When Noah's flood covered the deepest mountains, you may rest assured it covered the mole-hills; and when God's love covers the little sins it covers the big ones, and they are all gone at once! When a bill is receipted fully there is not an item which can be charged again, and when God pardons the sins of the believer there is not one single sin left; not even half-an-one can ever be brought to his remembrance again. Nay, more than this; when God forgives, he not only forgives all but once for all. Some tell us that God forgives men and yet they are lost. A fine god yours! They believe that the penitent sinner finds mercy, but that if he slips or stumbles in a little while he will be taken out of the covenant of grace and will perish. Such a covenant I could not and would not believe in; I tread it beneath my feet as utterly despicable. The God whom I love when he forgives never punishes afterwards. By one sacrifice there is a full remission of all sin that ever was against a believer, or that ever will be against him. Though you should live till your hair is bleached thrice over, till Methuselah's thousand years should pass over your furrowed brow, not a single sin shall ever stand against you, nor shall you ever be punished for a single sin; for every sin is forgiven, fully forgiven, so that not even part of the punishment shall be executed against you. "Well, but," saith one, "how is it that God does punish his children?" I answer, he does not. He chastises them as a father, but that is a different thing from the punishment of a judge. If the child of a judge were brought up to the bar, and that child were freely forgiven all that he had done amiss, if justice exonerated and acquitted him, it might nevertheless happen that there was evil in the heart of that child which the father, out of love to the child, might have to whip out of him. But there is a great deal of difference between a rod in the hand of the executioner, and a rod in a father's hand. Let God smite me, if I sin against him, yet it is not because of the guilt of sin, there is no punishment in it whatever, the penal clause is done away with. It is only that he may cure me of my fault, that he may fetch the folly out of my heart. Do you chasten your children vindictively because you are angry with them? No; but because you love them; if you are what parents should be, the chastisement is a proof of your affection, and your heart smarts more than their body pains, when you have to chasten them for what they have done amiss. God is not angry against his children, nor is there a sin in them which he will punish. He will whip it out of them, but punish them for it he will not. O glorious grace! It is a gospel worth preaching.

> "The moment a sinner believes,
> And trusts in his crucified God,
> His pardon at once he receives,
> Redemption in full through Christ's blood."

All is gone; every atom gone; gone for ever and ever; and well he knows it.

> "Now freed from sin I walk at large,
> My Saviour's blood my full discharge;
> At his dear feet my soul I lay,
> A sinner saved, and homage pay."

Having thus spoken of the pardon of sin as being fully commensurate with the grace of God, I will put this question to my hearer: My friend, are you a forgiven man? Are your sins all gone?

"No," saith one, "I cannot say they are, but I am doing my best to reform." Ah! you may do your best to reform, I hope you will, but that will never wash out your past sins. All the waters of the rivers of reformation can never wash away a single blood-red stain of guilt. "But," saith one, "may I, just I am, believe that my sins are forgiven?" No, but I tell thee what thou mayst do. If God help thee, thou mayst now cast thyself simply upon the blood and righteousness of Christ; and the moment thou dost that, thy sins are all gone, and gone so that they never can return again. "He that believeth on the Lord Jesus Christ shall be saved." Nay, he is saved in the moment of his faith. He is no more in the sight of God received as a sinner; Christ has been punished for him. The righteousness of Christ is wrapped about him, and he stands accepted in the beloved. "Well, but," saith one, "I can believe that a man, after he has been a long time a Christian, may know his sins to be forgiven, but I cannot imagine that I can know it at once." The knowledge of our pardon does not always come the moment we believe, but the fact of our pardon is before our knowledge of it, and we may be pardoned before we know it. But if thou believest on the Lord Jesus Christ with all thine heart, I will tell thee this: If thy faith be free of all self-trust thou shalt know to-day that thy sins are forgiven, for the witness of the Spirit shall bear witness with thy heart, and thou shalt hear that secret, still small voice, saying, "Be of good cheer; thy sins, which are many, are all forgiven." "Oh," saith one, "I would give all I have for that." And you might give all you have, but you would not have it at that price. You might give the firstborn for your transgression, the fruit of your body for the sin of your soul, you might offer rivers of oil, and ten thousand of the fat of fed beasts; you would not have it for money, but you may have it for nothing; it is freely brought to you; you are bidden to take it. Only acknowledge your sin, and put your trust in Christ, and there is not one man among you who shall hear aught about his sin in the day of judgment. It shall be cast into the depth of the sea—it shall be carried away for ever.

I will give you a picture, and then leave this subject. See, there stands the high-priest of the Jews. A goat is brought to him: it is called "the scape-goat." He puts his hands upon the head of this goat, and begins to make confession of sin. Will you come and do the like? Jesus

Christ is the scape-goat; come and lay your hand on his thorn-crown'd head by faith, and make confession of your sin, as the high-priest did of old. Have you done it? Is your sin confessed? Now believe that Jesus Christ is able and willing to take your sin away. Rest wholly and entirely on him. Now what happens? The high-priest takes the scape-goat, gives it into the hand of a trusty man, who leads it over hill and down dale, till he is many miles away, and then, suddenly loosing its bonds, he frightens it, and the goat flees with all its might. The man watches it till it is gone, and he can see it no more. He comes back, and he says, "I took the scape-goat away, and it vanished out of my sight; it is gone into the wilderness." Ah, my hearer, and if thou hast put thy sins on Christ by a full confession, remember he has taken them all away, as far as the east is from the west, they are gone, and gone eternally. Thy drunkenness, thy swearing is gone, thy lying, thy theft is gone, thy Sabbath-breaking, thy evil thoughts are gone—all gone, and thou shalt never see them again—

> "Plunged, as in a shoreless sea,
> Lost, as in immensity."

III. And now I conclude by noticing THE BLESSED PRIVILEGES WHICH ALWAYS FOLLOW THE FORGIVENESS WHICH IS GIVEN TO US ACCORDING TO THE GRACE OF GOD. I think there are a great many people who do not believe there is any reality in religion at all. They think it is a very respectable thing to go to church and to go to chapel, but as to ever enjoying a consciousness that their sins are all forgiven, they never think about that. And I must confess that, in the religion of these modern times, there does not seem to be much reality. I do not hear at this day that clear ringing distinct proclamation of the gospel that I want to hear. It is a grand thing to carry the gospel to all manner of men, to take it to the theatre, and the like, but we want to have the gospel undiluted—the milk must have a little less water with it. There must be a more distinct, palpable truth taught to the people, a something that they can really lay hold of, a something that they can understand, even if they will not believe it. I trust no man will misunderstand me this morning in what I have said. There is such a thing as having all our sins forgiven now. There is such a thing as knowing it and enjoying it. Now I will show you what will be the happiness resulting to you, should you obtain this blessing.

In the first place, you will have peace of conscience, that heart of yours that throbs so fast when you are alone will be quite still and quiet. You will be least alone when you are alone. That fear of yours which makes you quicken your step in the dark because you are afraid of something, and you do not know what, will all be gone. I have heard of a man who was so constantly in debt, and continually being arrested by the bailiffs, that once upon a time, when going by some area railings, having caught his sleeve upon one of the rails, he turned round and said, "I dont owe you anything, Sir." He thought it was a bailiff. And so it is with unforgiven sinners, wherever they are, they think they are going to be arrested. They can enjoy nothing. Even their mirth, what is it, but the colour of joy, the crackling of thorns under the pot; there is no solid steady fire. But when once a man is forgiven, he can walk anywhere, He says, "to me it is nothing whether I live or die, whether ocean depths engulf me, or whether I am buried beneath the avalanche, with sin forgiven, I am secure. Death has no sting to him. His conscience is at rest. Then he goes a step further. Knowing his sins to be forgiven he has joy unspeakable. No man has such sparkling eyes as the true Christian; a man then knows his interest in Christ, and can read his title clear. He is a happy man, and must be happy. His troubles, what are they? Less than nothing and vanity; for all his sins are forgiven. When the poor slave first lands in Canada, it may be he is without a single farthing in his purse, and scarcely anything but rags on his back; but he puts his foot on British soil, and is free; see him leap and dance, and clap his hands, saying, "Great God I thank thee, I am a free man." So it is with the Christian, he can say in his cottage when he sits down to his crust of bread, thank God I have no sin mixed in my cup—it is all forgiven. The bread may be dry, but it is not half so dry as it would be if I had to eat it with the bitter herbs of a guilty conscience, and with a terrible apprehension of the wrath of God. He has a joy that will stand all weathers, a joy that will keep in all climates, a joy that shines in the dark, and glitters in the night as well as in the day.

Then, to go further, such a man has access to God. Another man with unforgiven sin about him stands afar off; and if he thinks of God at all it is as a consuming fire. But the forgiven Christian looking up to God when he sees the mountains and the hills, and rolling streams and the roaring flood, he says, "My Father made them all;" and he clasps hands with the Almighty across the infinite expanse that sunders man from his Maker. His heart flies up to God. He dwells near to him, and he feels that he can talk to God as a man talketh with his friend.

Then another effect of this is that the believer fears no hell. There are solemn things in the Word of God, but they do not affright the believer. There may be a pit that is bottomless, but into that his foot shall never slide; it is true there is a fire that never shall be quenched, but it cannot burn him. That fire is for the sinner, but he has no sin imputed to him; it is all forgiven. The banded host of all the devils in hell cannot take him there, for he has not a single sin that can be laid to his charge. Daily sinning though he is, he feels those sins are all atoned for; he knows that Christ has been punished in his stead, and therefore Justice cannot touch him again.

Once more, the forgiven Christian is expecting heaven. He is waiting for the coming of the Lord Jesus Christ, for if death should intervene before that glorious advent, he knows that to him sudden death is sudden glory; and in the possession of a quiet conscience and of peace with God, he can go up to his chamber when the last solemn hour shall come; he can gather up his feet in his bed; he can bid farewell to his brethren and companions, to his wife and to his children, and can shut his eye in peace without a fear that he shall open them in heaven. Perhaps never does the joy of forgiven sin come out more brightly than it does on a dying bed. It has often been my privilege to test the power of religion when I have been sitting by the bedside of the dying. There is a young girl in heaven now, once a member of this our church. I went with one of my beloved deacons to see her when she was very near her departure. She was in the last stage of consumption. Fair and sweetly beautiful she looked, and I think I never heard such syllables as those which fell from that girl's lips. She had had disappointments, and trials, and troubles, but all these she had not a word to say about, except that she blessed God for them; they had brought her nearer to the Saviour. And when we asked her whether she was not afraid of dying, "No," she said, "the only thing I fear is this, I am afraid of living, lest my patience should wear out. I have not said an impatient word yet, sir, I hope I shall not. It is sad to to be so very weak, but I think if I had my choice I would rather be here than be in health, for it is very precious to me; I know that my Redeemer liveth, and I am waiting for the moment when he shall send his chariot of fire to take me up to him." I put the question, "Have you not any doubts?" "No, none, sir, why should I? I clasp my arms around the neck of Christ." "And have not you any fear about your sins?" "No, sir, they are all forgiven, I trust the Saviour's precious blood." "And do you think that you will be as brave as this when you come actually to die?" "Not if he leaves me, sir, but he will never leave me, for he has said, 'I will never leave thee nor forsake thee.'" There is faith, dear brothers and sisters, may we all have it and receive forgiveness of sins according to the riches of his grace.[1]

---

[1] Spurgeon, C. H. (1860). The Treasure of Grace. In *The New Park Street Pulpit*

A GOSPEL WORTH DYING FOR

A Sermon

Delivered on Lord's-Day Morning, August 12th, 1883, by

C. H. SPURGEON,

AT EXETER-HALL.

"To testify the gospel of the grace of God."—Acts 20:24.

PAUL says that, in comparison with his great object of preaching the gospel, he did not count even his life to be dear to himself; yet we are sure Paul highly valued life. He had the same love of life as other men, and he knew besides that his own life was of great consequence to the churches, and to the cause of Christ. In another place he said, "To abide in the flesh is more needful for you." He was not weary of life, nor was he a vain person who could treat life as though it were a thing to fling away in sport. He valued life, for he prized time, which is the stuff that life is made of, and he turned to practical account each day and hour, "redeeming the time because the days are evil." Yet he soberly said to the elders of the church at Ephesus that he did not regard his life as a dear thing in comparison with bearing testimony to the gospel of the grace of God. According to the verse before us the apostle regarded life as a race which he had to run. Now, the more quickly a race is run the better: certainly, length is not the object of desire. The one thought of a runner is how he can most speedily reach the winning-post. He spurns the ground beneath him; he cares not for the course he traverses except so far as it is the way over which he must run to reach his desired end. Such was life to Paul: all the energies of his spirit were consecrated to the pursuit of one object—namely, that he might everywhere bear testimony to the gospel of the grace of God; and the life which he lived here below was only valued by him as a means to that end. He also regarded the gospel, and his ministry in witnessing to it, as a sacred deposit which had been committed to him by the Lord himself. He looked upon himself "as put in trust with the gospel;" and he resolved to be faithful though it should cost him his life. He says he "desired to fulfil the ministry which he had received of the Lord Jesus Christ." Before his mind's eye he saw the Saviour taking into his pierced hands the priceless casket which contains the celestial jewel of the grace of God, and saying to him—"I have redeemed thee with my blood, and I have called thee by my name, and now I commit this precious thing into thy hands, that thou mayest take care of it, and guard it even with thy heart's blood. I commission thee to go everywhere in my place and stead, and to make known to every people under heaven the gospel of the grace of God." All believers occupy a somewhat similar place. We are none of us called to the apostleship, and we may not all have been called to the public preaching of the word of God; but we are all charged to be valiant for the truth upon the earth, and to contend earnestly for the faith once delivered to the saints. Oh, to do this in the spirit of the apostle of the Gentiles! As believers, we are all called to some form of ministry; and this ought to make our life a race, and cause us to regard ourselves as the guardians of the gospel, even as he that bears the colours of a regiment regards himself as bound to sacrifice everything for their preservation.

Paul was a true hero; a hero of even a nobler stamp than those brave Greeks whose stories still stir the blood and fire the soul. Their heroism to a large extent depended upon public note, the present approval of their fellow-citizens, or upon the animal excitement of the battle-field; but Paul's heroism, so far as man was concerned, was self-contained, deliberate, and as sure to display itself in the solitude of a dungeon as in the assembly of the faithful. He was parting with his weeping friends, and going forward to trials of unknown intensity, but he was altogether unmoved by fear, and advanced on his way without a question. His leave-taking of the elders irresistibly reminds me of the old historian's record of Epaminondas the Theban general who, when he was mortally wounded by a Spartan spear, the head of which remained in his flesh, bade his friends leave it alone a little, "for" said he, "I have lived long enough if I die unconquered;" and when they told him that the battle was won, and that his comrades were victorious, he bade them draw out the head of the spear, that his life might end. One observed to him that he had fallen but that he had not lost his shield, and that the victory was won; to which he replied with his last breath, "Your Epaminondas thus dying doth not die." So Paul has lived long enough if the gospel is prospering in its course, and though he lays down his life he does not die if his ministry is fulfilled. Let me read you his words, and you shall judge if they have not this heroic ring. "And now, behold, I go bound in the spirit unto Jerusalem, not knowing the things that shall befall me there: save that the Holy Ghost witnesseth in every city, saying that bonds and afflictions abide me. But none of these things move me, neither count I my life dear unto myself, so that I might finish my course with joy, and the ministry, which I have received of the Lord Jesus, to testify the gospel of the grace of God."

We shall this morning first of all inquire, *what was this gospel which Paul judged to be worth dying for?*—"the gospel of the grace of God." When we have made that inquiry, I think we shall be prepared for another; if we cannot die for it, *how can we live for it?* and then, thirdly, I shall press this consecration upon you by answering the question—*Why should we?* Oh, that the Holy Spirit may work in us the holy devotion and self-sacrifice of Paul!

I. First, then, our enquiry this morning is, WHAT WAS THIS GOSPEL FOR WHICH PAUL WOULD DIE? It is not everything called "gospel" which would produce such enthusiasm, or deserve it. For, my brethren, we have gospels nowadays which I would not die for, nor recommend anyone of you to live for, inasmuch as they are gospels that will be snuffed out within a few years. It is never worth while to die for a doctrine which will itself die out. I have lived long enough to see half-a-dozen new gospels rise, flourish, and decay. They told me long ago that my old Calvinistic doctrine was far behind the age, and was an exploded thing; and next I heard that evangelical teaching in any form was a thing of the past, to be supplanted by "advanced thought." I have heard of one improvement upon the old faith and then of another; and the philosophical divines are still improving their theology. They have gone on advancing and advancing, till heaven knows and perhaps hell knows what next they will advance to; but I am sure I do not. I would not die for any one of all the modern systems. I should like to ask broad church divines whether there is any positive doctrine in the Bible at all; and whether any form of teaching could for a moment be judged worth dying for; and whether the martyrs were not great fools to die for truths which might be valuable to them, but which the advance of thought has cast into disuse. Those men and women who went to Smithfield and were burnt quick to the death for Christ, were they not fools every one of them to die for a set of ideas which "modern thought" has quite exploded? I do verily think that to our modern divines there is no such thing as fixed truth, or that, if there be, they are not sure of having yet reached it. They have digged, and digged, and digged: look at the dark pits of unbelief which they have opened; but they have not come to the rock yet. Wait a little longer; they may one of these days find out something solid; but as yet they have only bored through layers of sand.

Yet there used to be a gospel in the world which consisted of facts which Christians never questioned. There was once in the church a gospel which believers hugged to their hearts as if it were their soul's life. There used to be a gospel in the world which provoked enthusiasm and commanded sacrifice. Tens of thousands have met together to hear this gospel at peril of their lives. Men, to the teeth of tyrants, have proclaimed it, and have suffered the loss of all things, and gone to prison and to death for it, singing psalms all the while. Is there not such a gospel remaining? Or are we arrived at cloud-land, where souls starve on suppositions, and become incapable of confidence or ardour? Are the disciples of Jesus now to be fed upon the froth of "thought" and the wind of imagination, whereon men become heady and high-minded? Nay, rather, will we not return to the substantial meat of infallible revelation, and cry to the Holy Ghost to feed us upon his own inspired word?

What is this gospel which Paul valued before his own life? It was called by him "the gospel of the grace of God." That which most forcibly struck the apostle in the gospel was that it was a message of *grace*, and of grace alone. Amid the music of the glad tidings one note rang out above all others and charmed the apostle's ear; that note was grace—the grace of God. That note he regarded as characteristic of the whole strain: the gospel was "the gospel of the grace of God." In these days that word "grace" is not often heard; we hear of moral duties, and scientific adjustments, and human progress; but who tells us of "the grace of God" except a few old-fashioned people who will soon be gone? As one of those antiquated folk I am here this morning, and I shall try to sound out that word "GRACE" so that those who know its joyful sound shall be glad, and those who despise it shall be cut to the heart. *Grace* is the essence of the gospel. *Grace* is the one hope for this fallen world! *Grace* is the sole comfort of saints looking forward for glory! Perhaps Paul had a clearer view of grace than even Peter, or James, or John; and hence he has so much larger space in the New Testament. The other apostolic writers excelled Paul in certain respects; but Paul as to his depth and clearness in the doctrine of grace stood first and foremost. We need Paul again, or at least the Pauline evangelism and definiteness. He would make short work of the new gospels, and say of those who follow them, "I marvel that ye are so soon removed from him that called you into the grace of Christ unto another gospel, which is not another; but there be some that trouble you, and would pervert the gospel of Christ."

Let me try to explain in a brief manner how the gospel is the good news of grace.

The gospel is an announcement that God is prepared to deal with guilty man on the ground of free favour and pure mercy. There would be no good news in saying that God is just; for, in the first place, that is not news,—we know that God is just; the natural conscience teaches man that. That God will punish sin and reward righteousness is not news at all; and if it were news, yet it would not be good news, for we have all sinned, and upon the ground of justice we must perish. But it is news, and news of the best kind, that the Judge of all is prepared to pardon transgression, and to justify the ungodly. It is good news to the sinful that the Lord will blot out sin, cover the sinner with righteousness, and receive him into his favour, and that not on account of anything he has done, or will ever do, but out of sovereign grace. Though we are all guilty without exception, and all most justly condemned for our sins, yet God is ready to take us from under the curse of his law, and give us all the blessedness of righteous men, as an act of pure mercy. Remember how David saw this and spake of it in the thirty-second Psalm:—"Blessed is he whose transgression is forgiven, whose sin is covered. Blessed is the man unto whom the Lord imputeth not iniquity, and in whose spirit there is no guile." This is a message worth dying for, that through the covenant of grace God can be just, and yet the justifier of him that believeth in Jesus; that he can be the righteous Judge of men, and yet believing men can be justified freely by his grace through the redemption that is in Christ Jesus. That God is merciful and gracious, and is ready to bless the most unworthy, is a wonderful piece of news, worth a man's spending a hundred lives to tell. My heart leaps within me as I repeat it in this Hall, and tell the penitent, the desponding, and the despairing that, though their sins deserve hell, yet grace can give them heaven, and make them fit for it: and *that* as a sovereign act of love, altogether independent of their character or deservings. Because the Lord hath said, "I will have mercy on whom I will have mercy, and I will have compassion on whom I will have compassion," there is hope for the most hopeless. Since "it is not of him that willeth, nor of him that runneth, but of God that showeth mercy" (Romans 9:16), there is an open door of hope for those who otherwise might despair. It is as though there had been held a great assize, and the judge had passed from county to county, and a number of prisoners had been condemned, and there remained nothing further in the course of justice but that their sentences should be carried into execution. Lo, suddenly, by the silver trumpets of messengers clothed in silken apparel, it is proclaimed that the king has discovered a method by which, without violating justice, he can deal with the condemned in pure mercy, and so grant them free pardon, immediate jail-delivery, and a place in his majesty's favour and service. This would be glad tidings in the condemned cells, would it not? Would you not be glad to carry such news to the poor prisoners? Ah, Paul, I can understand your getting into a holy excitement over such a revelation as that of free grace. I can understand your being willing to throw your life away that you might tell to your fellow sinners that grace reigns through righteousness unto eternal life.

But the gospel tells us much more than this, namely, that in order to his dealing with men upon the ground of free favour, God the Father has himself removed the grand obstacle which stood in the way of mercy. God is just; that is a truth most sure; man's conscience knows it to be so, and man's conscience will never rest content unless it can see that the justice of God is vindicated. Therefore, in order that God might justly deal in a way of pure mercy with men, he gave his only-begotten Son, that by his death the law might receive its due, and the eternal principles of his government might be maintained. Jesus was appointed to stand in man's stead, to bear man's sin, and endure the chastisement of man's guilt. How clearly doth Isaiah state this in his fifty-third chapter! Man is now saved securely, because the commandment is not set aside, nor the penalty revoked; all is done and suffered which could be exacted by the sternest justice, and yet grace has her hands untied to distribute pardons as she pleases. The debtor is loosed, for the debt is paid. See a dying Saviour, and hear the prophet say, "The chastisement of our peace was upon him, and with his stripes we are healed." Here, too, everything is of grace. Brethren, it was grace on God's part to resolve upon devising and accepting an atonement, and especially in his actually providing that atonement at his own cost. There is the wonder of it: he that was offended himself provides the reconciliation. He had but one Son, and sooner than there should be any obstacle in his way as to dealing with men on the footing of pure grace, he took that Son from his bosom, allowed him to assume our frail nature, and in that nature permitted him to die, the just for the unjust, to bring us to God. You admire Abraham's giving up his son to God; much more admire Jehovah's giving up his Son for sinners. "Herein is love, not that we loved God, but that he loved us, and sent his Son to be the propitiation for our sins." This, then, is the gospel of the grace of God—that God is able, without injustice, to deal with men in a way of pure mercy, altogether apart from their sins or their merits, because their sins were laid upon his dear Son Jesus Christ, who hath offered to divine justice a complete satisfaction, so that God is glorious in holiness and yet rich in mercy. Ah, beloved Paul, there is something worth preaching here.

In the gospel there is also revealed a motive for mercy which is in agreement with the grace of God. There is always needed in the action of every wise man a competent motive; men do not act without reason if they are reasonable men. The same is true with God, the highest of all intelligences: he acts upon the highest reasons. His motive for dealing with men on the footing of free grace is the revealing of his own glorious character. He says: "Not for your sakes do I this, saith the Lord God, be it known unto you: be ashamed and confounded for your own ways, O house of Israel." He works the wonders of his grace "to the intent that now unto the principalities and powers in heavenly places might be known by the church the manifold wisdom of God, according to the eternal purpose which he purposed in Christ Jesus our Lord." He finds a motive in his own nature and mercy since he could not find it anywhere else. He will deal with guilty men according to the sovereignty of his will, "to the praise of the glory of his grace wherein he hath made us accepted in the Beloved." He saves men that his own beloved Son Jesus Christ may be magnified and extolled, and be very high, and that his Holy Spirit may be honoured in the new-creating of rebellious natures. Listen to this, ye that feel your guilt: God is able without infringement of his justice to deal with you on the footing of pure grace, and he has found a reason for so doing, a reason which will apply as much to the worst of men as to the best. If it be for his own glory's sake that he saves guilty sinners, then is a window opened by which light can come to those who sit in the thickest gloom of despair.

In order to the accomplishment of the designs of grace it was necessary further that a gospel message should be issued full of promise, encouragement, and blessing; and truly that message has been delivered to us; for that gospel which we preach to-day is full of grace to the very brim. It speaks on this wise,—Sinner, just as you are, return unto the Lord, and he will receive you graciously and love you freely. God hath said, "I will be merciful to their unrighteousness, and their sins and their iniquities will I remember no more." For Christ's sake, and not because of any agonies, or tears, or sorrows on your part, he will remove your sins as far from you as the east is from the west. He saith, "Come now, and let us reason together: though your sins be as scarlet, they shall be as white as snow; though they be red like crimson, they shall be as wool." You may come to Jesus just as you are, and he will give you full remission upon your believing in him. The Lord says today, "Look not within, as though you would search for any merit there; but look unto me, and be ye saved. I will bless you apart from merit, according to the atonemeut of Christ Jesus." He says, "Look not within as though you looked for any strength for future life: I am become both your strength and your salvation; for when you were yet without strength, in due time Christ died for the ungodly." The gospel invitation is, "Ho, every one that thirsteth, come ye to the waters, and he that hath no money; come ye, buy, and eat; yea, come, buy wine and milk without money and without price." Come and welcome, ye lame, ye halt, ye blind, ye wandering, ye foul, ye miserable. You are invited, not because you are good, but because you are evil; not because you are hopeful, but because you are hopeless. The gospel message is of grace, because it is directed to those whose only claim is their need. The whole have no need of a physician, but they that are sick. Christ came not to call the righteous but sinners to repentance. Come, therefore, ye morally sick; ye whose brows are white with the leprosy of sin; come and welcome, for to you is this free gospel proclaimed by divine authority. Assuredly such a message as this is worth any exertion for its spreading, and it is so blessed, so divine, that we may gladly pour out our blood to proclaim it.

Further, brethren: that this gospel blessing might come within the reach of men, God's grace has adopted a method suitable to their condition. "How can I be forgiven?" saith one, "tell me truly and quickly!" "Believe in the Lord Jesus Christ, and thou shalt be saved." God asks of you no good works, nor good feelings either, but that you be willing to accept what he most freely gives. He saves upon believing. This is faith: that thou believe that Jesus Christ is the Son of God, and that thou trust thyself with him; "But as many as received him, to them gave he power to become the sons of God, even to them that believe on his name." If thou believest, thou art saved. Salvation "is of faith that it might be of grace, to the end the promise might be sure to all the seed."

Dost thou say, "But faith itself seems beyond my reach"? Then, in the gospel of the grace of God we are told that even faith is God's gift, and that he works it in men by his Holy Spirit; for apart from that Spirit they lie dead in trespasses and sins. Oh, what grace is this, that the faith which is commanded is also conferred! "But," saith one, "if I were to believe in Christ and have my past sins forgiven, yet I fear I should go back to sin; for I have no strength by which to keep myself for the future." Hearken! the gospel of the grace of God is this, that he will keep thee to the end—that he will preserve alive within thee the fire which he kindles, for he saith, "I give unto my sheep eternal life"; and again he saith, "The water that I shall give him shall be in him a well of water springing up unto everlasting life." The sheep of Christ shall never perish, neither shall any pluck them out of Christ's hand. Dost thou hear this, thou guilty one—thou who hast no claim upon God's grace whatever? His free grace comes to thee, even to thee; and if thou art made willing to receive it, thou art this day a saved man, and saved for ever beyond all question. I do say it again, this is a gospel so well worth the preaching that I can understand Paul saying, "Neither count I my life dear unto myself, so that I might finish my course with joy, and the ministry which I have received of the Lord Jesus, to testify the gospel of the grace of God." I read in an old book a dream of one who was under concern of soul. He fell asleep and dreamed that he was out in the wilds in a terrible storm. The lightnings flamed around him, and the voice of the thunder made the earth to rock beneath him. He looked eagerly around for a shelter. He ran to the first house before him, but he was denied admittance. He that dwelt there was named *Justice*, and he said in angry tones, "Get thee gone—I cannot shelter a criminal, a traitor to his King and God!" He fled to the next house, and it turned out to be the mansion of *Truth*. Truth came to the door with calm but stern countenance, and said, "Thou art full of falsehood, thou canst not sojourn here." He fled to the home of *Peace*, which stood near, and hoped that there perhaps he might be housed from the storm; but Peace said, "Begone! there is no peace, saith my God, unto the wicked." He could not then tell what to do, for the storm waxed yet more furious: when lo! he saw a portal over which was written "*Mercy*." "Ay," said he, "this is the place for me, for I am guilty." The door was open and he was welcomed there. To that house I invite you. Come in and be at rest. You who cannot as yet be harboured by justice, or peace, or truth, may come to mercy, and receive abundant grace.

 Do you seem inclined to accept the way and method of grace? Let me test you. Some men think they love a thing and yet they do not, for they have made a mistake concerning it. Do you understand that you are to have no claim upon God? He says, "I will have mercy on whom I will have mercy, and I will have compassion on whom I will have compassion." When it comes to pure mercy, then no one can possibly urge a claim; in fact, no claim can exist. If it be of grace it is not of debt, and if of debt it is not of grace. If God wills to save one man, and another be left to perish in his own wilful sin, that other cannot dare to dispute with God. Or if he do, the answer is—"Can I not do as I will with my own?" Oh, but you seem now as if you started back from it! See, your pride revolts against the sovereignty of grace. Let me beckon you back again. Though you have no claim, there is another truth which smiles upon you; for, on the other hand, there is no bar to your obtaining mercy. If no goodness is needed to recommend you to God, since all must be pure favour which he gives, then also no badness can shut you out from that favour. However guilty you may be, it may be God may show favour to you. He has in other cases called out the chief of sinners; why not in your case also? At any rate, no aggravation of sin, no continuance in sin, no height of sin, can be a reason why God should not look with grace upon you; for if pure grace and nothing else but grace is to have sway then the jet black transgressor may be saved. In his case there is room for grace to manifest its greatness. I have heard men make excuse out of the doctrine of election, and they have said, "What if I should not be elected?" It seems to me far wiser to say, "What if I should be elected?" Yea, I am elected if I believe in Jesus; for there never was a soul yet that cast itself upon the atonement of Christ but what that soul was chosen of God from before the foundation of the world.

This is the gospel of the grace of God, and I know that it touches the heart of many of you. It often stirs my soul like the sound of martial music, to think of my Lord's grace from old eternity, a grace that is constant to its choice, and will be constant to it when all these visible things shall disappear as sparks that fly from the chimney. My heart is glad within me to have to preach free grace and dying love: I can understand why crowds met at dead of night to hear of the grace of God. I can understand the Covenanters on the bleak hills listening, with sparkling eyes, as Cameron preached of the grace of the great King! There is something in a free-grace gospel worth preaching, worth listening to, worth living for, and worth dying for!

II. This brings me to the second head: you and I are not called to die for it just yet; let us see to-day that we live for it. HOW CAN WE LIVE FOR THIS GOSPEL OF THE GRACE OF GOD?

I answer, first, if anybody here is to live for this gospel, he must have received it from God, and he must have received a call to minister or serve for it. He must feel himself under bonds to hold and keep this gospel; not so much because he has chosen it, but because it has chosen him. I forget who it was, but a quaint old minister was once told that he could not preach in a certain pulpit if he held the doctrines of grace. "Well," said he, "I think I might be allowed to preach there, for I can truly say that I do not hold the doctrines of grace, the doctrines of grace hold me." That might be rather a quibble, but there is a grand truth in it. When a man picks and selects his creed, the probabilities are that by-and-by he will pick again, and will select another next time. There is about the love which constitutes our domestic bliss a something of necessity: our beloved one was chosen by us, but yet we could not help it, we were carried away and overborne, and so our marriage came to pass. It was not altogether choice, there was a mystic power that enchained our hearts; and I am sure it is so with the doctrines of grace if we believe them,—we chose them with a willing soul, but yet we were under constraint, and could do no other. To me there is but one form of doctrine; I know no other. Brethren, I cannot be of any other faith than that which I preached nearly twenty-nine years ago on this platform. I think I have read as much as most men, and I know most of the maunderings of advanced thinkers; but I have never come into their secret, and I never can. I abhor the very idea of an advance upon the gospel which Paul preached. I am to-day what I was when, as a youth, I preached to crowds in this Hall. I have progressed in my theology not so much as the tithe of an inch. I hope I preach better and with more experimental knowledge of the truth; but that which I preached thirty-three years ago I preach to-day. You know the story of the boy who stood upon the burning deck because his father said, "Stand you there"; and I desire to imitate his steadfastness. Other boys might be much wiser than he was, but his wisdom was obedience. I prefer obeying God to being wise with my own wisdom. The gospel which the Bible has revealed, and the Holy Ghost has taught me, I must preach, and no other. I am incapable of believing the novelties of the hour. I must abide in my old faith. I would say with Luther, "I cannot help it, so help me God!" I know no other gospel today than that which I knew when I first believed in Jesus. I know that by grace we are saved through faith, and that not of ourselves,—it is the gift of God: what more do I need to know? You shall leave this rock, if you like, my brother, for you may be able to swim; but I must stop where I am, for I should drown. When the crack of doom shall be heard, I shall be here, God helping me, believing the gospel of the grace of God and none other creed. I hope there is something in adhesiveness and pertinacity which will help to preserve, if not to spread the gospel. Steadfastness at this particular time has a special value, and I urge you to it; to the gospel which ye have received, to the gospel of the grace of God, I implore you to stand fast so long as you live.

But the next thing Paul did was to make it known. Wherever he went he published the gospel. This is what we must do. "Oh," says one, "I cannot make it known." Why not? "I could not tell out the gospel." Why not? "Why, I am a person of mean appearance, and I do not suppose people would pay me any respect." Just what they said about Paul—"his personal presence is weak." "Oh, but I am no speaker." Just so, that also is what they said of Paul—"His speech is contemptible." "Oh, but if I were to say anything, I could not adorn it with a figure of speech, or illustrate it with a simile; I could not even quote a bit of poetry, to make it fine." Paul also used home-spun. He says, "We use great plainness of speech." Many of the other teachers were great orators, but Paul always fought shy of oratory; he stood up and allowed the truth to flow out of his mouth freely, in its own way; and I do believe at the present moment we want a race of preachers who will not be fine, or scholarly, or rhetorical, or sensational; men of whom you will say when you have heard them—"I cannot make out why people flock to hear such a ministry. All that they can go for is *what* the man says; for he does not say it grandly, he does not seem as if he wanted to do so, he appears only concerned to get his message out of his own heart, and get it into the people's hearts." That is just what Paul did. Do you not think that you could tell the gospel out in his fashion? "Oh, but I have so many infirmities." Yes, Paul said he gloried in infirmities because the power of Christ the more clearly rested on him. When he had done preaching the people could not say, "Oh, we understand why we felt it so; you see Paul practises all the graces of manner. We quite understand why his speech penetrated our hearts; he has such a melodious, bell-like voice. We can understand why we like to hear him; he has such expressive eyes, they look into our souls." Now, Paul, in all probability, had weak eyes; according to his name he was a short man; and it is likely that he spoke very plainly. Yet he never felt sorry that it was so; on the contrary, he believed that in his weakness he was strong, for the power of Christ rested upon him. He hoped also that for this very reason their faith would not stand in the wisdom of man, but in the power of God. Brothers and sisters, we are all qualified, if this be the case, to go and tell to others the gospel of the grace of God.

Yet further, Paul desired to *testify* to the gospel. Now, to testify is something more than to proclaim; it means to bear personal witness to the truth. Paul was specially qualified to testify; was he not? When he preached he frequently told that story about the fierce persecutor who was on the way to Damascus, and was suddenly struck down—a persecutor who had never asked to be saved by grace, who had no freewill towards Christ, but who had a very strong will against him, and was haling men and women to prison, and compelling them to blaspheme, being exceeding mad against them. Oh how sweetly Paul told out the gospel of the grace of God when he said, "The Lord appeared to me by the way." "I obtained mercy, that in me first Jesus Christ might show forth all longsuffering for a pattern to them which should hereafter believe on him to life everlasting." Friend, cannot you tell of your conversion, and let men know how free grace came to you when you looked not for it?

Nor would Paul end there; for he would often tell his consolations, how the gospel had comforted him when he had been stoned, and tried by false brethren, and yet had been upheld by the grace of God. Paul could tell also of his heavenly joys: how often he had been exceedingly lifted up, and made to triumph in Christ by feeding upon the gospel of the grace of God. His personal experience of its power over himself was that which he used as the great instrument and argument for spreading the gospel—for this is the meaning of testifying.

My friend, if the gospel has done nothing for you, hold your tongue or speak against it; but if the gospel has done for you what it has done for some of us, if it has changed the current of your life, if it has lifted you up from the dunghill and made you to sit as on a throne, if it is to-day your meat and your drink, if to your life it is the very centre and sun,—then bear constant witness to it. If the gospel has become to you what it is to me, the light of my innermost heart, the core of my being, then tell it, tell it wherever you go; and make men know that even if *they* reject it it is to you the power of God unto salvation, and will be the same to every man that believeth.

III. My time is gone, but yet I must detain you a minute while I remind you of reasons WHY WE, MY BRETHREN, SHOULD LIVE TO MAKE KNOWN THE GOSPEL OF THE GRACE OF GOD.

First, because *it is the only gospel in the world*, after all. These mushroom gospels of the hour, which come and go like a penny newspaper, which has its day and then is thrown aside, have no claim on any man's zeal. These changing moons of doctrine, what are they doing for England? They are doing much evil in this city—they are alienating the mass of the people from going to any place of worship at all. Why should they come to hear uncertainties? Why should they come merely to be taught their duty, and to be moralized, and so on? Men are not led to assemble in multitudes by such poor attractions. I do not know that I should go across the street Sunday after Sunday merely to hear a moral essay. I might as well stay at home and read the paper. But to hear the gospel of the grace of God is worth many a mile's walk, and if it were plainly set forth in all our churches and chapels I warrant we should see very few empty pews: the people would come and hear it, for they always have done so. It is your graceless gospel which starves the flock till they forsake the pasture: it is your Socinian reasoning which leads men to treat ministry and public worship with contempt. The old gospel is a sweet savour which attracts the masses. When Whitefield sounded it forth, what common was big enough to hold the thousands? Man wants something that shall cheer his heart in the midst of his labour, and give him hope under a sense of sin. As the thirsty need water, so does man want the gospel of the grace of God. And there are no two gospels in the world any more than there are two suns in the heavens. There is but one atmosphere for us to breathe, and one gospel for us to live by. "Other foundation can no man lay than that which is laid, Jesus Christ the righteous." Therefore tell out the gospel, lest men die for lack of the knowledge of it.

Do it, next, because *it is for God's glory*. Do you not see how it glorifies God? It lays the sinner low; it makes man nobody, but God is all-in-all. It sets' God on a throne, and trails man in the dust; and then it sweetly leads men to worship and reverence the God of all grace, who passeth by transgression, iniquity, and sin—therefore spread it.

Spread it, because thus you will *glorify Christ*. Oh, if he should come on this platform this morning, how gladly would we all make way for him! how devoutly would we adore him! If we might but see that head, that dear majestic head, would we not all bow in worship? And if he then spoke, and said, "My beloved, I have committed to you my gospel; hold it fast as ye have received it! Give not way to the notions and inventions of men, but hold fast the truth as ye have received it; and go and tell my word, for I have other sheep that are not yet of my fold, who must be brought in; and you have brothers that yet are prodigals, and they must come home": I say, if he looked you each one in the face, and addressed you so, your soul would answer, "Lord, I will live for thee! I will make thee known! I will die for thee if needs be to publish the gospel of Jesus Christ."

Now, if you and I arouse ourselves this day, and God's Holy Spirit shall help us so to do, and we begin to proclaim the gospel of the grace of God, do you know what I think is sure to happen? I prophesy the best results. They tell us that all sorts of evils are growing strong, and brethren, darkly prophetic, tell us that awful times are coming—I cannot tell you how dreadful they are to be. Popery is to come back according to some, and once again the harlot of the Seven Hills is to dominate over all the earth. Is she? We shall see. If you boldly proclaim the gospel I tell you it will not be so. If the gospel of the grace of God be fully and fairly preached it cannot be so. Listen to what John saw—"I saw another angel fly in the midst of heaven having the everlasting gospel to preach unto them that dwell on the earth, and to every nation, and kindred, and tongue, and people, saying with a loud voice, fear God and give glory to him." Do you see that angel? Observe what follows! Close behind him flies another celestial herald. "And there followed another angel, saying, Babylon is fallen, that great city, because she made all nations drink of the wine of the wrath of her fornication." Fly, angel of the everlasting gospel! Fly, for as surely as thou dost speed thy flight, that other angel will follow who shall proclaim the downfall of Babylon, and of every other system that opposeth itself to the grace of the Lord God Almighty! The Lord stir you up for his name's sake. Amen.

PORTIONS OF SCRIPTURE READ BEFORE SERMON—Psalm 32; Romans 3:9–31; 4:1–8.

HYMNS FROM "OUR OWN HYMN BOOK"—100, 980, 546.[2]

---

[2] Spurgeon, C. H. (1883). A Gospel Worth Dying for. In *The Metropolitan Tabernacle Pulpit Sermons* (Vol. 29, pp. 433–444). London: Passmore & Alabaster.

THE WATER OF LIFE

A Sermon

DELIVERED BY

C. H. SPURGEON,

AT THE METROPOLITAN TABERNACLE, NEWINGTON.

"The woman saith unto him, Sir, give me this water."—John 4:15.

YOU will remember that our Saviour had been speaking to the woman of Samaria concerning living water. He had endeavoured to catch her attention by using a metaphor to her work and her position. Water was uppermost in her thoughts, and Jesus sanctified the element to his own gracious end. Sitting at the well's mouth, I think I can see his earnest face, and note the woman's wondering eyes while he talked to her as she had never been spoken to before, concerning water which caused a man never to thirst again. At first the woman raised questions: the sceptical part of her nature took its turn, and cavilled, and carped, and argued. "Sir, thou hast nothing to draw with, and the well is deep," and so on. Do you not see all the elements of the infidel in her? But she is in good hands, and soon she has passed from the period of questioning into that of petitioning, and she cries this time, "Sir, give me this water." She was still, I am afraid, very ignorant. She did not even understand her own petition. That is clear from the words which follow the text, "That I thirst not, neither come hither to draw." She was giving a material meaning to a spiritual utterance. She was thinking of the water that could moisten the lips, when Christ was speaking of that living water, his own grace and love, which touches the heart, and the heart only. Her eyes were dark, but her face was turned the right way; and, best of all, Jesus was there, who can lead the blind in a way which they know not. It will be all well with her, you may leave her alone, and think of yourselves.

I hope I am now conversing with some here who have got clear of this woman's ignorance, and have passed away also, as she did, from the period of questioning; you know best who you are and where you are, but I hope you are desirous to partake of the grace which saveth. You have got away from raising difficulties. You have had enough of that unprofitable hair-splitting and cobweb-making. You feel that you get no good by constantly insinuating doubts as to the possibility of your salvation, and questioning whether Christ is a Saviour or not, and so you are about to leave the sceptical business, and try another line of things. You are now arrived at the point of desiring, not, I hope, the terminus of the line, but only the first or second station. Glad am I that you have come so far. If there be grace to be had, you are saying, "O that I might have it!" If there be pardon, peace, eternal life, you believe all that Jesus Christ says of it, and you want to possess it. You are stretching out your hands, like the drowning man who is ready to catch at the plank. Your desires are awake; your better thoughts are no longer slumbering. You have broken away from indifference and obstinacy, and you are now anxious and desirous to obtain salvation by Jesus Christ.

It is to you that I wish to speak this evening, and I shall first take the text, *and try to use it to excite your desire still further by a description of the water spoken of in the text;* secondly, I shall *try to assure your hearts by some remarks upon the likelihood of your obtaining this water;* and then we shall close *by urging you not to leave this house until the prayer has been registered in heaven,* "Lord, give me this water; give me this water to-night!"

I. To begin, then, I am TO TRY TO EXCITE YOUR DESIRE BY A DESCRIPTION OF THE WATER SPOKEN OF IN THE TEXT.

Water is an essential element in the natural world. There is a spiritual world, in describing which, we are obliged to use analogies taken from the natural world; and the grace of God in the mental and the spiritual world, is just what water is in the natural World. You want water as a man; you must have it; on certain occasions it becomes an imperative necessity: you must drink or die. You want grace as a man, not for your body, but for your soul, and it is imperative that you should have it, or else your soul will first be in pain here, and at death the pangs of remorse will seize it, and afterwards an everlasting thirst, an unsatisfied want, will be the second death to you.

The grace of God is like water in no less than eight senses. But let me not alarm you. I will not weary you; be sure of that, for I long to win you, and weariness will not serve my purpose. I shall only mention the eight parallels with a few remarks, and pass rapidly on from each one.

1. Water, first, *is thirst-removing*, and so is the grace of God. The man who drinks water, thirsts not, his bodily want is removed; the man who receives the grace of God in his heart, gets that which his nature is wanting, and his painful longings are over. Man by nature is so foolish that he does not know what his nature wants, but he feels that it wants something. Awakened men talk to themselves in this fashion, "I want—I do not know what I want—but I know I want something which the world cannot give me, which I cannot find within myself, which my fellow men cannot bestow upon me; I want a something: O my God, what is it? Tell me what it is!" Friend, if you are in this condition, the gospel of our Lord Jesus Christ is just the thing for you, for in it the Lord not only tells you what you want, but he presents it to you. He tells you that you need his love; that if his grace be shed abroad in your heart, and your sin be pardoned, and you be made to be his child, and accepted through Christ Jesus, then will your soul say, "Now I have what I wanted; now I want no, more; I can sit still and say, Blessed be God that my desires are full. The aching void which the world could never fill, is now filled to overflowing; and my soul has what it was always wanting, though it did not know what it really wanted. I can sit down now perfectly content!" It is a grand thing for a man to be able to say, "I am satisfied," but the genuine believer in Christ can say that. "Thou hast satisfied my mouth with good things; so that my youth is renewed as the eagle's." Believers in Jesus carry the pearl of content in their bosoms. Jesus takes away the restless spirit, and gives us rest. Jesus is the door that fits the heart, and when he is near to us he shuts out the world's cold and heat, and gives us sweet content. O ambitious man, thou that runnest after something, and thou canst not tell what it is that can gratify thine immortal spirit, turn to the cross, for at the foot of it there springs a sacred fount of soul-satisfying delight, and if thou wilt but stoop and drink, thine ambition

shall be over, and thou shalt want no more. There is satisfaction for the deepest longings of heart, and head, and conscience, in the fount which springs from the wounds of Jesus. Faith is the silver cup. Dip it into the overflowing stream and drink. O Holy Spirit, put the cup to my poor thirsty brother's lip!

2. Secondly, water is also *life-preserving*. In the wilderness, where there is no water, the lip becomes chapped; the skin is dried; the tongue is like a firebrand, and the mouth is like an oven; and the weary traveller must drink or die. O for a draught of water there! A bag of diamonds could not buy a flagon there! Priceless is the life-draught. And far out on the salt, salt sea, with

> "Water, water everywhere,
> But not a drop to drink,"

the mariner, though he may seek to satisfy himself with the brine around him, feels that it will be death sooner or later to him unless he can get some pure, clear, refreshing drops of water to drink. Drop, ye heavens in pity, or let some friendly bark espy the castaways. Such is the grace of God to the soul of man. The whole world over, there is nothing that can save a soul apart from the grace of God. Your good works can no more save you than the salt sea can give the sailor drink. Ceremonies can no more fill your heart with peace and give it life, than the hot sand of the wilderness can quench the thirst of the weary traveller. God must lead you to the river of eternal life flowing out of the Rock that was smitten. You must get grace through Jesus Christ, or hope shall never dawn upon you, but despair's midnight shall be your everlasting portion, where lost spirits wail out their undying lives in one endless death. O soul, if thou gettest God's grace, thou shalt never die! Believest thou this? If that grace of God shall come flowing into thy soul, thou shalt possess eternal life, an immortal principle which shall bid defiance to the grave, and make thee sing in the very jaws of death, for he that drinketh of this water, shall live in Christ for ever. "He that liveth and believeth in me shall never die." "He that believeth in me, though he were dead, yet shall he live." This grace of God, then, is life-preserving, as well as thirst-quenching: Have you found it so? for, friend, I cannot afford to let you hear me, and yet escape a squeeze or two. If you forget this sermon, it shall not be because I did not press you to remember it.

3. Water, in the third place, *is filth-purging*. Man seeks no more than to get to the stream to wash when he is defiled. Many and many a time in passing through a country, the poor traveller comes to a brook so clear that he can see his face reflected in it, and he stoops down and laves his brow again and again, and takes his bath, and goes his way all bright and shining, as though he had exchanged sorrow for gladness, and received the oil of joy for mourning. Now, the guilty sinner, and such are we all by nature, however foul he may be, has but to stoop down at the river of eternal grace and wash, and he shall be clean. This stream can take out spots which nothing else can remove. Our sin is of such a crimson dye, naturally, that it might incarminate the Atlantic before it should be washed away, but this water of life can do it; it takes away the stain of blasphemy and lust; it removes the pollution of theft and murder. All manner of sin shall be forgiven unto that man who comes to the cross and trusts in Jesus. Whosoever believeth in the world's great Redeemer, shall find full and complete pardon for every offence that he has committed. O try it, thou blackest of the black, if thou be here! Thou who hast gone to the greatest extent of sin, cast thy guilty soul into this fountain, and see if thou dost not rise from it with thy flesh like unto that of a little child, clean and pure, and not a spot remaining on thee. This filth-removing is the grace of God streaming from the cross, where Jesus suffered in our stead the wrath which was due to us for our transgressions.

> "Calvary's wonders let us trace,
> Justice magnified in grace;
> Mark the purple streams, and say,
> Thus my sins were washed away."

Friend, can you do this by faith, trusting for pardon to the blood of God's dear Son?

4. Water, again, is well known very frequently *to be softening*. There are some things which, when laid in water, soon lose their hardness, and are soft and pliable. This water of the grace of God, which it is my longing desire to commend to you, has a marvellous

softening power. Adamant, millstone, ay, the nether millstone, northern iron and steel, have been melted when laid asoke in this fount. The hardest heart yields before the power of the love of God revealed in Christ Jesus. I think I hear one of you exclaim, "That is good news for me; I know that Christ can pardon me, but I cannot feel my sin as I ought: I am such a stiff-necked sinner, so hardened, so perverse, I cannot feel my need as I would wish to." Soul, if the grace of God shall flow upon thy heart, it shall turn the stone, by a wondrous transformation, into flesh at once. There is no stubbornness which the grace of God cannot overcome. What a blessed thing it is for the preacher that he has not to give his hearers soft hearts, nor even to find tender hearts in them to begin with; how delightful it is for him to remember that he preaches a gospel which works wonders, wonders even greater than the rod of Moses; for when with the gospel we smite even a rock, penitential streams gush forth, and yet more, the rocky soul is itself dissolved under a sense of sin. O that some Saul of Tarsus might be washed by this stream now! He would no longer be the enemy of God's church, but would seek out some poor disciple to ask him what he must do to be saved. It is a heart-softening water. May the Lord give it to every one of us who have hard hearts remaining; fain would I bathe in it anew, that I might the more tenderly feel for you. Friend, will you never feel for yourself?

    5. In the fifth place, this water has the property, like earthly water, *of being fire-quenching*. There is nothing like water after all, with all your new inventions, for putting out fire. We run for the engines, and turn on the main, what can we do better? But there are fires that burn within the human heart, deep volcanic fires fed from the depths of hell, furious flames which roar within the inner man, and anon roll over in torrents of sin-lava in his daily life—these are fires which never will be put out except by heavenly water. Oh, that fire of lust! How many a man has been consumed by it! It has devoured him as the fire devoureth the stubble. But when the grace of God comes, how soon that fire is damped, and even quenched for ever! And there are other fires which burn in the soul—the fire of envy and of malice, the flames of anger and of unholy desire—how these will rage and glow until the grace of God comes! I know it puzzles many a man to know how he

could live without such-and-such sins. "Oh," says he, "I could not live without them, I have fallen into the habit of them, and I must have them." Ah! but you shall be made a new man, such a new man, that if you were to meet your old self, you would avoid the wretch or struggle with him in deadly hand to hand encounter, out of sheer hatred to so mean a thing. Let me tell you you will never be on good terms with your old self so long as you live. You will hate that old self of yours, and it will be your daily desire to kill him. You will try to drive the nails through his hands and feet, and crucify him upon the cross of Jesus; and you will not be content unless you can kill him daily, mortifying him with his affections and his lusts. Oh, mighty grace of God that can put out the flames of sin! O sinner, the very flames of hell are put out by this grace of God; I mean so far as the saved soul is concerned: for the soul that is washed in this fountain, there is no hell in which God can punish it. How can he punish a pardoned sinner? How can he that is in Christ Jesus be cast into the flames?

> "No condemnation now I dread,
> For justice smote my Surety's head."

"Who shall lay anything to the charge of God's elect?" He that has Christ to be his substitute is beyond all fear of hell. He can look down into that dread abyss, and feel that there is not a burning coal there for him, and that whoever may perish, yet he, being in Christ Jesus, can never die. Friend, have the fires in your soul met with this glorious antagonist? Are the engines of grace casting their floods upon thy soul? Let conscience give its reply, and let it have thine ear.

6. A sixth property is one that is not found in ordinary water, and that is, that it is a *spring-creating water*. Wherever the water of life falls, it makes a new spring, which begins to bubble up directly. By this I mean that if the grace of God enters into a man's heart, it is an immortal principle, and, as the Saviour says, "Out of the midst of him shall flow rivers of living water." "The water that I shall give him shall be in him a well of water springing up into everlasting life." What a great difference there is between a pool and a running spring! Frequently in crossing the Alps, when one has been very faint and thirsty, it has been a sweet rest to sit down by a running spring, and

wash one's face and feet, or bathe one's self in it. You may have walked till you are very footsore—you sit down to bathe your feet, and if you have found a mere pool, you will stir the bottom of it, and it will soon be very filthy; but when it is a running spring, you can sit and wash, and wash, and wash again, and if you do stir the sand at the bottom, the earth is all gone in a moment, because the water still comes bubbling up fresh and fresh, and therefore it is always clean. So it is with the grace of God in a Christian: it never gets flat, and dull, and dead; and the daily pollutions, and washing of our feet, do not stain it, because it is a living spring, and arises from those "fresh springs" which David sings about which he rejoiced to find in the Lord his God. It is very hard work to play the part of a Christian if you have not a spring within you. For a man to have to keep up year after year a profession without life, why, it must be slavish work. Do you think that I would come and take a seat in this place, or in any other place of worship, and occupy it merely because it was respectable to do so, if I had no care for it? I would as soon be a slave! Base is the man who even in his religion is the serf of tyrant fashion. To come up to the house of God because you love to be there, and to sing because you cannot help singing, and to unite with God's people because "birds of a feather" must "flock together," and you love to be among them—why there is something in that, something which tastes of reality and sincerity. He who has no great deeps of godliness in his soul makes a bondage of religion, he lives the life of a dog, and does not even get the crumbs from under the table as his portion. Mark you, brethren, it is harder to preach without this spring than it is to hear without it, because if you have not a spring in you, you may go foraging this dead man's books, and that other dead man's stores, to find a subject, but you will soon run dry; but if God the Holy Ghost is a spring within you, you may remain full of precious truth, and pour it out so long as God shall give you utterance, and you shall not run dry. What a blessing it is when the living water makes a spring within the Christian! What a curse to be one of the stagnant ponds of formality exhaling the putridity of hypocrisy. Friend, where are you, I must have my hand on you again, what are you in this matter as in the sight of God?

7. Seventhly, it is *fruit-producing water*. What fruit would there be upon the trees, what pasture in the meadows, what harvest in the field, if it were not for the rain? Everything would be barren without water, and even where there is fruit, if there be not also a fair share of water, what poor stuff it is! When I was in the country in June, and there were some heavy showers, I could not help thinking what good they were doing. There was the wheat just wanting plumping out, and the rain came to fill it, and to make the ears full. It might have been wheat of course without it, but the ear is likely to be more full of grain when the drought is gone. So, brethren, we may produce some little fruit when we have but little grace; but if we had more grace, how that fruit would plump out! how would our fruit be more rich, and fat, and mellow! How would our service to God be improved and perfected if we had more of this fruit-producing water! You cannot serve God without his grace. You cannot give him true praise, nor true prayer, nor true service, nor anything that is acceptable, unless he first shall give you of the rain of his grace, grace for grace. "By their fruits shall ye know them:" friend, what fruit have you? O that grace may turn the barren fig-tree into a good fruit-bearing tree!

8. And, lastly upon this point; *it is heaven-ascending water*. You know there is a rule of this sort in hydrostatics, that water will rise to its own level. Not long ago, I thought such things were gone out. I was riding along where the road was in a little cutting, and a spout was actually taken over the road to carry water from one field to the other, it was dripping fast upon the passengers, and making an ugly place in the road. Now, they might easily have taken the little stream under the road, and up again in a pipe; but, I suppose, when the spout was made, it was not known to those who made it that water will rise as high as its source. Now, the grace of God will rise as high as its source. If you and I have grace that began with us, it will never get higher than we are. If you have grace that the priest gave you when you were christened, it will never get higher than the priest; but if you get the true grace of God which descends from heaven, it will take you as high as the New Jerusalem, from which it came. High up in the throne of God are the everlasting springs of divine mercy; at the foot of divine sovereignty it wells up a spring, clear as crystal, pure without a stain,

and it flows down to earth, leaping down by the way of the cross. And it will ascend as high as its source. It will go up to the throne again, that is where it came from, and it will rise to its own level, and it will float you up there with it. If, by the grace of God, you have been taken up by the stream of Jesu's dying love, it will take you up to its own source, and where God is, there you shall be. Because you have been made to taste, to feel, and to be saturated with the grace that came from God, from a divine source, you shall also have a divine portion for ever. The rivers go to the sea because they originally came from the sea. Did not the sun kiss the sea, and make it ascend to him in clouds, that it might descend in rain? And so, all the rivers of grace in us shall flow into the sea, whence they came, the bottomless, shoreless sea of everlasting love, because that is the eternal source and fountain of them all. Clouds of suffering went up from the heart of Jesus to return to earth in showers of mercy for poor sinners. Friend, do you know anything about this in your very soul?

Now, I have thus spoken of the grace of God which is revealed in Jesus Christ. I only hope that some one here may say, "I wish I were washed in it! I wish my thirst were satisfied with it! I wish that my soul were made to overflow with it! I wish that I might be lifted up to heaven though its energy!" Oh! then, soul, I am glad you have the desire. Turn it into a prayer, and let the prayer be the text, "Give me this water!"

II. And now, with great brevity indeed, we shall take the second point, that is, TO CHEER YOUR HEARTS WITH SOME REFLECTIONS UPON THE LIKELIHOOD OF YOUR GETTING THIS LIVING WATER.

I am supposing now that you really want it. If you say, "Sir, give me this water," you will have it; and I will tell you why I think you will have it—because, in the first place, *I do not think that an ordinary man would deny another water.* If I stood by a well, and you approached me, and said, "Sir, give me this water," I should say, "As much as you like of it." Who would not give water? It is the very commonest of gifts. Even in the East, with all the value that is attached to water there, the Saviour mentions that as one of the most ordinary acts of benevolence. "Whosoever shall give to drink unto one of these little ones a cup of cold water only in the name of a disciple, verily I say unto you, He shall in no wise lose his reward." Who will deny another a glass of water? Then note, that according to our text, the giving of saving grace is to the great Redeemer no more than the giving of water to you! Grace is a priceless boon for you to receive, but to Jesus it is a delight to give it. If you give water, you have a little less water left, but if Christ gives grace, he has not any grace the less. He still has as much grace in the inexhaustible fulness which dwells in his adorable person. As the sun is just as bright for all its shining, and the ocean still full notwithstanding all the clouds exhaled from it, so Jesus is as abundant as ever in pardoning mercy and saving power. I tell you that for Jesus Christ to be gracious, is as much according to his nature as it is for you and for me to be generous enough to give away water. The blessing of poor needy souls is no labour with Jesus, no loss to him, no tax upon him; all the pain and cost he has borne long ago, and now to save the guilty is his reward in which he sees the recompense of his travail. Now, if in this place the grace of God had been compared to gold, that metaphor would have suited well to express its value; but you would have said, "Who gives gold away?" But here it is compared with water, water which man freely gives, and which our Lord Jesus never denies to those who seek it of him. I do not believe, then, if an ordinary man will give away water—and Christ compares his grace with water, that he will let you say, "Sir, give me this water!" and then send you away without it. Friend, be not so unbelieving as to think that the Lord Jesus is ungenerous and unkind, but ask for the living water, and it shall be given you.

Again, *if you would refuse water to some persons, I am very sure that you would not refuse it to a thirsty person*. If you saw him panting, and the hot sweat starting to his brow, and if he could scarcely speak, but had only strength enough to gasp out, "Sir, if you would but give me a cup of water, I would bless you for it with all my heart," why, you would run and bring out the sparkling crystal, and feel a great pleasure in seeing him drink. Would you not? I am sure you would. Now, if you are a thirsty soul, I am quite sure Christ will give you the water of life. He will give it to any that ask, for he refuses none; but to you he will give it so quickly, that he will seem to give it twice over. He will not let you thirst in vain, for has he not promised, "When the poor and needy seek water, and there is none, and their tongue faileth for thirst, I the Lord will hear them, I the God of Israel will not forsake them. I will open rivers in high places, and fountains in the midst of the valleys: I will make the wilderness a pool of water, and the dry land springs of water." "Oh," says one, "how I desire to be saved! How I long to have Christ!" Thou mayst have him then, for Jesus Christ never did deny a thirsty sinner, never did refuse to give of his substance to the poor, his clothes to the naked, or his medicine to the sick. He came on purpose to bless such. I say, there are all likelihoods that you shall have the blessing if you will but pray earnestly, "Lord, give me this water;" nay, more, there is a certainty of it.

Another reason gives me comfort for you, and that is—*there certainly is a plenty of it*, for the apostle John says he saw "a *river of* the water of life." Now, nobody is afraid, when there is a deep, broad, flowing river to draw from. Who fears to exhaust the Thames or drain the Danube by his thirst? Moreover, as John Bunyan reminds us, a river is free to everybody to drink. The source of it is private. Many rivers rise in a park or private grounds, but the river itself is public. As soon as it becomes a considerable stream, it becomes a public highway, and a universal water-supply. It is free, it flows the way it wills. Rivers possess a sort of sovereignty, you cannot bid them flow in a straight line, or order them by rules or geometry; they will have their own sweet will. If the river chooses to go by one town and not by another, it will have its way, try to stop it who may? But while it is sovereign in its course and direction, yet it is free for public use; the cattle come to drink, and even a poor dog is not refused when he gets to the river's brink; if he wants to lap and cool his feverish tongue in the dog days, who shall say him nay? And you, poor sinner, you shall find the grace of God free to you, for there is enough of it; it is up to the banks; nay, it overflows the banks; there is a flood of it, such a flood that there never can by any possibility be any lack, though all men should come. Though ten thousand times ten thousand should come, there would still be found sufficient grace in Jesus to meet the case of all, for whom the Lord brings, the Lord can provide for in Christ Jesus. The grace of God is sovereign in its choice, and discriminating in its course, but still it is free to all thirsty ones who long to partake of its everlasting fulness.

I am comforted, also, by another thought, namely, *that this river flows on purpose* for the thirsty. I am sure I do not know what there is mercy in the world for, unless it is for those who want it because of their sin and misery. What could Christ have made an atonement for, except for sinners? It is not possible that the beloved Physician came all the way from heaven to heal those who were well and needed no medicine. It is not likely that he opens his great granaries to feed the nations who have a harvest of their own; it must be that our Joseph has stored up the wheat for hungry perishing ones. O ye that need, come and welcome, for the fountain is opened especially for you; it flows, that such as you may come and drink. Friend, shall our invitations have no power with you? O Holy Spirit, make men willing in this the day of thy power!

I feel sure, too, that you who seek the Lord, will find his grace, *because there never has been one refused yet*. A dear brother, who, I believe, is now present, told me that he owed his conversion in early life to hearing a sentence or two of a sermon from a man whose name he never knew, but whom he heard preach standing on a log of wood on a village green. He had never gone to listen to the gospel anywhere, but happened to be straying through the village, and he heard the man say that there never was a soul that sincerely sought God through Jesus Christ, but what ultimately, sooner or later, it was brought into a state of peace. And let me say to you all—it may sink into some heart, and one day yield it comfort—it shall not be said by you in eternity, that you sought the Lord and he would not hear you. I recollect what comfort this gave to me when I heard my mother say, that she had heard many wicked things in the world, but she never heard a man wicked enough to say, that he had sincerely sought God through Jesus Christ, and yet had been refused. When I heard that, I thought I would say it, for I was confident that I had sought the Lord, but I had had no comfortable answer. But I have never said it, I have never had cause to say it, for before I could be driven to that state of despair, I looked unto him and was lightened, and so I am persuaded it shall be with you.

There never was one refused who said, "Give me this water," and you shall not be the first.

To close this point, *it is to Jesus Christ's glory to give of his saving mercy, and therefore be certain that he will not withhold it*. It cannot make Christ more glorious to deny a poor sinner his mercy. It cannot be to his profit to shut his door in a seeking sinner's face. It is impossible that the bleeding Lamb should cease to be pitiful to poor bleeding hearts. By everything that can make the name of the great Physician glorious, by every pang of his soul on account of sinners, I am persuaded that he will not deny you. Why, the more a physician cures, the greater is his fame; the more the Saviour saves, the higher is his honour; the more Jesus Christ can bless, the more lofty will be the praise, and the more exalted that mighty shout of "Hallelujah!" that shall go up from ten thousand times ten thousand of sinners, who have been washed in his blood. Come, then, seeking sinner, come thou now, and by humble faith trust in the Mediator's sacrifice. Wipe those eyes of thine. Be of good cheer. Be bold in heart. He calleth thee. There is room at his table. The door is open. There is room in his heart, he died for those who rest in him. If thou wishest for Christ, he wishes for thee. If thou longest to go to the feast, he wants guests as much as thou wantest the feast. Only trust thou him! God help thee to trust him by his Spirit, and thou shalt live.

III The last thing was to be this: to urge you to-night, before you leave this house—but my urging will be of no service unless God the Holy Spirit own it—TO URGE YOU TO PRAY THE PRAYER OF THE TEXT.

A desire is like seed in the bag, but prayer sows it in the furrow. A desire is like water in the bottle, but prayer drinks thereof. Now, I commend to you the prayer of my text—"Sir, give me this water." Begin, then, your prayer *by honouring Christ*. Do not call him "Sir," but call him "Lord." She gave him the highest title that her respect could accord. She did not know him in any other capacity, but she called him "Sir." Now, call Jesus "Lord," for thou wilt get no mercy if thou dishonourest Christ. Think thou of him as God's only Son suffering for sinners. Call him "Lord." Canst thou do that? If thou rejectest his divinity, thou dost shut thyself out of his kingdom. He must be owned as Lord and God as well as Saviour. "Oh!" sayest thou, "I have long age called him Lord, I know him to be divine; I rejoice in the thought of his eternal power and Godhead; I would honour him with all that I have." Well, then, thou hast well begun, but may grace make thee go further.

Now, in the next place, if thou wouldst pray this prayer aright, notice it, and *confess thine undeservingness*. It is not, "Sir, sell me this water," but, "Sir, *give* me this water." Confess that it is a gift. Thou shalt never have it otherwise. Away with thy merit-mongering. Away with thy trusting in thy prayers, and thy tears, and thy sense of need. Mercy must be given, or else thou shalt never have it. "Sir, *give* me, *give* me, *give* me this water. O Lord, give me grace, or else I die; give it me of thy free mercy, because thou hast promised to save the chief of sinners; give it me, Lord. I have done with boasting; I have done with the Pharisee's thanking thee that I am not as other men are; I come empty-handed; I come naked, poor, and miserable; give it me; I have nought to buy it with. Oh! give me, without money and without price, thy salvation." Friend, does your pride kick at this? Be wise, I pray thee, and bow thy neck to the yoke of grace.

Take care, too, that you make it *a personal prayer*—"Lord, give it *me*." Never mind your neighbours just now. Care for them when you are saved. Look after their salvation when your own is secure; but just now you have first to do with yourself. Your children? Ay, pray for them. Your relatives? Yes, consider them. But, meanwhile, now it is *yourself*, your own proper self that is concerned. Do not think of the whole congregation. Think now personally of your own soul, and say, "Lord, give *me* this water." I mean you, Mary, and you, Thomas, and you, John, let the prayer come from your own lips, as distinctly being from yourself. As you sit or stand now in this house, silently breathe the petition—"Lord, give thy grace to *me, even me*."

> "Pass me not, O gracious Father,
> Sinful though my heart may be;
> Thou might'st curse me, but the rather
> Let thy mercy light on me,
> Even me.
>
> Pass me not, O tender Saviour!
> Let me love and cling to thee;

> I am longing for thy favour;
> When thou comest, call for me,
> Even me."

Once more, I want you to offer this prayer *in the present tense*—not "Give me this water to-morrow;" but "To-night give it me; Lord, save my soul now." The worst of most of men is this: they would be saved, but it must be when they die. You would serve the devil all your life, and then cheat him of your soul at the last! Mean, miserable thought! If God be God, serve him, serve him now; and may the Lord have us in life, as we hope he may have us in our death. "Give me this water." But you are going out next Wednesday; that will be awkward! "Yes," said some young woman at a revival meeting, who was in much concern, "but I am going to a ball to-morrow;" and so everything good was put off for that; but she dropped down dead at the ball! God grant there may be no such cases of postponing here, lest we postpone ourselves into eternity, where there are no acts of pardon past. May we have Christ *now*. We may not live to see to-morrow's sun. Albeit that the sun is well-nigh gone down, yet the light of this evening may not have gone before our life may be ended. How near to death we stand, and yet we scarcely think of it! Right on the edge of our graves sometimes we are, and yet we sport and laugh as though we had a lease of life! You forget death, most of you. The cemetery is so far out of town, but still you should not quite forget, for the hearse goes to and fro with awful regularity, and the church-bell that tolls is not rusty, and those words, "Earth to earth, dust to dust, ashes to ashes," are still familiar to the ears of some of us. It will soon be your turn to die. You, too, must gather up your feet in the bed, and meet your father's God; God grant that you may then be found right with him. Little do I know for whom these sentences may have a special bearing; but they may have a bearing, dear friend, upon you. I see some of you dressed in black; you have had to go to the grave mourning because of others: that black will be worn by others soon for you, and the place that now knows you shall know you no more for ever. Oh! by the frailty of life, by the near approach of the Master, or by the certainty of death, I pray you see to it that you breathe the prayer, "Lord give me of thy grace." The Lord help you to pray it. Amen.

PORTION OF SCRIPTURE READ BEFORE SERMON—Revelation 7:9–17.[3]

---

[3] Spurgeon, C. H. (1867). The Water of Life. In *The Metropolitan Tabernacle Pulpit Sermons* (Vol. 13, pp. 505–516). London: Passmore & Alabaster.

SALVATION ALL OF GRACE

A Sermon

Delivered on Lord's Day Morning, August 4th, 1872, by

C. H. SPURGEON,

AT THE METROPOLITAN TABERNACLE, NEWINGTON.

"By grace are ye saved."—Ephesians 2:8.

OTHER Divine attributes are manifest in salvation. The wisdom of God devised the plan; the power of God executes in us the work of salvation; the immutability of God preserves and carries it on—in fact, all the attributes of God are magnified in the salvation of a sinner: but at the same time the text is most accurate, since grace is the fountain-head of salvation, and is most conspicuous throughout. Grace is to be seen in our election; for "there is a remnant according to the election of grace, and if by grace then it is no more of works." Grace is manifestly revealed in our redemption, for ye know therein the grace of our Lord Jesus Christ, and it is utterly inconceivable that any soul could have deserved to be redeemed with the precious blood of Christ. The mere thought is abhorrent to every holy mind. Our calling is also of grace, too, for "He hath saved us, and called us with an holy calling, not according to our works, but according to his own purpose and grace, which was given us in Christ Jesus before the world began." By grace also we are justified; for over and over again the apostle insists upon this grand and fundamental truth. We are not justified before God by works in any measure or in any degree, but by faith alone; and the apostle tells us "it is of faith, that it might be by grace." We see a golden thread of grace running through the whole of the Christian's history, from his election before all worlds, even to his admission to the heaven of rest. Grace, all along, "reigns through righteousness unto eternal life," and "where sin aboundeth, grace doth much more abound." There is no point in the history of a saved soul upon which you can put your finger and say, "In this instance he is saved by his own deservings." Every single blessing which we receive from God, comes to us by the channel of free favour, revealed to us in Christ Jesus our Lord. Boasting is excluded, because deservings are excluded. Merit is an unknown word in the Christian church; it is banished once for all; and our only shoutings over foundation or top stone are, "Grace, grace unto it!" Perhaps the apostle is the more earnest in insisting upon this truth here, and in many other places, because this is a point against which the human heart raises the greatest objection. Every man by nature fights against salvation by grace. Though we have nothing good in ourselves, we all think we have; though we have all broken the law, and have lost all claim upon divine regard, yet we are all proud enough to fancy that we are not quite so bad as others; that there are some mitigating circumstances in our offences, and that we can, in some measure, appeal to the justice as well as to the compassion of God. Hence the apostle puts it so strongly, "By grace are ye saved, through faith, and that not of yourselves, it is the gift of God; not of works, lest any man should boast."

The statement of the text means just this, that we all need saving—saving from our sins, and saving from the consequences of them; and that if we are saved it is not because of any works which we have already performed. Who among us, upon looking back at his past life, would dare to say that he deserves salvation? Neither are we saved on account of any works foreseen which are yet to be performed by us. We have made no bargain with God that we will give him so much service for so much mercy; neither has he made any covenant with us of this character; he has freely saved us, and if we serve him in the future, as we trust we shall, with all our heart and soul and strength, even then we shall have no room for glorying, because our works are wrought in us of the Lord. What have we even then which we have not received? We are saved, not because of any mitigating circumstances with regard to our transgressions, nor because we were excusable on account of our youth, or of our ignorance, or any other cause; we are not saved because there were some good points in our character, which ought not to be overlooked, or some hopeful indications of better things in the future. Ah, no; "By grace are ye saved." That clear and unqualified statement sweeps away all supposition of any deserving on our part, or any thought of deserving. It is not a case of a prisoner at the bar who pleads "not guilty," and who escapes because he is innocent; far from it, for we are guilty beyond all question. It is not even a case of a prisoner who pleads "guilty," but at the same time mentions certain circumstances which render his offence less heinous; far from it, for our offence is heinous to the last degree, and our sin deserves the utmost wrath of God. But ours is the case of a criminal confessing his guilt and owning that he deserves the punishment, offering no extenuation and making no apology, but casting himself upon the absolute mercy of the judge, desiring him for pity's sake to look upon his misery and spare him in compassion. As condemned criminals we stand before God when we come to him for mercy. We are not in a state of probation, as some say; our probation is over: we are already lost, "condemned already," and our only course is to cast ourselves upon the sovereign mercy of God in Christ Jesus; not uttering a syllable of claim, but simply saying, "Mercy, Lord, I crave, undeserved, mercy according to thy lovingkindness, and thy grace in Christ Jesus." "By grace are ye saved." This is true of every saint on earth and every saint in heaven, altogether true without a single sentence of qualification. No man is saved except as the result of the free favour and unbought mercy of God, not of deserving, not of debt, but entirely and altogether because the Lord "will have mercy on whom he will have mercy," and he wills to bestow his favour on the unworthy sons of men.

I. This simple truth we do not mean to work out this morning, doctrinally or controversially, but to use it for practical purposes, and the first is this—THIS GREAT DOCTRINE SHOULD INSPIRE EVERY SINNER WITH HOPE. If salvation be altogether of the free favour and grace of God, then—who among us dare despair? "Who in this place shall be so wicked as to sit down in sullenness and say, "It is impossible for me to be saved"?

For first, my brethren, if salvation be of mercy only, it is clear that *our sin is by no means an impediment to our salvation*. If it were of justice our transgression of the law would render our salvation utterly impossible; but if the Lord deals with us upon quite another footing, and says, "I will forgive them freely," that very promise presupposes sin. If the Lord speaks of mercy, that very word takes it for granted that we are guilty, or else there would be no room for mercy at all. The very statement that we are saved by grace implies that we are fit objects for grace; and who are fit objects for grace but the guilty, the wretched, the condemned. O sons of men, the law stops your mouths, and makes you silently own that you are guilty before God, but the gospel opens the mouth of the dumb by declaring that "Christ died for the ungodly," and that "he came into the world to save sinners." If mercy come into the field, sin is swallowed up in forgiveness, and unworthiness ceases to be a barrier for love. Is not this both clear and comforting?

Now, observe, that *this prevents the despair which might arise in any heart on account of some one especial sin.* I meet with many whose terror of conscience arises from one particular crime. Had they not committed that crimson sin, they consider that they might have been pardoned, but now they are in an evil case. "Surely," say they, "that sin, like an iron bolt, has fast closed the gates of heaven against me." And yet it cannot be so if salvation be of grace. Whatever the sin may be, its greatness will only serve to illustrate the great grace of God. Undeserved mercy can pardon one sin as well as another, if the soul confess it. If God acted on the rule of merit with us, then no sin would be pardonable under any circumstances; but when he deals with us in a way of grace he can pass by any offence for which we seek forgiveness. The great sinner is so much the fitter object for great mercy. He who hath but little sin, can, as it were, but draw forth little mercy from God to blot it out; but he who is guilty of some great, crowning, damning sin, he it is to whom the heights and depths of divine mercy may be displayed; and if I speak to such an one this morning I would look upon him with joyful eyes. Sorrowful as he is, I am thankful to have found out such an one. Thou art a rare platform on which my Lord's love may display itself, because thou knowest thyself to be so utterly lost a sinner. Thou art but a black foil to set forth the brilliant diamond of my Master's grace. Thy foulness shall but illustrate the virtue of his precious blood, and thy crimson sin, by yielding in a moment to the precious blood, shall only show how great is his power to save.

It is clear, too, that *if the sinner's despair should arise from the long continuance, multitude, and great aggravation of his sins, there is no ground for it.* For if salvation be of pure mercy only, why should not God forgive ten thousand sins as well as one? "Oh," sayest thou, "I see why he should not." Then thou seest more than is true; for once come to grace, you have done with bounds and limits. Know, moreover, that "his thoughts are not your thoughts. And as the heavens are higher than the earth so are his thoughts higher than your thoughts and his ways than your ways." To blot out ten thousand sins is with him no effort of grace, for "he is plenteous in mercy." He has been forgiving the sons of men ever since the first sinner crossed the threshold of Paradise, and he delights to do it; so that, guilty ones, I see in the multitude of your sins only so much the more room for the Lord to exercise his own delightful attribute of mercy. If he delights to blot out one sin, then he delights ten thousand times more to blot out ten thousand sins. If thou wilt look at it in that light, though thy transgressions may be as many as the hairs on thy head or as the sands on the sea shore, innumerable, thou needest not for a moment think thou art cast away from hope. The Lord's mercy is a sea which cannot be filled, though mountains of sin be cast into its midst; it is like Noah's flood, which covers all and drowns even the mountain-tops of heaven-defying sins. I wish to speak right home to the hearts of those who are in trouble and seeking mercy, and to them I say,—do you not see that if salvation be of grace alone, then *the depravity of thy nature does not shut thee up in despair?* What though thy nature be inclined to sin, and especially inclined to some sins; what if thou be naturally angry and passionate, or if thou be proud and covetous; what if thou be in thy natural disposition sceptical or lustful, yet from the grace of God hope flows even for thee. If the Lord were to deal with thee according to thy constitution and nature, then, indeed, it were a hopeless case with thee: but if he blesses thee, not because thou art good, but because thou needest to be blest; if he looks upon thee in mercy, not because thou art beautiful, but because thou art sick unto death, and defiled, and needest to be healed and cleansed; if it be thy misery and not thy merit which he considers, then thou art yet in the land of hope. However fallen thou mayest be, thou mayest yet be raised up. Why should not the Lord take the most depraved, and abandoned, and obstinate among us, and renew his nature and make of him a miracle of grace? Would it not magnify his mercy if he should make of such an one the opposite of what he now is, tender in heart, holy in spirit, devout in character, ardent in love, and fervent in prayer? He can do it. Glory be to his name, he can do it; and now that he deals with us in grace let us hope he will do it in the case of many.

Remember, too, that *any spiritual unfitness which may exist in a man should not shut him out from a hope, since God deals with us in mercy.* I hear you say, "I believe God can save me, but I am so impenitent." Yes, and I say it again, if thou wert to stand on terms of debt with God, thy hard heart would shut thee out of hope. How could he bless such a wretch as thou art, whose heart is a heart of stone? But if he deal with thee entirely upon another ground, namely, his mercy, why I think I hear him say, "Poor hard-hearted sinner, I will pity thee, and take away thy heart of stone, and give thee a heart of flesh." Dost thou say, "I cannot repent?" I know the criminality of that sad fact. It is a great sin not to be able to repent; but then the Lord will not look upon thee from the point of what thou oughtest to be, but he will consider what he can make thee, and he will give thee repentance. Has not his Son gone up to heaven, "exalted on high, to give repentance and remission of sins"? Do I hear thee confess that thou canst not believe? Now, the absence of faith from thee is a great evil, yea a horrible evil; but then the Lord is dealing with thee on terms of grace, and does not say, "I will not smite thee because thou dost not believe," but he saith, "I will give thee faith," for faith is "not of yourselves, it is the gift of God." He works our faith in us, and has pity upon us, and takes away the unbelieving heart, and gives the tender heart, the believing heart, in the presence of the cross of Christ. Oh, though I were black as the devil with past sin, and vile as the devil with innate depravity, yet, if the Lord's mercy looked upon me could he not forgive the past and change my nature, and make me, as bright a seraph as Gabriel before his throne? "Is anything too hard for the Lord?" O sinner, what a door of hope there ought to be open to thee in this truth, that salvation is altogether of grace.

For now, to sum up all in a word, there is no supposable circumstance or incident, or anything connected with any man, that can shut him out of hope if he seek forgiveness through the Saviour's blood. Whoever thou mayest be, and whatever thou mayest have done, grace can come and save thee. I say again, if thy character be the question at issue, thou art a lost man; if thy power to amend thy character be the hinge of the business, thou art a lost man; but if the grace that pardons and the power that amends both come from God, why shouldest thou be a lost man? Why should the harlot perish? Why should the thief perish? Why should the adulterer perish? Why should the murderer perish? "Let the wicked forsake his way, and the unrighteous man his thoughts, and let him turn unto the Lord, and he will have mercy upon him, and to our God for he will abundantly pardon." Ye have heaped up your sins, but God will heap up his mercies; ye have highly aggravated your transgressions; ye have sinned against light and knowledge; ye have done evil with both hands greedily; but, thus saith the Lord, "I have blotted out, as a thick cloud, thy transgressions, and, as a cloud, thy sins: return unto me; for I have redeemed thee." "Come now, and let us reason together, saith the Lord: though your sins be as scarlet, they shall be white as snow; though they be red like crimson, they shall be as wool."

Thus much upon the first statement, that this doctrine ought to give hope to the sinner.

II. Secondly, THIS DOCTRINE AFFORDS DIRECTION TO THE SINNER, as to how to act before his God in seeking mercy. Clearly, O soul, if salvation be of grace alone, it would be a very wrong course of action to plead that thou art not guilty, or to extenuate thy faults before God: that were to go upon the wrong tack altogether. If salvation be by thy merit, or by an absence of demerit, then thou wouldst be right enough to set up a good character as a plea, though I believe that in the trial thou wouldest mightily break down, for thou art as full of sin as an egg is of meat, and thy sin is as damnable as hell itself, and therefore it were vain for thee to plead innocence; but if thou couldest plead it, it is the wrong plea. If salvation be of grace, then go to the Lord and confess thy sin and transgression, and ask for grace. Do not for a moment attempt to show that thou hast no need of grace, for that were folly indeed.

What more foolish than for a beggar to plead that he is not in want? Do not shut the door of grace in thine own face. To say, "I am not guilty," is to say "I do not want mercy;" to say "I have not transgressed," is to say, "I do not need to be forgiven," and how better couldest thou commit spiritual suicide than by such pleading?

Neither, O sinner, hope to propitiate the Lord with gifts and sacrifices. If salvation be of grace, how durst thou think to buy it? If he saith he gives it freely, bring not with thee any bribe in thy hand; for in so doing thou wilt insult and anger him. Indeed, what couldest thou bring to him when Lebanon is not sufficient to burn, nor the beasts thereof for a burnt sacrifice? If thou couldest give him rivers of oil that should deluge a continent, or seas of sacrificial blood broad as the Pacific, yet couldest thou not for a moment render thyself acceptable with him. Try it not therefore. Venture on no ceremonies. Rest not in rituals. If salvation be of grace, accept it as a free gift, and bless the giver. Do not think to dress thyself in garments of outward religiousness, or to borrow virtue from a fellow-man who claims to be a priest; but since salvation is of free mercy, go and cast thyself on that free mercy. That is to act according to the dictates of prudence. Thy true course is this. Since God is willing to show his mercy, go and confess that thou needest that mercy. Aggravate thy sin in the confession, if thou canst. Instead of trying to make it appear white, try to see its unutterable blackness. Say that thou art without excuse, justly condemned, for thy transgressions. I warrant thee thou shalt never go beyond the truth in stating thy sin, for that were quite impossible. A man lying on the field of battle wounded, when the surgeon comes round, or the soldiers with the ambulance, does not say, "Oh, mine is a little wound," for he knows that then they would let him lie; but he cries out, "I have been bleeding here for hours, and am nearly dead with a terrible wound," for he thinks that then he will gain speedier relief; and when he gets into the hospital he does not say to the nurse, "Mine is a small affair; I shall soon get over it"; but he tells the truth to the surgeon in the hope that he may set the bone at once, and that double care may be taken. Ah, sinner, do thou so with God. The right way to plead is to plead thy misery, thine impotence, thy danger, thy sin. Lay bare thy wounds before the Lord, and as Hezekiah spread Sennacherib's letter before the Lord, spread thy sins before him with many a tear and many a cry, and say, "Lord, save me from all these; save me from these black and foul things, for thy infinite mercy's sake." Confess thy sin; wisdom dictates that thou shouldest do so, since salvation is of grace. And then yield thyself up to God; capitulate at discretion; make no terms with him, but say, "Here I stand before thee, O my Maker; I have offended thee; I yield to thee, because thou hast said thou wilt deal with me on terms of grace; behold I cast myself at thy feet; the weapons of my rebellion I cast from my hands for ever; I desire that thou wouldest take me and make me what thou wouldest have me to be; and seeing thou art a God of grace, I beseech thee to have pity upon me. Thou hast appointed a way of salvation by Jesus Christ, Oh, save me in that way, I entreat thee."

Now, mark, I want to dwell upon this next point,—because salvation is of grace it directs the guilty as to how to plead before God. When we are praying and pleading we sometimes feel we want a help to guide us in the pleading. Let this guide you. Take care that all your pleas with God are consistent with the fact that he saves by his grace. Never bring a legal plea, or a plea that is based upon self, for it will be an offence to God; whereas, if thine argument be based on grace, it will have a sweet savour to him. Let me teach thee, seeking sinner, for a moment how to pray. Let it be in this way. Plead with God thy miserable and undone condition; tell him thou art utterly lost if he do not save thee. Tell him thou art already lost, so that thou canst not help thyself hand or foot in this matter, if he do not come to thy rescue with the fulness of his power and love. Tell him that thou art afraid to die and to come before his righteous bar, for unless he save thee hell will be thy portion. Plead with him and ask him whether it will delight him that thou shouldest make thy bed in hell. Say to him, "Shall the dead praise thee? Shall the condemned set forth thy praise?" Show him the imminence of thy danger. He knows it, but let him see that thou knowest it, and this will be good pleading with his mercy. "Save me, O Lord, for if ever soul needed saving, if ever soul were in the jaws of destruction, I am that soul, therefore have pity upon me." Thus pour out your heart before him. Then humbly urge the suitableness of his mercy to you. "Lord, thou art merciful, thy mercy will find ample scope in me. Does thy grace seek out sin to purge it away? It is here, Lord; I teem with it; my heart swarms with evils. If thou art pitiful, here is a heart which bleeds and is ready to perish. Oh, if thou be indeed a physician, here is a sick soul that wants thee; if thou art ready to forgive, here are sins that need forgiving. Come to me, Lord, for thy mercy will find a grievousness of misery in me. Besides, is not thy mercy free. It is true I do not deserve it, but thou dost not give it to men because of their deserving, else were it no grace and mercy at all. Let thy free mercy light on me. Why shouldest thou pass me by? If I be the vilest of the sons of men thou wilt be the more gracious if thou dost look upon me. What though I have forgotten thee these many years and have even despised thy love, will it not be the greater mercy on thy part to turn and give thy free grace to me, even to me?" Then argue with him the plenteousness of his grace. Say to him, "Lord, thy mercy is very great, I know it is. 'According to the multitude of thy tender mercies, blot out my transgressions.' If thou wert a little God and thou hadst but little mercy, I should have but little hope in thee; but oh, thou art so great and glorious, thou can'st cast my transgressions behind thy back. By the greatness of thy compassion, then, look thou on me."

It is well also to return to the first plea and repeat it, saying, "Lord, because thou hast this great mercy and I need it, look on my impotence this day. I am so weak, I cannot come to thee unless thou come to me. Thou biddest me repent, but see how hard my heart is; thou commandest me to believe in Jesus, but my unbelief is very strong; thou tellest me to look to thy dear Son upon the cross, but I cannot see him for my tears, which blind these weary eyes. Master, come to the rescue, come and help thy servant, for thou art strong, though I be weak. Thou canst break my heart though I cannot break it, and thou canst open my poor bleared eyes, though I cannot as yet see as I would see the Saviour Jesus Christ. Oh! by thy power and mercy save a weak, dead sinner."

And then, if you feel as if you wanted some other plea, begin to plead his promises. Say:

> "Thou hast promised to forgive
> All who on thy Son believe;

Lord, I know thou canst not lie;
Give me Christ or else I die."

"Thou hast said that if the wicked forsake his way and turn unto thee he shall live. Lord, I turn to thee. Receive me. Thou hast said that all manner of sin and of blasphemy shall be forgiven unto men. Thou hast declared that the blood of Jesus Christ thy Son cleanseth from all sin. Go not back from thy word, O God. Since thou art dealing with men on terms of grace, keep thy promise and let thy rich, free mercy come to me."

I know what all this means by experience. I have gone over all these pleas by the week together, and pleaded with God that he would have mercy upon me. "This poor man cried, and the Lord heard him, and delivered him from all his fears." Therefore, bear I testimony unto you, O seeking souls, that this is the way to move his heart. Go upon the plan of grace, and plead his love. Not your deservings, but your undeservings; not your profession of what you hope to do, but your acknowledgment of your misery, will have power with him.

I have found it sweet work sometimes to plead with God his mercy in the gifts of Christ. Let me help thee, sinner, to do it, and may the Spirit help thee. Say thou unto God thus, "Lord, thou hast given thine only begotten Son to die; surely he need not have died for the righteous; he died for the guilty; I am such an one; Lord, wilt thou give thy Son for sinners, and then cast sinners away? Didst thou nail him to the cross only for a mockery, that we might come to that cross, and not find pity? O thou God of mercy, in the gift of thy Son thou hast done so much that thou canst not draw back; thou must save sinners, now that thou hast given Jesus to die for them."

Then plead with Jesus the compassion of his heart. Tell him that he said he would not break the bruised reed nor quench the smoking flax. Pluck him by the sleeve, and say, "Thou hast said 'Him that cometh unto me, I will in no wise cast out.' " Tell him that it was written of him, "This man receiveth sinners and eateth with them." Tell him that thou hast heard that "this is a faithful saying, and worthy of all acceptation, that Christ Jesus came into the world to save sinners;" and say to him, "Hast thou lost thy compassion, Saviour? Wilt thou not dart a glance of love on me, even me? Thou didst heal lepers, heal my leprosy. Thou didst permit the woman, whom thou didst call a dog, to come and receive blessings at thy hands; and although I be a dog, yet give the crumbs of thy mercy to me, even me." This is the style of plea that will win the day.

And then I would advise thee, if thou failest still in prayer, to go to God thus, and say to him, "Lord, thou hast sworn with an oath—'As I live, saith the Lord, I have no pleasure in the death of him that dieth, but had rather that he would turn to me and live.' I know that thou meanest this, my God; wilt thou take pleasure then in my death, and spurn me now that I turn to thee?" Tell him that he has saved other sinners like thyself. Remind him of thy wife, or child, or friend; tell him of Saul of Tarsus; tell him of the woman that was a sinner; tell him of Rabab; and say unto him, "Lord, dost thou not delight to save great, big, black sinners? and I am just such an one. Thou hast not changed. By all that thou hast done for others, I pray thee do the like for me." And then say to him again, "I thank thee, O God, that thou hast permitted me even to pray to thee; I bless thy grace that thou hast moved me to come to thee; and as thou hast given me grace to feel my sin in a measure, wilt thou leave me to perish after all? Oh, by the grace I have received in being spared so long, in being permitted to hear thy gospel, I beseech thee to give me more grace." Then throw yourself down before him, and if you perish, perish there. Go to the cross with such pleas as these, and resolve that if it can be that a sinner may die at the cross' foot, you will die there, but nowhere else. As the Lord my God liveth, before whom I stand, there shall never a soul perish that can cast itself upon the sovereign grace of God through Jesus Christ his Son.

III. Now, to turn away from that to a third point. A FULL CONVICTION OF THIS TRUTH WILL RECONCILE OUR HEARTS TO ALL DIVINE ORDINANCES WITH REGARD TO SALVATION. I feel in my own heart, and I think every believer here does, that if salvation be of grace, God must do as he wills with his own. None of us can say to him, "What doest thou?" If there were anything of debt, or justice, or obligation, in the matter, then we might begin to question God; but as there is none, and the thing is quite out of court as to law, and far away from rights and claims, as it is all God's free favour, we will henceforth stop our mouths and never question him. As to the persons whom he chooses to save, let him save whom he wills. His name shall be had in honour for ever, let his choice be what it may. As to the instrument by whom he saves, let him save by the coarsest speaker, or by the most eloquent; let him do what seemeth him good. If he will save by the Bible, without ministers, we will be glad to hold our tongues; and if he will save souls by one of our brethren, and not by us, we will grieve to think that we are so little fitted for his service; but still, if after doing all we can, he uses another more than us, we will say, "Blessed be his name." We will not envy our brethren. The Lord shall distribute his grace by what hands he pleases. Send, Lord, by whomsoever thou wilt send.

And here I come to the sinner again: with the two great gospel commands we will raise no dispute. Hath he said, "He that believeth and is baptised shall be saved"? We will never raise a question against either the believing or the baptism. If the Lord chooses to say, "I will save those who trust in Christ," it is both so natural a thing that he should claim our faith, and so gracious a thing that he should give us the faith he claims of us, that we cannot question it. And even if it were not so, he has a right to make what rules he pleases. If God permits entrance only by one door, let us enter by it and raise no contention. The Lord bids thee trust in Jesus; say not in thy heart, "I would rather do or feel some wonderful matter." If he had bidden thee do some great thing wouldst thou not have done it? How much rather now that he saith to thee, simply trust in Jesus and be saved. I know if I were authorised to preach this morning that every man who would sail round the world should be saved, you would begin saving your money to make the great excursion; but when the gospel comes to you there in those very pews and aisles, and bids you now turn your eyes to the crucified Saviour and only look to him, I know if you have not learned the truth, that salvation is of grace, you will kick at that divine command; but if you know it is of grace, and only grace, you will say, "Sweet is the command of God; Lord, enable me now to trust myself with thy dear Son."

And, then, you will not quarrel with the ordinance of baptism either. I know it is very natural that you should say, "What is there in it?" I also would say, what is there in it? What can there be in a mere washing in water? If you thought there were any salvation by it meritoriously, you would have missed the track altogether; but the Lord hath put it, that "he that believeth and is baptised, shall be saved," and therefore you obey. I do not attempt to justify my Lord for so commanding, for he needs no defence from me, but if he so chooses to put it, the true heart will yield a prompt obedience to his will. If it were of merit, I could see no merit in baptism or in the believing, for surely it cannot be meritorious to believe what is true, or to have one's body washed with pure water. But salvation is of grace; and if the Lord chooses to put it so, let him put it as he wills. I am such a sinner, I will take his mercy, let him present it in what way he pleases.

As to the manner in which the Lord may be pleased to reveal himself to any one of us, I am sure that if we know that salvation is of grace, we shall never quarrel about that any more. To some of us, the Lord revealed himself on a sudden. We know when we were converted to a day. I know the place to a yard. But many others do not. The day breaks on them gradually; first twilight, then a brighter light, and afterwards comes the noon. Do not let us quarrel about that. So long as I get a Saviour, I do not mind how I get him; so long as he blots out my sins, I will not cavil about the way in which he manifests his love to me. If it be of grace, that silences everything; Jew and Gentile shut their mouths without a murmuring word, and all together sit, down at the foot of the cross, no more to question, but reverently to adore.

IV. I pass over this point rapidly, for time flies. I fain would clip his wings. But I must needs introduce to you the next fact,—that the doctrine that salvation is of grace furnishes to those who receive it A MOST POWERFUL MOTIVE FOR FUTURE HOLINESS.

A man who feels that he is saved by grace says, "Did God of his free favour blot out my sins? Then, oh, how I love him. Was it nothing but his love that saved an undeserving wretch? Then my soul is knit to him for ever," Great sin becomes in such a case no barrier to great holiness, but rather a motive for it; for he who has had much forgiven loves much, and loving much he begins at once to be in earnest in the service of him whom he loves. I put it to thee, sinner, if the Lord this morning were to appear to thee and say, "All thy sins have been blotted out," wouldst thou not love him? Ay, methinks a dog would love such a Master as that. Wouldst thou not love him? Ay, I know thou wouldst. I know you proud, self-righteous people, would not; but you real sinners, if pardon were to come to you, would you not love God with all your hearts? Assuredly you would, and then your soul would begin to burn with a desire to honour him. You would want to tell the next person you met—"The Lord has had mercy upon me; wonder of wonders, he has had mercy upon me." And then you would desire to put away everything that would displease him. Away ye sins, away ye sins; how can I defile myself with you again? And then you would desire to practise all his will, and say, "For the love I bear his name no duty shall be too difficult, no command too severe." There are none that love God like those who are saved by grace. The man who thinks to save himself by works does not love God at all; he loves himself; he is a servant working for wages, and that is the kind of servant who would turn to another master tomorrow if he could get better paid, and if the wages do not suit him he will strike. The old-fashioned servants were the best servants in the world, for they loved their masters, and if paid no wages at all would have stuck to the family for love's sake. Such are the servants of God who are saved by his grace. "Why," say they, "he has already pardoned me and saved me, and therefore my ear is bored and fastened to the door of his house to be his servant for ever; and my glory is, 'I am thy servant, I am thy servant, and the son of thy handmaid, thou hast loosed my bonds.'" Such a man feels that he must perfect holiness in the fear of the Lord. He will not stop short with a measure of grace; he wants immeasurable grace. He will not say, "There are some sins in me which I cannot overcome;" but by God's grace he will seek to drive out all the Amalekites. He will not say, "Up to this point I am commanded to go, but beyond that I have a licence to say, "That is my besetting sin; I cannot get rid of it." No, but loving God with all his heart he will hate sin with all his heart, and war with sin with all his might, and will never put sword in scabbard till he is perfected in the image of Christ. The Lord fires us with such ardent love as this, and I know no way by which to get it except by coming to him on terms of grace, confessing sin, receiving mercy, feeling love kindle in the heart in consequence, and thus the whole soul becomes consecrated to the Lord.

V. Lastly, I would I could handle my text as I desire and as it handles me; but the truth of my text will be A TEST FOR THIS CONGREGATION.

The way you treat this text shall well reveal what you are. It will be either a stone of stumbling to you this morning, or else a foundation stone on which you build. Is it a stone of stumbling? Did I hear you murmur, "Why, the man does not hold up morality and good works; he preaches salvation for the guilty and the vile: I do not want such a religion"? Alas! thou hast stumbled at this stumbling stone, and shalt be broken upon it. Thou shalt perish, for thou dost insult thy God by thinking thyself wiser than his word, and by fancying that thy righteousness is purer than the righteousness of Christ. Thou dost imagine thou canst force thy way to heaven by a road that is most effectually blocked up; thou dost despise the path which the Lord has opened. Beware of self-righteousness. The black devil of licentiousness destroys his hundreds, but the white devil of self-righteousness destroys his thousands. But dost thou accept this text as a foundation stone? Dost thou say, "I need grace indeed for I am guilty;" then come and take all the blessings of the covenant, for they are thine. "He hath put down the mighty from their seat, and he hath exalted them of low degree. He hath filled the hungry with good things, but the rich he hath sent empty away." Art thou guilty? Come and trust thy Saviour. Art thou empty? Come and be filled out of the fulness which is treasured up in Christ Jesus. Believe in Jesus now, for one act of faith sets thee free from all sin. Do not tarry for a moment, nor raise questions with thy God. Believe him capable of infinite mercy, and through Jesus Christ rest thou in him. If thou be the worst soul in the world to thine own apprehension, and the one odd man that would be left out of every catalogue of grace, now write not such things against thyself; or even if thou do, come and cast thyself upon thy God. He cannot reject thee; or if he should, thou wouldst be the first that ever trusted in him and was confounded. Come and try. Oh! that his Spirit may bring thee to Jesus at this very moment, and that in heaven there may be joy in the presence of the angels of God because a soul has confided in the grace of God and found immediate pardon, instantaneous salvation, through the precious blood of Christ. The Lord bless every one of you.

Oh, how I would like that every soul here should be washed in the blood of Christ this morning. Would God that every one of you were robed in the righteousness of Christ this day, and prepared to enter into his rest. Pray for it, Christian brethren and sisters. Why should we not have it? Why, this congregation, great as it may seem comparatively, is very little to God. Why should there be one left out? Let your prayers encircle the whole house and bear the entire audience up to God, and lay it before him and say, "By thy mercy and by thy loving-kindness, save all this gathered company, for Christ's sake." Amen.

PORTION OF SCRIPTURE READ BEFORE SERMON.—Romans 10.[4]

[4] Spurgeon, C. H. (1872). Salvation All of Grace. In *The Metropolitan Tabernacle Pulpit Sermons* (Vol. 18, pp. 433–444). London: Passmore & Alabaster.

LESSONS ON DIVINE GRACE

A Sermon

INTENDED FOR READING ON LORD'S-DAY, MAY 31ST, 1903,

DELIVERED BY

C. H. SPURGEON,

AT THE METROPOLITAN TABERNACLE, NEWINGTON

On a Lord's-day Evening, in the summer of 1861.

"But by the grace of God I am what I am."—1 Cor. 15:10.

THIS confession, suitable in the lips of Paul, is equally appropriate in the mouth of each one of us who have known and proved the grace of God. We must consider Paul, according to his own account of himself, as being "not meet to be called an apostle,"—though "not a whit behind the very chiefest apostles,"—because he had persecuted the Church of God. In respect of personal merit, he knew that he did not deserve to be accounted of at all; yet, when the sole ground of approbation was not the service he had rendered to his Sovereign, but the favour which his Sovereign had bestowed upon him, he could say, "By the grace of God I am what I am." Take the meanest lamb in Jesu's fold, the feeblest heir of grace, the most timid and fearing, the most hopeless and helpless of all disciples, the man most devoid of talent, the man who stands the very lowest on the list of the saints of God, surely he may and must say that "by the grace of God" he is what he is, so far as he is in Christ, a believer, with all the privileges that believers have a gracious right to claim. Let this be thy comfort, thou little one, that the same grace that made an apostle of Paul has made a Christian of thee. The selfsame power that hath quickened the mightiest man in the army of the Lord of hosts hath quickened thee also; the grace that saves the greatest saves the least. If the largest and brightest gem in the crown of Christ reflects his grace, and glorifies his love, even so shalt thou though thou be as the smallest pearl that shall be set in his glorious diadem of honour.

Then, next, take the apostle Paul in the other way, as he describes himself in our text. In the preceding verse, he says he is the least of the apostles, yet he also says, "I laboured more abundantly than they all." It is equally true, whether you put him in the meanest place among converts, or in the very forefront of the army of faithful soldiers of Christ,—among the feeblest of pensioners or the most zealous of all the labourers in the vineyard of the Master,—the acknowledgment must be made, "By the grace of God I am what I am." Be our attainments never so eminent, our knowledge never so extensive, our usefulness never so great, yet still we stand, in the sight of God, on the same footing as the very meanest member of the Church of Christ. The song, which begins among the little and the timid, gathers strength among the great and the brave. It is not altered in the slightest degree; the language is the same, the strain the same, the song the same, "By the grace of God," we all of us must say, "we are what we are."

I am going to speak of my text, first, *doctrinally;* secondly, *experimentally;* and, thirdly, *practically.*

I. First, DOCTRINALLY. Each one of us, who is a believer in the Lord Jesus Christ, can take this sentence as his creed, and say, "By the grace of God I am what I am."

That is to say, first, I am not what I am *as the result of something good which God foresaw would be in me.* God has not vouchsafed his love, his favour, his mercy, to me because he foresaw that I should repent of my sin, and trust in his dear Son. No, there is a deeper cause for his love than anything that could be found in me. Indeed, there is nothing that could be found in me, that is lovely in his sight, but it would be proved, immediately, that he had, first of all, freely given that lovely thing to me, or himself created it within me. If I am a child of God, an heir of heaven, the well-spring of God's love to me is in his own sovereign grace. Nothing in my disposition or character could move his heart to me. His heart must have moved spontaneously; it must have welled up, because of its own deep love; and it must have flowed towards me, in its own divine channel, simply because God in his sovereignty would have it so. "By the grace of God," I am elected unto eternal life.

> "Grace first inscribed my name,
> In God's eternal book."

'Twas grace which set me apart, in distinguishing love, before the stars were made; 'twas grace that separated me from the mass of mankind; 'twas grace that laid hold of me while I was but as a pebble in the brook, and ordained that I should be a bright diamond in Christ's crown. It was God who, in the beginning, by his own grace, decreed that I should be what I am; and, therefore, to begin there, we take this as our creed, "By the grace of God,"—as manifested in eternity, and by that alone,—have I been caused to be "what I am."

Then, next, my text also means, I am not what I am *as the result of any creature strength, or any means of my own*. I am not what I am because I chose to be what I am; for if I had been what I chose to be, I should still have been "dead in trespasses and sins." If I had followed my poor, blind free-will, it would have been, to this day, leading me to hell; but it would never have led me to heaven. If I had made it my guide, I should have wandered further, and further, and further away from God. With my back to the Saviour, I should never have moved towards God. It is the same with all of us; if there is anything good in any of us, we must confess that God himself put it there. He taught our souls to pray. He made us feel our need of grace. He stripped us of our boastful pride. He delivered us from our refuges of lies. He levelled the legality of our hearts by bringing us low with labour, exhausting all our strength. 'Twas he who cast the first ray of hope into our soul. He opened our blind eyes to see the beauty of Christ. He gave us the first glimmering of faith; he enabled us to see that our sins were washed away by the precious blood of Jesus; and he has kept us alive unto this day, and will not let us go.

We will maintain this truth against all comers, that saints are what they are "by the grace of God," and not by their own free-will. I have sometimes heard men preach doctrines contrary to this. They have said that men are what they are as the result of the improvement of universal grace, and that the distinction which is apparent in them is made by themselves; God gave them a grace which they were to use,—not a grace which operated upon them, but a grace which they operated upon. According to that teaching, grace is given to men as a tool with which they are to work, not as a seal which God sets upon a man; grace is subservient to him, but he is not subservient to grace. Yet I must say that, although I have heard such doctrine as that preached from the pulpit, I have never known it to be practically received in the heart of a child of God. When you come to the point, and ask a true believer, "Why are you now a child of God, and an heir of heaven?" he tells you, once for all, "God made the difference." He will, perhaps, tell you that men can do much towards their own conversion, but he will deny that he has done anything towards his own; he will loyally put the crown on the head of Christ, even though—being beclouded in his understanding,—he may have talked as if he denied the truth. But, brethren, what we hold is the doctrine of the effectual working of God in the hearts of his chosen ones, as the Lord said to Zerubbabel, "Not by might, nor by power, but by my Spirit, saith the Lord of hosts;" and as Paul wrote to the Ephesians, "according to the working of his mighty power, which he wrought in Christ, when he raised him from the dead, and set him at his own right hand in the heavenly places."

Now let us look at our text in another aspect. *Some suppose that, even if divine grace begins the work, we must at least carry it on.* It cannot be denied that the living child of God has power, but it must not be forgotten that the power of the living child of God is not in himself, but in his Heavenly Father. For it is as true of him as of any sinner "dead in trespasses and sins" that, without Christ, he can do nothing. The living child of God is still as powerless as the dead sinner apart from the constant indwelling of the Holy Spirit, and the constant inflowing of the divine life into his soul. "By the grace of God" we not only are what we are, but we also remain what we are. We should long ago have ruined ourselves, and damned ourselves, if Christ had not kept us by his almighty grace. There has not been one hour in our whole Christian experience in which we have preserved ourselves; we cannot look back to any stage in our history, and say, "Here I wrought mighty marvels by my own unaided power." We dare not say, when we have been made to stand on our high places, that we stood there by our own wisdom; nor can we say, when we have run without weariness, that we did it in our own strength. Nay, beloved, whenever we discover our own strength in our pilgrimage, it is in going backward, and in tumbling down, but never in going forward, or in mounting upward. With the psalmist, we have to say to the Lord, "All my springs are in thee;" and, as all the springs are in the Lord, so are all the streams as well. As for myself, I must continually sing,—

> "Oh, to grace how great a debtor
> Daily I'm constrained to be!"

Not only am I debtor to grace once for all, but each day adds to the debt, and each hour the bulk of my obligation grows. I must still say, "By the grace of God I am what I am." Some of you could say this twenty years ago, but you can say it with even greater emphasis now; and when you get grey-headed, and totter down to Jordan's brink, you will not be able to say, "By my own goodness I am what I am." Even there must you give all the glory to that grace which, having been the Alpha, will also be the Omega,—which, having been the beginning, will also be the end.

So, doctrinally, I state the truth of my text thus, "By the grace of God I am what I am." I am elect;—my election is of grace. I am redeemed;—redemption is a mighty masterpiece of grace. I am called,—called by grace. I am preserved,—preserved by grace; and whatever there is in me that is commendable and virtuous,—whatever there is in me which the Son of God can admire, and which gives to my own soul real comfort,—must be all of grace, and of grace alone. I have spoken so much in the first person because the text is in the first person. Will every one of you also speak in the first person, and say in your heart, "By the grace of God I am what I am," endorsing the text from your own experience, setting your seal to this part of God's Word, and declaring it to be true, and going forth with this motto emblazoned on your banner as the doctrine which you will hear, and which, if you are called to the ministry, you will preach, "By the grace of God I am what I am"?

II. Now, in the second place, I am going to take the text EXPERIMENTALLY.

By this I mean that there are times, in our experience, when this truth starts up in letters of light, and we recognize it as an indisputable fact, not only taught to us as a Scriptural doctrine, but proved to us by our own personal experience. Let me just narrate a few instances.

Brethren and sisters, have you ever had times *when the fountains of the great deep of your depravity have been broken up?* Have you ever been taken into the chambers of imagery, and has the Spirit of God there said to you, "Son of man, I will show you greater abominations than these;" and has he taken you first into one room, and then into another, and made you stand aghast while he has shown you the idols of your heart, the deep depravity that still remaineth in you, the pride, and sloth, and various forms of sin which still lurk and find shelter there? Have you ever had the filthy rags unrolled before your eyes? Have you heard the chattering of the unclean birds in the cage of your heart? Have you ever been fully conscious of the stench arising from your Old Adam nature? Has your spirit sickened at the very thought of the depravity of manhood in general, and of yourself in particular? Have you ever had your secret sins set in the light of God's countenance? Have you ever been made to see the blackness of your own sin side by side with the brightness of divine favour? Have you ever been made to taste the exceeding bitterness of your sin even at the communion table,—even while you realized the preciousness of the blood of Christ, and renewed your former fellowship with him? If so, then I know that my text has been true to you, as it has been also to me, and that you have said, as I have often been compelled to say, "By the grace of God I am what I am." You have looked at your heart, and you have seen its barren soil; and if there has been any wheat growing upon it, you have said, "This is the result of the grace of God." You have looked at the huge black rock of your Old Adam nature, and when you have seen rivers of living water flowing out of the very midst of it, you have been obliged to say, "This mighty miracle could only have been wrought by the grace of God." Flimsy views of human depravity lead to very indistinct ideas of the grace of God. There is nothing but deep sub-soil ploughing that ever makes a man sound in the doctrines of grace; and I will defy any man, who has had a deep experience of his own odious depravity, to believe any other doctrines but the doctrines of grace, which are commonly called Calvinism. Nay, more than that, the mind, unless it be most graciously taught by the Spirit of God, will be apt to go beyond the true Scriptural doctrine, and to push the term beyond its legitimate sphere.

There have been other occasions on which you and I have been forced to cry, "By the grace of God I am what I am;" namely, *after some strong and terrible temptation.* Have you never known what it is to feel some old lust, which you thought was dead, suddenly come upon you with a whirlwind power, and drive you before it, like a sere leaf of the forest, that could not resist its might? I have, sometimes, had this trying experience. When quietly meditating upon the things of God, some fierce and fearful impulse to sin has assailed me, as if a giant had seized me by the neck, and pushed me onward until, at last, I came to the very brink of some awful iniquity, and looked down upon it; and, just as it seemed as if I must plunge into it, my eyes have been opened, and I have seen the horror of great darkness, and I have exclaimed, "O God! how is it that I have not committed that sin? How is it that thou hast come to save me just in the nick of time, and stretched out thy hand to rescue me just when 'my feet were almost gone,'—when 'my steps had well-nigh slipped'?" Not only had I thought of slipping, but "my steps had well-nigh slipped. Then, thy mercy, O God, held me up!" I do not know whether you have had strong impulses of that kind; many of God's people have, and especially those who, before conversion, plunged deeply into sin. You have sometimes had almost on your lips the oath which you have hated in your inmost heart; iniquity has come before you in a fascinating guise, and although you abhorred it, yet, for the moment, a strange hallucination of dazzling bewitchery seemed to lay hold of your spirit, and if you had yielded to it, you would have been like Samson when he fell into the hands of the Philistines. So it is that we are often compelled to say, as we look back upon marvellous providences and divine interpositions, "Truly, by the grace of God we are what we are, and by that grace alone have we been preserved from falling into sin."

I think, too, that this truth has often been brought home to us *when we have witnessed the fall of others*. You have, perhaps, walked to and from the house of God with some notable professor of religion, and he has instructed you on many points. He seemed to be a man of deep experience and devout life. Your heart has been knit to him, and you have said, "Here is a brother indeed;" and you have, possibly, envied him his great attainments and his fluent speech. Then, on a sudden, you heard that he had fallen into some terrible sin; you made enquiries, and you found that it was only too true. You were present, one night, at the church-meeting, when the solemn sentence of excommunication was pronounced upon him; and while the minister uttered it, all the members wept, and prayed that the poor fallen one might be brought to repentance, and that his soul might not be the prey of Satan. At such a time as that, you have said, "By the grace of God I am what I am," and you have said, with good John Newton,—

> "When any turn from Zion's way,
>   (Alas, what numbers do!)
> Methinks I hear my Saviour say,
>   'Wilt thou forsake me too?'

> "Ah, Lord! with such a heart as mine,
>   Unless thou hold me fast,
> I feel I must, I shall decline,
>   And prove like them at last."

Such instances may act as beacons to warn us of pride, and to teach us again the lesson that by the grace of God we are what we are.

Then, brethren, I think there are other seasons when we learn this lesson; that is, *in times of great dulness in spiritual matters*. Heavenly trade is not always brisk, even in the best market, that is, in the breast of the believer. Spiritual mariners do not find that the wind always blows; and thus, though we should always have our sails up, (which, alas! is not always the case with us,) even then the wind would not always blow, for it "bloweth where it listeth." Like the sea, we have our ebb as well as our flood-tide. Do you not know what it is to go to the throne of grace, when—as for words, you can find plenty of them; but as for heart, and soul, and vigour in prayer,—if your salvation depended upon your fervency, you must perish? Have you not gone to the mercy-seat, and groaned there—and groaned most of all because you could not groan as you ought? You have taken your wants to the throne of grace, but you have had to bring them away again. You have gone up to the house of God; and though you could find no fault with the sermon, there was, somehow or other, nothing in it for you. You went home to read your Bible; and though you knew that it was a precious book, it did not seem precious to you. It might be like a honeycomb, but you could not get any of the honey out of it. You had lost all spiritual appetite, and you felt as if you were drawing near to the gates of death. You remember, too, how you then sought the society of the godly, yet you received no consolation from them. Heavenly things seemed to be but dreams, the substantial things of eternity did not affect your spirit as they should have done; and you could only cry, with the psalmist, "My soul cleaveth unto the dust: quicken thou me according to thy word." And at such times, and especially if your prayer has been graciously heard, you have been compelled to say, "It is my natural state to be cold and dull; and if, at any time, I run swiftly in the heavenly race,—if my sails are filled, and my bark is wafted towards paradise,—surely this is by the grace of God."

Just one more remark upon this point. *Times of great mercy* often operate upon some of us so as to bring us very low, and to make us feel, "By the grace of God we are what we are." Simon Peter had this experience. When his boat was full of fish, so that it began to sink, he fell on his knees before his Master, and said, "Depart from me, for I am a sinful man, O Lord." The greatness of God's mercy to him convinced him of his own undeservedness; and it has been the same with some of us. The more the glory of God's grace has been revealed to our souls, the humbler have we been made to lie at his feet. When the Lord has piled up his mercies till they were like the great mountains, and his faithfulness has been like the bottomless depths, then have we been obliged to say, "These great things are indeed of God, they could not have come of man." At such times, we have felt that we could sit before the Lord, as David did, and say, "Who am I, O Lord God? and what is my house, that thou hast brought me hitherto?" God sometimes overwhelms his children with mercy quite as completely as he ever does with affliction. Pride may be overcome in two ways. It is sometimes overcome by trouble that crushes a man; but, at other times, the same result is produced by almighty grace, which, in overwhelming waves of love, rushes in upon the man's spirit, till, submerged in love and mercy, he can only resign himself to its depths, and feel—yet ever feel that he cannot feel enough—the wonders of God's grace, and his own littleness in comparison with God's amazing favour. God sometimes humbles his children by putting them in the dark, but he sometimes does it in another way, as David said, "When I consider thy heavens, the work of thy fingers, the moon and the stars which thou hast ordained; what is man, that thou art mindful of him? and the son of man, that thou visitest him?" How often have we also had to say, with David, "How precious also are thy thoughts unto me, O God! how great is the sum of them!" So I hope it will be with each one of us, that the greatness of God's mercy to us, as a church, and as individuals, will lead us to say, "By the grace of God we are what we are."

III. Now, in closing, let us consider our subject PRACTICALLY. What is the practical use of this text, "By the grace of God I am what I am."

Surely, as I have already reminded you, it is designed *to keep us humble*. Depend upon it, if we do not take this text for our motto every day, there is the rod of the covenant ready for us. He will soon be in a storm who does not see God's grace in the sunshine. If his mercies surround us, and our days roll happily along, but we begin to ascribe our greatness and our riches to ourselves, it will not be long before God will bring us down. It may be so in your experience, especially if you soar upon the wings of self-confidence. As surely as you begin to get strong in your own strength, there is an hour of weakness close at hand. Whenever you are full of self, it will not be long before you learn your own emptiness; for he who begins to grow rich in himself is next door to poverty; nay, he is already clothed in rags. No, my brethren, there is no safe walking unless we make this the staff on which we lean, "By the grace of God we are what we are." While we stick to this as our hourly, daily, weekly, monthly, yearly, everlasting motto, we shall not go astray, nor shall we experience those terrible down-castings which are the inevitable result of our up-flyings in self-confidence. Come then, beloved, from this day let us learn humility, let us tread our pride in the dust, and say, "Why should we be proud? By the grace of God we are what we are."

Then, in the light of our text, *let us learn charity*. Why should I be harsh towards those who are not what I am? I wish that some persons, who think themselves very sound in doctrine, would recollect our text. If another brother is thought to be unsound, they are ready to cut him in pieces; it would be better if they were to say, before using their sword for such a purpose, "By the grace of God we are what we are." Though you should be never so sound and right yourselves, be gentle with the brother who has not received so much grace as you have. Good John Newton used to say that, for a Calvinist to be proud, was the most inconsistent thing in the world; because, by his own profession, there were truths which no man could receive or understand of himself; so, why should he boast of his own attainments, and why should he blame others for not doing what he knows they cannot do of themselves? If our brethren cannot see as well as we can, why should we be angry with them because our eyes are better than theirs? I see no reason for being angry with a blind man because he cannot see; that is the very reason why we should pity his infirmity. So, let us seek to relieve those who are burdened, to bring back those who have wandered, to strengthen the weak hands, and confirm the feeble knees, and, to the best of our power, to lead others into that glorious light in which we ourselves are walking, for by the grace of God we are what we are.

Moreover, this should teach us *hopefulness concerning other men*. There is a drunken man; you think he can never be converted, but why not? The grace that saved you is sufficient to save him. You sometimes meet with an infidel; perhaps you have one in your family,—a father, or brother, or sister,—and you are apt to say, "Well, it is no use trying to get such an one to go to the house of God; all he would do would be to mock and jeer. If the minister should make a mistake, he would seize upon it, and use it as his stock-in-trade for the abuse of a week. If there be a fault among God's children, he is sure to notice it, and to make it the theme of his reproach, so he had better be kept away from them." But again I say, the grace that saved you is sufficient to save him; never give anyone up, even as God did not give you up. I always think that, as God has converted me by his grace, he can convert anybody; the conversion of any other sinner is not any more difficult to omnipotence, neither is it any easier, for omnipotence knows nothing of degrees. What marvellous things Christ has done, and done in some of us, too! Some of you must weep over that verse in which the apostle says. "And such were some of you, but ye are washed;" and you say, "Yes, and to God be all the glory that he hath made us what we are." Therefore, let us continue to look after those whom Satan has ensnared, even the most hard-hearted sinners, and seek to bring them under the saving influence of the grace of God.

Then, lastly, if we are what we are "by the grace of God," this should *teach us greater thankfulness*. Children of the Heavenly King, never forget to praise your God. We sometimes fail in this duty. We have had many meetings for prayer, to ask God to bless us in our manifold labours; now let us have some meetings for praise, to bless the Lord for his great goodness to us. I have heard that, in some parts of New England, there used to be a day of fasting every month, to mourn for the iniquity of the land, and so on; and, at last, some senator proposed that they should have a feast, and thank God for the mercies which they had received; and, truly, he was in the right. It is not good always to be fasting, we must feast sometimes. An old Puritan says that we take in breath by prayer,—by a sort of heavenly inspiration,—and that we breathe it out again by praise. Dear brethren and sisters, if you and I were to sing as heartily as we ought to sing, what a joyous song of praise there would be! If our voices could but be tuned to the deservings of God, what songs and sonnets would make glad this wilderness! You remember Ralph Erskine's sonnet on the battle in heaven,—the great contention of the bards in paradise. He pictures them all contending as to who should have the lowest place, and which should most loudly praise the Lord. There were the babes snatched from their mothers' breasts; they claimed the lowest place because they had gone straight to heaven without any trials or troubles. But the grey-headed men, who had been divinely supported under the afflictions of many years, said that they owed the most to sovereign grace. Then came those who had been converted in their early years, and who said that they had already had a heaven below, so they could sing the loudest of all. Then came the penitent thief, who said that he had the greatest cause to praise the Lord for he had been converted at the last. While some declared that they must praise God most because they had been the blackest sinners, others said that they would praise him most for the restraining grace which had kept them from sin; and so the strife went on until they agreed, each one, to sing with all his might to the praise of that everlasting love which inscribed their names in the Lamb's book of life, that great love which bought them with Jesu's precious blood, and that omnipotent love which attended them all their journey through, and landed them at last in heaven.[5]

---

[5] Spurgeon, C. H. (1903). Lessons on Divine Grace. In *The Metropolitan Tabernacle Pulpit Sermons* (Vol. 49, pp. 253–262). London: Passmore & Alabaster.

LAW AND GRACE

A Sermon

Delivered on Sabbath Morning, August 26, 1855, by the

REV. C. H. SPURGEON,

AT NEW PARK STREET CHAPEL, SOUTHWARK.

"Moreover the law entered, that the offence might abound. But where sin abounded, grace did much more abound."—Romans 5:20.

THERE is no point upon which men make greater mistakes than upon the relation which exists between the law and the gospel. Some men put the law instead of the gospel: others put the gospel instead of the law; some modify the law and the gospel, and preach neither law nor gospel: and others entirely abrogate the law, by bringing in the gospel. Many there are who think that the law is the gospel, and who teach that men by good works of benevolence, honesty, righteousness, and sobriety, may be saved. Such men do err. On the other hand, many teach that the gospel is a law; that it has certain commands in it, by obedience to which, men are meritoriously saved; such men err from the truth, and understand it not. A certain class maintain that the law and the gospel are mixed, and that partly by observance of the law, and partly by God's grace, men are saved. These men understand not the truth, and are false teachers. This morning I shall attempt—God helping me to show you what is the design of the law, and then what is the end of the gospel. The coming of the law is explained in regard to its objects: "Moreover the law entered, that the offence might abound." Then comes the mission of the gospel: "But where sin abounded, grace did much more abound."

I shall consider this text in two senses this morning." First, *as it respects the world at large and the entrance of the law into it*; and then afterwards, *as respecting the heart of the convinced sinner, and the entrance of the law into the conscience.*

I. First, we shall speak of the text as CONCERNING THE WORLD. The object of God in sending the law into the world was "that the offence might abound." But then comes the gospel, for "where sin abounded, grace did much more abound." First, then, in reference to the entire world. *God sent the law into the world "that the offence might abound."* There was sin in the world long before God sent the law. God gave his law that the offence might be seen to be an offence; ay, and that the offence might abound exceedingly more than it could have done without its coming. There was sin long before Sinai smoked; long ere the mountain trembled beneath the weight of Deity, and the dread trumpet sounded exceeding loud and long, there had been transgression. And where that law has never been heard, in heathen countries where that word has never gone forth, yet there is sin,— because, though men cannot sin against the law which they have never seen, yet they can all rebel against the light of nature, against the dictates of conscience, and against that traditional remembrance of right and wrong, which has followed mankind from the place where God created them. All men, in every land, have consciences, and therefore all men can sin. The ignorant Hottentot, who has never heard anything of a God, has just so much of the light of nature, that in the things that are outwardly good or bad he will discern the difference; and though he foolishly bows down to stocks and stones, he has a judgment which, if he used it, would teach him better. If he chose to use his talents, he might know there is a God; for the Apostle, when speaking of men who have only the light of nature, plainly declares that "the invisible things of him, from the creation of the world, are clearly seen, being understood by the things that are made, even his eternal power and Godhead; so that they are without excuse." Rom. 1:20. Without a divine revelation men can sin, and sin exceedingly— conscience, nature, tradition, and reason, being each of them sufficient to condemn them for their violated commandments. The law makes no one a sinner; all men are such in Adam, and were so practically before its introduction. It entered that "the offence might *abound.*" Now this seems a very terrible thought at first sight, and many ministers would have shirked this text altogether. But when I find a verse I do not understand, I usually think it is a text I *should* study; and I try to seek it out before my heavenly Father, and then when he has opened it to my soul, I reckon it my duty to communicate it to you, with the holy aid of the Spirit. "The law entered that the offence might abound." I will attempt to show you how the law makes offences "abound."

1. First of all, the law tells us that *many things are sins which we should never have thought to be so if it had not been for the additional light.* Even with the light of nature and the light of conscience, and the light of tradition, there are some things we should never have believed to be sins had we not been taught so by the law. Now what man by the light of conscience, would keep holy the Sabbath-day—suppose he never read the Bible, and never heard of it? If he lived in a South Sea island he might know there was a God, but not by any possibility could he find out that the seventh part of his time should be set apart to that God. We find that there are certain festivals and feasts among heathens, and that they set apart days in honour of their fancied gods; but I should like to know where they could discover that there was a certain *seventh* day to be set apart to God, to spend the time in his house of prayer. How could they, unless indeed, tradition may have handed down the fact of the original consecration of that day by the creating Jehovah. I cannot conceive it possible that either conscience or reason could have taught them such a command as this: "Remember the Sabbath-day to keep it holy. Six days shalt thou labour, and do all thy work; but the seventh day is the Sabbath of the Lord thy God; in it thou shalt not do any work, thou, nor thy son, nor thy daughter, thy manservant, nor thy maidservant, nor thy cattle, nor thy stranger that is within thy gates." Moreover, if in the term "law" we comprehend the ceremonial ritual, we can plainly see that many things, in appearance quite indifferent, were by it constituted sins. The eating of animals that do not chew the cud and divide the hoof, the wearing of linsey-woolsey, the sitting on a bed polluted by a leper—with a thousand other things, all seem to have no sin in them, but the law made them into sins, and so made the offence to abound.

2. It is a fact which you can verify by looking at the workings of your own mind, *that law has a tendency to make men rebel.* Human nature rises against restraint. I had not known lust except the law had said, "Thou shalt not covet." The depravity of man is excited to

rebellion by the promulgation of laws. So evil are we, that we conceive at once the desire to commit an act, simply because it is forbidden. Children, we all know, as a rule, will always desire what they may not have, and if forbidden to touch anything, will either do so when an opportunity serves, or will long to be able to do so. The same tendency any student of human nature can discern in mankind at large. Is then the law chargeable with my sin? God forbid. "But sin, taking occasion by the commandment, wrought in me all manner of concupiscence. For sin taking occasion by the commandment deceived me, and by it slew me." Rom. 7:7, 8, 11. The law is holy, and just, and good, *it* is not faulty, but *sin* uses it as an occasion of offence, and rebels when it ought to obey. Augustine placed the truth in a clear light when he wrote—"The law is not in fault, but our evil and wicked nature; even as a heap of lime is still and quiet until water be poured thereon, but then it begins to smoke and burn, not from the fault of the water, but from the nature and kind of the lime which will not endure it." Thus, you see, this is a second sense in which the entrance of the law causes the offence to abound.

3. Yet again, the law *increases the sinfulness of sin, by removing all excuse of ignorance*. Until men know the law, their crimes have at least a palliation of partial ignorance, but when the code of rules is spread before them, their offences become greater, since they are committed against light and knowledge. He who sins against conscience shall be condemned; of how much sorer punishment shall he be thought worthy who despises the voice of Jehovah, defies his sacred sovereignty, and wilfully tramples on his commands. The more light the greater guilt—the law affords that light, and so causes us to become double offenders. Oh, ye nations of the earth who have heard the law of Jehovah, your sin is increased, and your offence abounds.

Methinks I hear some one say, "How unwise it must have been that a law should come to make these things abound!" Does it not, at first sight, seem very harsh that the great author of the world should give us a law which will not justify, but indirectly cause our condemnation to be greater? Does it not seem to be a thing which a gracious God would not reveal, but would have withheld? But, know ye, "that the foolishness of God is wiser than men;" and understand ye that there is a gracious purpose even here. Natural men dream that by a strict performance of duty they shall obtain favour, but God saith thus: "I will show them their folly by proclaiming a law so high that they will despair of attaining unto it. They think that works will be sufficient to save them. They think falsely, and they will be ruined by their mistake. I will send them a law so terrible in its censures, so unflinching in its demands, that they cannot possibly obey it, and they will be driven even to desperation, and come and accept my mercy through Jesus Christ. They cannot be saved by the law—not by the law of nature. As it is, they have sinned against it. But yet, I know, they have foolishly hoped to keep my law, and think by works of the law they may be justified; whereas I have said, 'By the works of the law no flesh living can be justified;' therefore I will write a law—it shall be a black and heavy one—a burden which they cannot carry; and then they will turn away and say, 'I will not attempt to perform it; I will ask my Saviour to bear it for me.'" Imagine a case—Some young men are about to go to sea, where I forsee they will meet with a storm. Suppose you put me in a position where I may cause a tempest before the other shall arise. Well, by the time the natural storm comes on, those young men will be a long way out at sea, and they will be wrecked and ruined before they can put back and be safe. But what do I? Why, when they are just at the mouth of the river, I send a storm, putting them in the greatest danger, and precipitating them ashore, so that they are saved. Thus did God. He sends a law which shows them the roughness of the journey. The tempest of law compels them to put back to the harbour of free grace, and saves them from a most terrible destruction, which would otherwise overwhelm them. The law never came to save men. It never was its intention at all. It came on purpose to make the evidence complete that salvation by works is impossible, and thus to drive the elect of God to rely wholly on the finished salvation of the gospel. Now, just to illustrate my meaning, let me describe it by one more figure. You all remember those high mountains called the Alps. Well, it would be a great mercy if those Alps were a little higher. It would have been, at all events, for Napoleon's soldiers when he led his large, army over, and caused thousands to perish in crossing. Now, if it could have been possible to pile another Alps on their summit, and make them higher than the Himalaya, would not the increased difficulty have deterred him from his enterprise, and so have adverted the destruction of thousands? Napoleon demanded, "Is it possible?" "Barely possible," was the reply. "*Avancez*," cried Buonaparte; and the host were soon toiling up the mountain side. Now, by the light of nature, it *does seem possible* for us to go over this mountain of works, but all men would have perished in the attempt, the path even of this lower hill being too narrow for mortal footsteps. God, therefore, puts another law, like a mountain, on the top; and now the sinner says, "I cannot climb over that. It is a task beyond Herculean might. I see before me a narrow pass, called the pass of Jesus Christ's mercy—the pass of the cross—methinks I will wend my way thither." But if it had not been that the mountain was too high for him, he would have gone climbing up, and climbing up, until he sank into some chasm, or was lost under some mighty avalanche, or in some other way perished eternally. But the law comes that the whole world might see the impossibility of being saved by works.

Let us turn to the more pleasing, part of the subject—the *superabundance* of grace. Having bewailed the devastations and injurious deeds of sin, it delights our hearts to be assured that "grace did much more abound."

1. *Grace excels sin in the numbers it brings beneath its sway*. It is my firm belief that the number of the saved will be far greater than that of the damned. It is written that in all things Jesus shall have the pre-eminence; and why is this to be left out? Can we think that Satan will have more followers than Jesus? Oh, no; for while *it is* written that the redeemed are a number that no man can number; it *is not* recorded that the lost are beyond numeration. True, we know that the visible elect are ever a *remnant*, but then there are others to be added. Think for a moment of the army of infant souls who are now in heaven. These all fell in Adam, but being all elect, were all redeemed and all regenerated, and were privileged to fly straight from the mother's breasts to glory. Happy lot, which we who are spared might well envy. Nor let it be forgotten that the multitudes of converts in the millennial age will very much turn the scale. For then the world will be exceedingly populous, and a thousand years of a reign of grace might

easily suffice to overcome the majority accumulated by sin during six thousand years of its tyranny. In that peaceful period, when all shall know him, from the least even unto the greatest, the sons of God shall fly as doves to their windows, and the Redeemer's family shall be exceedingly multiplied.

What though those who have been deluded by superstition, and destroyed by lust, must be counted by thousands—grace has still the pre-eminence. Saul has slain his thousands, but David his ten-thousands. We admit that the number of the damned will be immense, but we do think that the two states of infancy and millennial glory will furnish so great a reserve of saints that Christ shall win the day. The procession of the lost may be long; there must be thousands, and thousands, and thousands, of those who have perished, but the greater procession of the King of kings shall be composed of larger hosts than even these. "Where sin abounded, grace did much more *abound*." The trophies of free grace will be far more than the trophies of sin.

Yet again. Grace doth "*much* more abound,"—because a time shall come when the world shall be all full of grace; whereas there has never been a period in this world's history when it was wholly given up to sin. When Adam and Eve rebelled against God, there was still a display of grace in the world; for in the garden, at the close of the day, God said, "I will put enmity between thee and the woman, and between thy seed and her seed; it shall bruise thy head, and thou shalt bruise his heel;" and since that first transgression, there has never been a moment when grace has entirely lost its footing in the earth. God has always had his servants on earth; at times they have been hidden by fifties in the caves, but they have never been utterly cut off. Grace might be low; the stream might be very shallow, but it has never been wholly dry. There has always been a salt of grace in the world to counteract the power of sin. The clouds have never been so universal as to hide the day. But the time is fast approaching when grace shall extend all over our poor world and be universal. According to the Bible testimony, we look for the great day when the dark cloud which has swathed this world in darkness shall be removed, and it shall shine once more like all its sister planets. It hath been for many a long year clouded and veiled by sin and corruption; but the last fire shall consume its rags and sackcloth. After that fire, the world in righteousness shall shine. The huge molten mass now slumbering in the bowels of our common mother shall furnish the means of purity. Palaces, and crowns, and peoples, and empires, are all to be melted down; and after like a plague-house, the present creation has been burned up entirely, God will breathe upon the heated mass, and it will cool down again. He will smile on it as he did when he first created it, and the rivers will run down the new-made hills, the oceans will float in new-made channels; and the world will be again the abode of the righteous for ever and for ever. This fallen world will be restored to its orbit; that gem which was lost from the sceptre of God shall be set again, yea, he shall wear it as a signet about his arm. Christ died for the world; and what he died for, he will have. He died for the whole world, and the whole world he will have, when he has purified and cleansed it, and fitted it for himself. "Where sin abounded, grace did much more abound;" for grace shall be universal, whereas sin never was.

One thought more. Hath the world lost its possessions by sin? It has gained far more by grace. True, we have been expelled a garden of delights, where peace, love and happiness found a glorious habitation. True, Eden is not ours, with its luscious fruits, its blissful bowers, and its rivers flowing o'er sands of gold, but we have through Jesus a fairer habitation. He hath made us sit together in heavenly places—the plains of heaven exceed the fields of paradise in the ever-new delights which they afford, while the tree of life, and the river from the throne render the inhabitants of the celestial regions more than emparadised. Did we lose natural life and subject ourselves to painful death by sin? Has not grace revealed an immortality for the sake of which we are too glad to die? Life lost in Adam is more than restored in Christ. We admit that our original robes were rent in sunder by Adam, but Jesus has clothed us with a divine righteousness, far exceeding in value even the spotless robes of created innocence. We mourn our low and miserable condition through sin, but we will rejoice at the thought, that we are now more secure than before we fell, and are brought into closer alliance with Jesus than our standing could have procured us. O Jesus! thou hast won us an inheritance more wide than Adam ever lost by his folly; thou hast filled us a coffer with greater riches than our sin has ever lavished. Thy grace has overtopped our sins. "Grace doth much more abound."

II. Now we come to the second part of the subject, and that is THE ENTRANCE OF THE LAW INTO THE HEART. We have to deal carefully when we come to deal with internal things; it is not easy to talk about this little thing, the heart. When we begin to meddle with the law of their soul, many become indignant, but we do not fear their wrath. We are going to attack the hidden man this morning. The law entered their hearts that sin might abound, "but where sin abounded, grace did much more abound."

1. The law causes the offence to abound by *discovering sin to the soul*. When once God the Holy Ghost applies the law to the conscience, secret sins are dragged to light, little sins are magnified to their true size, and things apparently harmless become exceedingly sinful. Before that dread searcher of the hearts and trier of the reins makes his entrance into the soul, it appears righteous, just, lovely, and holy; but when he reveals the hidden evils, the scene is changed. Offences which were once styled peccadilloes, trifles, freaks of youth, follies, indulgences, little slips, &c., then appear in their true colour, as breaches of the law of God, deserving condign punishment.

John Bunyan shall explain my meaning by an extract from his famous allegory: "Then the Interpreter took Christian by the hand and led him into a very large parlour that was full of dust, because never swept; in which after he had reviewed it a little while, the Interpreter called for a man to sweep. Now, when he began to sweep, the dust began so abundantly to fly about, that Christian had almost therewith been choked. Then said the Interpreter to a damsel that stood by, 'Bring hither water, and sprinkle the room;' the which when she had done, it was swept and cleansed with pleasure. Then said Christian, 'What means this?' The Interpreter answered, 'This parlour is the heart of a man that was never sanctified by the sweet grace of the gospel. The dust is his original sin and inward corruptions that have defiled the whole man. He that began to sweep at first, is the law; but she that brought the water and did sprinkle it, is the gospel. Now, whereas thou sawest that as soon as the first began to sweep, the dust did so fly about, that the room could not by him be cleansed, but that thou wast almost choked therewith; this is to show thee, that the law, instead of cleansing the heart (by its working) from sin, doth revive, Rom. 7:9, put strength into, 1 Cor. 15:56, and increase it in the soul, Rom. 5:20, even as it doth discover and forbid it, for that doth not give power to subdue. Again, as thou sawest the damsel sprinkle the room with water, upon which it was cleansed with pleasure; this is to show thee, that when the gospel comes in the sweet and precious influences thereof to the heart, then, I say, even as thou sawest the damsel lay the dust by sprinkling the floor with water, so is sin vanquished and subdued, and the soul made clean, through the faith of it, and consequently fit for the King of glory to inhabit.' "

The heart is like a dark cellar, full of lizards, cockroaches, beetles, and all kinds of reptiles and insects, which in the dark we see not, but the law takes down the shutters and lets in the light, and so we see the evil. Thus sin becoming apparent by the law, it is written the law makes the offence to abound.

2. Once again. *The law, when it comes into the heart, shows us how very black we are.* Some of us know that we are sinners. It is very easy to say it. The word "sinner" hath only two syllables in it, and many there be who frequently have it on their lips, but who do not understand it. They see their sin, but it does not appear exceedingly sinful till the law comes. We think there is something sinful in it; but when the law comes, we detect its abomination. Has God's holy light ever shone into your souls? Have you had the fountains of your great depravity and evil broken up, and been wakened up sufficiently to say, "O God! I have sinned?" Now, if you have your hearts broken up by the law, you will find the heart is more deceitful than the devil. I can say this of myself, I am very much afraid of mine, it is so bad. The Bible says, "The heart is deceitful above all things." The devil is one of the things; therefore, it is worse than the devil—"and desperately wicked." How many do we find who are saying, "Well, I trust I have a very good heart at the bottom. There may be a little amiss at the top, but I am very good-hearted at bottom." If you saw some fruit on the top of a basket that was not quite good, would you buy the basket because they told you, "Ay, but they are good at the bottom?" "No, no," you would say, "they are sure to be the best at the top, and if they are bad there,

they are sure to be rotten below." There are many people who live queer lives, and some friends say, "He is good hearted at bottom; he would get drunk sometimes, but he is very good-hearted at the bottom." Ah! never believe it. Men are seldom estimated better than they seem to be. If the outside of the cup or platter is clean, the inside may be dirty, but if the outside is impure, you may always be sure the inside is no better. Most of us put our goods in the window—keep all our good things in the front, and bad things behind. Let you and I, instead of making excuses about ourselves, about the badness of our hearts, if the law has entered into your soul, bow down and say, "O the sin—O the uncleanness—the blackness—the awful nature of our crimes!" "The law entered that the offence may abound."

3. The law reveals the exceeding abundance of sin, *by discovering to us the depravity of our nature*. We are all prepared to charge the serpent with our guilt, or to insinuate that we go astray, from the force of ill example—but the Holy Spirit dissipates these dreams by bringing the law into the heart. Then the fountains of the great deep are broken up, the chambers of imagery are opened, the innate evil of the very essence of fallen man is discovered.

The law cuts into the core of the evil, it reveals the seat of the malady, and informs us that the leprosy lies deep within. Oh! how the man abhors himself when he sees all his rivers of water turned into blood, and loathsomeness creeping over all his being. He learns that sin is no flesh wound, but a stab in the heart; he discovers that the poison has impregnated his veins, lies in his very marrow, and hath its fountain in his inmost heart. Now he loathes himself, and would fain be healed. Actual sin seems not half so terrible as in-bred sin, and at the thought of what he is, he turns pale, and gives up salvation by works as an impossibility.

4. Having thus removed the mask and shown the desperate case of the sinner, the relentless law causes the offence to abound yet more by *bringing home the sentence of condemnation*. It mounts the judgment seat, puts on the black cap, and pronounces the sentence of death. With a harsh unpitying voice it solemnly thunders forth the words, "Condemned already." It bids the soul prepare its defence, knowing well that all apology has been taken away by its former work of

conviction. The sinner is therefore speechless, and the law, with frowning looks, lifts up the veil of hell, and gives the man a glimpse of torment. The soul feels that the sentence is just, that the punishment is not too severe, and that mercy it has no right to expect; it stands quivering, trembling, fainting, and intoxicated with dismay, until it falls prostrate in utter despair. The sinner puts the rope around his own neck, arrays himself in the attire of the condemned, and throws himself at the foot of the King's throne, with but one thought, "I am vile;" and with one prayer, "God be merciful to me a sinner."

5. Nor does the law cease its operations even here, for it renders the offence yet more apparent *by discovering the powerlessness occasioned by sin*. It not only condemns but it actually kills. He who once thought that he could repent and believe at pleasure, finds in himself no power to do either the one or the other.

When Moses smites the sinner he bruises and mangles him with the first blow, but at a second or a third, he falls down as one dead. I have myself been in such a condition that if heaven could have been purchased by a single prayer I should have been damned, for I could no more pray than I could fly. Moreover, when we are in the grave which the law has digged for us, we feel as if we did not feel, and we grieve because we cannot grieve. The dread mountain lies upon us which renders it impossible to stir hand or foot, and when we would cry for help our voice refuses to obey us. In vain the minister cries "Repent," Our hard heart will not melt; in vain he exhorts us to believe; that faith of which he speaks seems to be as much beyond our capacity as the creation of a universe. Ruin is now become ruin indeed. The thundering sentence is in our ears, "CONDEMNED ALREADY," another cry follows it, "DEAD IN TRESPASSES AND SINS," and a third more awful and terrible, mingles its horrible warning, "*The wrath to come—the wrath to come*" In the opinion of the sinner he is now cast out as a corrupt carcase, he expects each moment to be tormented by the worm that never dies and to lift up his eyes in hell. Now is mercy's moment, and we turn the subject from condemning law to abounding grace.

Listen, O heavy laden, condemned sinner, while in my Master's name, I publish superabounding grace. *Grace excels sin in its measure and efficacy.* Though your sins are many, mercy hath many pardons.

Though they excel the stars, the sands, the drops of dew in their number, one act of remission can cancel all. Your iniquity, though a mountain, shall be cast into the midst of the sea. Your blackness shall be washed out by the cleansing flood of your Redeemer's gore. Mark! I said YOUR sins, and I meant to say so, for if you are now a law-condemned sinner, I know you to be a vessel of mercy by that very sign. Oh, hellish sinners, abandoned profligates, off-casts of society, outcasts from the company of sinners themselves, if ye acknowledge your iniquity, here is mercy, broad, ample, free, immense, INFINITE. Remember this, O sinner,—

> "If all the sins that men have done,
> In will, in word, in thought, in deed,
> Since worlds were made, or time began,
> Were laid on one poor sinner's head,
> The stream of Jesus' precious blood
> Applied, removes the dreadful load."

Yet again, grace excelleth sin in another thing. *Sin shows us its parent, and tells us our heart is the father of it, but grace surpasseth sin there, and shows the Author of grace—the King of kings.* The law traces sin up to our heart; grace traces its own origin to God, and

> "In his sacred breast I see
> Eternal thoughts of love to me."

O Christian, what a blessed thing grace is, for its source is in the everlasting mountains. Sinner, if you are the vilest in the world, if God forgives you this morning, you will be able to trace your pedigree to him, for you will become one of the sons of God, and have him always for your Father. Methinks I see you a wretched criminal at the bar, and I hear mercy cry, "Discharge him!" He is pallid, halt, sick, maimed—heal him. He is of a vile race—lo, I will adopt him into my family. Sinner! God taketh thee for his son. What, though thou art poor, God says, "I will take thee to be mine for ever. Thou shalt be my heir. There is thy fair brother. In ties of blood he is one with thee—Jesus is thy actual brother!" Yet how came this change? Oh! is not that an act of mercy? "Grace did much more abound."

"Grace hath put me in the number
Of the Saviour's family."

Grace outdoes sin, for it lifts us higher than the place from which we fell.

And, again, "where sin abounded grace did much more abound;" *because the sentence of the law may be reversed, but that of grace never can.* I stand here and feel condemned, yet, perhaps, I have a hope that I may be acquitted. There is a dying hope of acquittal still left. But when we are justified, there is no fear of condemnation. I cannot be condemned if I am once justified; *fully* absolved I am by grace. I defy Satan to lay hands on me, if I am a justified man. The state of justification is an unvariable one and is indissolubly united to glory. "Who shall lay anything to the charge of God's elect? It is God that justifieth. Who is he that condemneth? It is Christ that died, yea, rather, that is risen again, who is even at the right hand of God who also maketh intercession for us. Who shall separate us from the love of Christ? Shall tribulation, or distress, or persecution, or famine, or nakedness, or sword? Nay, in all these things we are more than conquerors through him that loved us. For I am persuaded that neither death, nor life, nor angels, nor principalities, nor powers, nor things present, nor things to come, nor height, nor depth, nor any other creature, shall be able to separate us from the love of God, which is in Christ Jesus our Lord." Oh! poor condemned sinner, doth not this charm thee, and make thee in love with free grace? And all this is YOURS. Your crimes, if once blotted out, shall never be laid to your charge again. The justification of the gospel is no Arminian sham, which may be reversed if you should in future turn aside. No; the debt once paid, cannot be demanded twice—the punishment, once endured, cannot again be inflicted. Saved, saved, saved, entirely saved by divine grace, you may walk without fear the wide world o'er.

And yet, once more. Just as sin makes us sick, and grievous, and sad, so does grace make us *far more joyful and free.* Sin causeth one to go about with an aching heart, till he seems as if the world would swallow him, and mountains hang above ready to drop upon him. This is the effect of the law. The law makes us sad; the law makes us miserable. But poor sinner, grace removeth the evil effects of sin upon your spirit, if thou dost believe in the Lord Jesus Christ, thou shalt go out of this place with a sparkling eye and a light heart. Ah! Well do I remember the morning when I stepped into a little place of worship, as miserable almost as hell could make me—being ruined and lost. I had often been at chapels where they spoke of the law, but I heard not the gospel. I sat down the pew a chained and imprisoned sinner; the Word of God came, and I went out free. Though I went in miserable as hell, I went out elated and joyful. I sat there black; I went away whiter than driven snow. God had said, "Though your sins be as scarlet, they shall be whiter than snow." Why not this be thy lot, my brother, if thou feelest thyself a sinner now? It is all he asks of thee, to feel thy need of him, this thou hast, and now the blood of Jesus lies before thee. "The law has entered that sin might abound." Thou art forgiven, only believe it; elect, only believe it; 'tis the truth that thou art saved.

And now, lastly, poor sinner, has sin made thee unfit for heaven? Grace shall render thee a fit companion for seraphs and the just made perfect. Thou who art to-day lost and destroyed by sin, shalt one day find thyself with a crown upon thy head, and a golden harp in thine hand, exalted to the throne of the Most High. Think, O drunkard, if thou repentest, there is a crown laid up for thee in heaven. Ye guiltiest, most lost and depraved, are ye condemned in your conscience by the law? Then I invite you, in my Master's name, to accept pardon through his blood. He suffered in your stead, he has atoned for your guilt and you are acquitted. Thou art an object of his eternal affection, the law is but a schoolmaster, to bring thee to Christ. Cast thyself on him. Fall into the arms of saving grace. No works are required, no fitness, no righteousness, no doings. Ye are complete in him who said, "It is finished."

> "Ye debtors whom he gives to know,
> That you ten thousand talents owe,
> When humble at his feet you fall,
> Your gracious God forgives them all.

"Slaves, that have borne the heavy chain
Of sin, and hell's tyrannic reign,
To liberty assert your claim,
And urge the great Redeemer's name.

"The rich inheritance of heaven,
Your joy, your boast, is freely giv'n;
Fair Salem your arrival waits,
With golden streets, and pearly gates.

"Her blest inhabitants no more
Bondage and poverty deplore!
No debt, but love immensely great;
Their joy still rises with the debt."[6]

SOVEREIGN GRACE AND MAN'S RESPONSIBILITY

A Sermon

DELIVERED ON SABBATH MORNING, AUGUST 1, 1858, BY THE

REV. C. H. SPURGEON,

AT THE MUSIC HALL, ROYAL SURREY GARDENS.

"But Esaias is very bold, and saith, I was found of them that sought me not; I was made manifest unto them that asked not after me. But to Israel he saith, all day long I have stretched forth my hands unto a disobedient and gainsaying people."—Rom. 10:20–21.

DOUBTLESS these words primarily refer to the casting away of the Jews, and to the choosing of the Gentiles. The Gentiles were a people who sought not after God, but lived in idolatry; nevertheless, Jehovah was pleased in these latter times to send the gospel of his grace to them: while the Jews who had long enjoyed the privileges of the Word of God, on account of their disobedience and rebellion were cast away. I believe, however, that while this is the primary object of the words of our text, yet, as Calvin says, the truth taught in the text is a type of a universal fact. As God did choose the people who knew him not, so hath he chosen, in the abundance of his grace, to manifest his salvation to men who are out of the way; while, on the other hand, the men who are lost, after having heard the Word, are lost because of their wilful sin; for God doth all the day long "stretch forth his hands unto a disobedient and gainsaying people."

The system of truth is not one straight line, but two. No man will ever get a right view of the gospel until he knows how to look at the two lines at once. I am taught in one book to believe that what I sow I shall reap: I am taught in another place, that "it is not of him that willeth nor of him that runneth, but of God that showeth mercy." I see

---

[6] Spurgeon, C. H. (1855). Law and Grace. In *The New Park Street Pulpit Sermons* (Vol. 1, pp. 285–292). London: Passmore & Alabaster.

in one place, God presiding over all in providence; and yet I see, and I cannot help seeing, that man acts as he pleases, and that God has left his actions to his own will, in a great measure. Now, if I were to declare that man was so free to act, that there was no presidence of God over his actions, I should be driven very near to Atheism; and if, on the other hand, I declare that God so overrules all things, as that man is not free enough to be responsible, I am driven at once into Antinomianism or fatalism. That God predestines, and that man is responsible, are two things that few can see. They are believed to be inconsistent and contradictory; but they are not. It is just the fault of our weak judgment. Two truths cannot be contradictory to each other. If, then, I find taught in one place that everything is fore-ordained, *that is true;* and if I find in another place that man is responsible for all his actions, *that is true;* and it is my folly that leads me to imagine that two truths can ever contradict each other. These two truths, I do not believe, can ever be welded into one upon any human anvil, but one they shall be in eternity: they are two lines that are so nearly parallel, that the mind that shall pursue them farthest, will never discover that they converge; but they do converge, and they will meet somewhere in eternity, close to the throne of God, whence all truth doth spring.

Now, this morning I am about to consider the two doctrines. In the 20th verse, we have taught us *the doctrines of sovereign grace*—"But Esaias is very bold, and saith, I was found of them that sought me not; I was made manifest unto them that asked not after me." In the next verse, we have *the doctrine of man's guilt in rejecting God*. "To Israel he saith, all day long I have stretched forth my hands unto a disobedient and gainsaying people."

I. First, then, DIVINE SOVEREIGNTY AS EXEMPLIFIED IN SALVATION. If any man be saved, he is saved by Divine grace, and by Divine grace alone; and the reason of his salvation is not to be found in him, but in God. We are not saved as the result of anything that we do or that we will; but we will and do as the result of God's good pleasure, and the work of his grace in our hearts. No sinner can prevent God; that is, he cannot go before him, cannot anticipate him; God is always first in the matter of salvation. He is before our convictions, before our desires, before our fears, before our hopes. All that is good or ever will be good in us, is preceded by the grace of God, and is the effect of a Divine cause within.

Now in speaking of God's gracious acts of salvation, this morning, I notice first, that they are entirely *unmerited*. You will see that the people here mentioned certainly did not merit God's grace. They found him, but they never sought for him; he was made manifest to them, but they never asked for him. There never was a man saved yet who merited it. Ask all the saints of God, and they will tell you that their former life was spent in the lusts of the flesh; that in the days of their ignorance, they revolted against God and turned back from his ways, that when they were invited to come to him they despised the invitation, and, when warned, cast the warning behind their back. They will tell you that their being drawn by God, was not the result of any merit before conversion; for some of them, so far from having any merit, were the very vilest of the vile: they plunged into the very kennel of sin; they were not ashamed of all the things of which it would be a shame for us to speak; they were ringleaders in crime, very princes in the ranks of the enemy; and yet sovereign grace came to them, and they were brought to know the Lord. They will tell you that it was not the result of anything good in their disposition, for although they trust that there is now something excellent implanted in them, yet in the days of their flesh they could see no one quality which was not perverted to the service of Satan. Ask them whether they think they were chosen of God because of their courage; they will tell you, no; if they had courage it was defaced, for they were courageous to do evil. Question them whether they were chosen of God because of their talent; they will tell you, no; they had that talent, but they prostituted it to the service of Satan. Question them whether they were chosen because of the openness and generosity of their disposition; they will tell you that that very openness of temper, and that very generosity of disposition, led them to plunge deeper into the depths of sin, than they otherwise would have done, for they were "hail fellow, well met," with every evil man, and ready to drink and join every jovial party which should come in their way. There was in them no reason whatever why God should have mercy upon them, and the wonder to them is that he did not cut them down in the midst of their sins, blot out their names from the book of life, and sweep them into the gulf where the fire burneth that shall devour the wicked. But some have said that God chooses his people because he foresees that after he chooses them, they will do this, that, and the other, which shall be meritorious and excellent. Refer again to the people of God, and they will tell you that since their conversion they have had much to weep over. Although they can rejoice that God has begun the good work in them, they often tremble lest it should not be God's work at all. They will tell you that if they are abundant in faith yet there are times when they are superabundant in unbelief; that if sometimes they are full of works of holiness, yet there are times when they weep many tears to think that those very acts of holiness were stained with sin. The Christian will tell you that he weeps over his very tears; he feels that there is filth even in the best of desires; that he has to pray to God to forgive his prayers, for there is sin in the midst of his supplications, and that he has to sprinkle even his best offerings with the atoning blood, for he never else can bring an offering without spot or blemish. You shall appeal to the brightest saint, to the man whose presence in the midst of society is like the presence of an angel, and he will tell you that he is still ashamed of himself. "Ah!" he will say, "you may praise me, but I cannot praise myself; you speak well of me, you applaud me, but if you knew my heart you would see abundant reason to think of me as a poor sinner saved by grace, who hath nothing whereof to glory, and must bow his head and confess his iniquities in the sight of God." Grace, then, is entirely unmerited.

Again, the grace of God is *sovereign*. By that word we mean that God has an absolute right to give that grace where he chooses, and to withhold it when he pleases. He is not bound to give it to any man, much less to all men; and if he chooses to give it to one man and not to another, his answer is, "Is thine eye evil because mine eye is good? Can I not do as I will with mine own? I will have mercy on whom I will have mercy." Now, I want you to notice the sovereignty of Divine grace as illustrated in the text: "I was found of them that sought me not, I was made manifest to them that asked not after me." You would imagine that if God gave his grace to any he would wait until he found them earnestly seeking him. You would imagine that God in the highest heavens would say, "I have mercies, but I will leave men alone, and when they feel their need of these mercies and seek me diligently with their whole heart, day and night, with tears, and vows, and supplications, then will I bless them, but not before." But, beloved, God saith no such thing. It is true he doth bless them that cry unto him, but he blesses them before they cry, for their cries are not their own cries, but cries which he has put into their lips; their desires are not of their own growth, but desires which he has cast like good seed into the soil of their hearts. God saves the men that do not seek him. Oh, wonder of wonders! It is mercy indeed when God saves a seeker; but how much greater mercy when he seeks the lost himself! Mark, the parable of Jesus Christ concerning the lost sheep; it does not run thus: "A certain man had a hundred sheep, and one of them did go astray. And he tarried at home, and lo, the sheep came back, and he received it joyfully and said to his friends, rejoice, for the sheep that I have lost is come back." No; he *went after* the sheep: it never would have come after him; it would have wandered farther and farther away. He went after it; over hills of difficulty, down valleys of despondency he pursued its wandering feet, and at last he laid hold of it; he did not drive it before him, he did not lead it, but he carried it himself all the way, and when he brought it home he did not say, "the sheep is come back," but, "I have *found* the sheep which was lost." Men do not seek God first; God seeks them first; and if any of you are seeking him today it is because he has first sought you. If you are desiring him he desired you first, and your good desires and earnest seeking will not be the cause of your salvation, but the effects of previous grace given to you. "Well," says another, "I should have thought that although the Saviour might not require an earnest seeking and sighing and groaning, and a continuous searching after him, yet certainly he would have desired and demanded that every man, before he had grace, should ask for it." That, indeed, beloved, seems natural, and God *will* give grace to them that ask for it; but mark, the text says that he was manifested "to them that asked not for him." That is to say, before we ask, God gives us grace. The only reason why any man ever begins to pray, is because God has put previous grace in his heart which leads him to pray. I remember, when I was converted to God, I was an

Arminian thoroughly. I thought I had begun the good work myself, and I used sometimes to sit down and think, "Well. I sought the Lord four years before I found him," and I think I began to compliment myself upon the fact that I had perseveringly entreated of him in the midst of much discouragement. But one day the thought struck me, "How was it you came to seek God?" and in an instant the answer came from my soul, "Why, because he led me to do it; he must first have shown me my need of him, or else I should never have sought him; he must have shown me his preciousness, or I never should have thought him worth seeking;" and at once I saw the doctrines of grace as clear as possible. God must begin. Nature can never rise above itself. You put water into a reservoir, and it will rise as high as that, but no higher if let alone. Now, it is not in human nature to seek the lord. Human nature is depraved, and therefore, there must be the extraordinary pressure of the Holy Spirit put upon the heart to lead us first to ask for mercy. But mark, we do not know anything about that, while the Spirit is operating; we find that out afterwards. We ask as much as if we were asking all of ourselves. Our business is to seek the Lord as if there were no Holy Spirit at all. But although we do not know it, there must always be a previous motion of the Spirit in our heart, before there will be a motion of our heart towards him.

> "No sinner can be beforehand with thee,
> Thy grace is most sovereign, most rich, and most free."

Let me give you an illustration. You see that man on his horse surrounded by a body of troopers. How proud he is, and how he reins up his horse with conscious dignity. Sir, what have you got there? What are those despatches you treasure up with so much care? "Oh, sir, I have that in my hand that will vex the church of God in Damascus. I have dragged the fellows into the synagogue, both men and women; I have scourged them, and compelled them to blaspheme; and I have this commission from the high priest to drag them to Jerusalem, that I may put them to death." Saul! Saul! have you no love for Christ? "Love to him! No. When they stoned Stephen, I took care of the witnesses' clothes, and I rejoiced to do it. I wish I had had the crucifying of their Master, for I hate them with perfect hatred, and I breathe out threatenings and slaughter against them." What do you say of this man? If he be saved, will you not grant that it must be some Divine sovereignty that converts him? Look at poor Pilate, how much there was that was hopeful in him. He was willing to save the Master, but he feared and trembled. If we had had our choice, we should have said, "Lord, save Pilate, he does not want to kill Christ, he labours to let him escape; but slay the bloodthirsty Saul, he is the very chief of sinners." "No," says God, "I will do as I will with mine own." The heavens open, and the brightness of glory descends—brighter than the noon-day sun. Stunned with the light he falls to the ground, and a voice is heard addressing him, "Saul, Saul, why persecutest thou me? it is hard for thee to kick against the pricks." He rises up; God appears to him: "Lo, I have made thee a chosen vessel to bear my name among the Gentiles." Is not that sovereignty—sovereign grace, without any previous seeking? God was found of him that sought not for him; he manifested himself to one that asked him not. Some will say, that was a miracle; but it is one that is repeated every day in the week. I knew a man once, who had not been to the house of God for a long time; and one Sunday morning, having been to market to buy a pair of ducks for his Sunday dinner, he happened to see a house of God opened as he was passing by. "Well," he thought, "I will hear what these fellows are up to." He went inside; the hymn that was being sung struck his attention; he listened to the sermon, forgot his ducks, discovered his own character, went home, and threw himself upon his knees before God, and after a short time it pleased God to give him joy and peace in believing. That man had nothing in him to begin with, nothing that could have led you to imagine he ever would be saved, but simply because God would have it so, he struck the effectual blow of grace, and the man was brought to himself. But we are, each of us who are saved, the very people who are the best illustrations of the matter. To this day, my wonder is, that ever the Lord should have chosen me. I cannot make it out; and my only answer to the question is, "Even so, Father, for so it seemed good in thy sight."

I have now, I think, stated the doctrine pretty plainly. Let me only say a few words about it. Some people are very much afraid of this truth. They say, "It is true, I dare say, but still you ought not to preach it before a mixed assembly; it is very well for the comfort of God's people, but it is to be very carefully handled, and not to be publicly preached upon." Very well, sir, I leave you to settle that matter with my Master. He gave me this great book to preach from, and I cannot preach from anything else. If he has put anything in it you think is not fit, go and complain to him, and not to me. I am simply his servant, and if his errand that I am to tell is objectionable, I cannot help it. If I send my servant to the door with a message, and he delivers it faithfully, he does not deserve to be scolded. Let *me* have the blame, not the servant. So I say; blame my Master, and not me, for I do but proclaim his message. "No," says one, "it is not to be *preached*." But it is to be preached. Every word of God is given by inspiration, and it is profitable for some good end. Does not the Bible say so? Let me tell you, the reason why many of our churches are declining is just because this doctrine has not been preached. Wherever this doctrine has been upheld, it has always been "Down with Popery." The first reformers held this doctrine and preached it. Well said a Church of England divine to some who railed at him, "Look at your own Luther. Do you not consider him to be the teacher of the Church of England? What Calvin and the other reformers taught is to be found in his book upon the freedom of the will." Besides, we can point you to a string of ministers from the beginning even until now. Talk of apostolic succession! The man who preaches the doctrines of grace has an apostolic succession indeed. Can we not trace our pedigree through a whole line of men like Newton, and Whitfield, and Owen, and Bunyan, straight away on till we come to Calvin, and Luther, Zwingle; and then we can go back from them to Savonarola, to Jerome of Prague, to Huss, and then back to Augustine, the mighty preacher of Christianity; and from St. Augustine to Paul is but one step. We need not be ashamed of our pedigree; although Calvinists are now considered to be heterodox, we are and ever must be orthodox. It is the old doctrine. Go and buy any puritanical book, and see if you can find Arminianism in it. Search all the book stalls over, and see if you can find one large folio book of olden times that has anything in it but the doctrine of the free grace of God. Let this once be brought to bear upon the minds of men, and away go the doctrines of penance and confession, away goes paying for the pardon of your sin. If grace be free and sovereign in the hand of God, down goes the doctrine of priestcraft, away go buying and selling indulgences and such like things; they are swept to the four winds of heaven, and the efficacy of good works is dashed in pieces like Dagon before the ark of the Lord. "Well," says one, "I like the doctrine; still there are very few that preach it, and those that do are very high." Very likely; but I care little what anybody calls me. It signifies very little what men call you. Suppose they call you a "hyper," that does not make you anything wicked, does it? Suppose they call you an Antinomian, that will not make you one. I must confess, however, that there are some men who preach this doctrine who are doing ten thousand times more harm than good, because they don't preach the next doctrine I am going to proclaim, which is just as true. They have this to be the sail, but they have not the other to be the ballast. They can preach one side, but not the other. They can go along with the high doctrine, but they will not preach the whole of the Word. Such men caricature the Word of God. And just let me say here, that it is the custom of a certain body of Ultra-Calvinists, to call those of us who teach that it is the duty of man to repent and believe, "Mongrel Calvinists." If you hear any of them say so, give them my most respectful compliments, and ask them whether they ever read Calvin's works in their lives. Not that I care what Calvin said or did not say; but ask them whether they ever read his works; and if they say "No," as they must say, for there are forty-eight large volumes, you can tell them, that the man whom they call "a Mongrel Calvinist," though he has not read them all, has read a very good share of them, and knows their spirit; and he knows that he preaches substantially what Calvin preached—that every doctrine he preaches may be found in Calvin's Commentaries on some part of Scripture or other. We are TRUE Calvinists, however. Calvin is nobody to us. Jesus Christ and him crucified, and the old fashioned Bible, are our standards. Beloved, let us take God's Word as it stands. If we find high doctrine there, let it be high; if we find low doctrine, let it be low; let us set up no other standard than the Bible affords.

II. Now then for the second point. "There now," says my ultra friend, "he is going to contradict himself." No, my friend, I am not, I am only going to contradict *you*. The second point is MAN'S RESPONSIBILITY.

"But to Israel he saith, All day long I have stretched forth my hands unto a disobedient and gain-saying people. Now, these people whom God had cast away had been wooed, had been sought, had been entreated to be saved; but they would not, and inasmuch as they were not saved, it was the effect of their disobedience and their gainsaying. That lies clearly enough in the text. When God sent the prophets to Israel, and stretched forth his hands, what was it for? What did he wish them to come to him for? Why, to be saved, "No," says one, "it was for temporal mercies." Not so, my friend; the verse before is concerning spiritual mercies, and so is this one, for they refer to the same thing. Now, was God sincere in his offer? God forgive the man that dares to say he was not. God is undoubtedly sincere in every act he did. He sent his prophets, he entreated the people of Israel to lay hold on spiritual things, but they would not, and though he stretched out his hands all the day long, yet they were "a disobedient and gainsaying people," and would not have his love; and on their head rests their blood.

Now let me notice the wooing of God and of what sort it is. First, it was the most *affectionate* wooing in the world. Lost sinners who sit under the sound of the gospel are not lost for the want of the most affectionate invitation. God says he stretched out his hands. You know what that means. You have seen the child who is disobedient and will not come to his father. The father puts out his hands, and says, "Come, my child, come; I am ready to forgive you." The tear is in his eye, and his bowels move with compassion, and he says, "Come, come." God says this is what *he* did—"*he* stretched out his hands." That is what he has done to some of you. You that are not saved to-day are without excuse, for God stretched out his hands to you, and he said, "Come, come." Long have you sat beneath the sound of the ministry, and it has been a faithful one, I trust, and a weeping one. Your minister has not forgotten to pray for your souls in secret or to weep over you when no eye saw him, and he has endeavoured to persuade you as an ambassador from God. God is my witness, I have sometimes stood in this pulpit, and I could not have pleaded harder for my own life than I have pleaded with you. In Christ's name, I have cried, "Come unto me all ye that are weary and heavy laden, and I will give you rest." I have wept over you as the Saviour did, and used his words on his behalf, "O

Jerusalem, Jerusalem, how often would I have gathered thy children together as a hen gathereth her chickens under her wings, and ye would not." And you know that your conscience has often been touched; you have often been moved; you could not resist it. God was so kind to you; he invited you so affectionately by the Word; he dealt so gently with you by his providence; his hands were stretched out, and you could hear his voice speaking in your ears, "Come unto me, come: come, now let us reason together; though your sins be as scarlet they shall be as wool; though they be red like crimson they shall be whiter than snow." You have heard him cry, "Ho every one that thirsteth, come ye to the waters." You have heard him say with all the affection of a father's heart, "Let the wicked forsake his way, and the unrighteous man his thoughts, and let him turn unto the Lord, and he will have mercy upon him, and unto our God, for he will abundantly pardon." Oh! God does plead with men that they would be saved, and this day he says to every one of you, "Repent, and be converted for the remission of your sins. Turn ye unto me. Thus saith the Lord of hosts; consider your ways." And with love divine he woos you as a father woos his child, putting out his hands and crying, "Come unto me, come unto me." "No," says one strong-doctrine man, "God never invites all men to himself; he invites none but certain characters." Stop, sir, that is all you know about it. Did you ever read that parable where it is said, "My oxen and my fatlings are killed, and all things are ready: come unto the marriage." And they that were bidden *would not come.* And did you never read that they all began to make excuse, and that they were punished because they did not accept the invitations. Now, if the invitation is not to be made to anybody, but to the man who will accept it, how can that parable be true? The fact is, the oxen and fatlings are killed; the wedding feast is ready, and the trumpet sounds, "Ho every one that thirsteth, come and eat, come and drink." Here are the provisions spread, here is an all-sufficiency; the invitation is free; it is a great invitation without limitation. "*Whosoever will*, let him come and take of the water of life freely." And that invitation is couched in tender words, "Come to me, my child, come to me." "All day long I have stretched forth my hands."

And note again, this invitation was very *frequent*. The words, "all the day long," may be translated "daily"—"Daily have I stretched forth my hands." Sinner, God has not called you once to come, and then let you alone, but every day has he been at you; every day has conscience spoken to you; every day has providence warned you, and every Sabbath has the Word of God wooed you. Oh! how much some of you will have to account for at God's great bar! I cannot now read your characters, but I know there are some of you who will have a terrible account at last. All the day long has God been wooing you. From the first dawn of your life, he wooed you through your mother, and she used to put your little hands together, and teach you to say,

> "Gentle Jesus meek and mild,
> Look upon a little child,
> Pity my simplicity;
> Suffer me to come to thee."

And in your boyhood God was still stretching out his hands after you. How your Sunday-school teacher endeavoured to bring you to the Saviour! How often your youthful heart was affected; but you put all that away, and you are still untouched by it. How often did your mother speak to you, and your father warn you; and you have forgotten the prayer in that bed-room when you were sick, when your mother kissed your burning forehead, knelt down and prayed to God to spare your life, and then added that prayer, "Lord, save my boy's soul!" And you recollect the Bible she gave you, when you first went out apprentice, and the prayer she wrote on that yellow front leaf. When she gave it, you did not perhaps know, but you may *now*; how earnestly she longed after you, that you might be formed anew in Christ Jesus; how she followed you with her prayers, and how she entreated with her God for you. And you have not yet surely forgotten how many Sabbaths you have spent, and how many times you have been warned. Why you have had waggon-loads of sermons wasted on you. A hundred and four sermons you have heard every year, and some of you more, and yet you are still just what you were.

But sinners, sermon hearing is an awful thing unless it is blessed to our souls. If God has kept on stretching out his hands every day and all the day, it will be a hard thing for you when you shall be justly condemned not only for your breaches of the law, but for your wilful rejection of the gospel. It is probable that God will keep on stretching out his hands to you until your hairs grow grey, still continually inviting you: and perhaps when you are nearing death he will still say, "Come unto me, come unto me." But if you still persist in hardening your heart, if still you reject Christ, I beseech you let nothing make you imagine that you shall go unpunished. Oh! I do tremble sometimes when I think of that class of ministers who tell sinners that they are not guilty if they do not seek the Saviour. How they shall be found innocent at God's great day I do not know. It seems to be a fearful thing that they should be lulling poor souls into sleep by telling them it is not their duty to seek Christ and repent, but that they may do as they like about that, and that when they perish they will be none the more guilty for having heard the Word. My Master did not say that. Remember how he said, "And thou, Capernaum, which art exalted unto heaven, shalt be brought down to hell: for if the mighty works, which have been done in thee, had been done in Sodom, it would have remained until this day. But I say unto you. That it shall be more tolerable for the land of Sodom in the day of judgment, than for thee." Jesus did not talk thus when he spoke to Chorazin and Bethsaida; for he said, "Woe unto thee, Chorazin! woe unto thee, Bethsaida! for if the mighty works, which were done in you, had been done in Tyre and Sidon, they would have repented long ago in sack-cloth and ashes. But I say unto you, It shall be more tolerable for Tyre and Sidon at the day of judgment, than for you." It was not the way Paul preached. He did not tell sinners that there was no guilt in despising the cross. Hear the apostle's words once more: "For if the word spoken by angels was stedfast, and every transgression and disobedience received a just recompence of reward, *how shall we escape, if we neglect so great salvation*, which at the first began to be spoken by the Lord, and was confirmed unto us by them that heard him." Sinner, at the great day of God thou must give an account for every warning thou hast ever had, for every time thou hast read thy Bible, ay, and for every time thou hast neglected to read it; for every Sunday when the house of God was open and thou didst neglect to avail thyself of the opportunity of hearing the Word, and for every time thou didst hear it and didst not improve it. Ye who are careless hearers, are tying faggots for your own burning for ever. Ye that hear and straightway forget, or hear with levity, are digging for yourselves a pit into which ye must be cast. Remember, no one will be responsible for your damnation but yourself, at the last great day. God will not be responsible for it. "As I live saith the Lord"—and that is a great oath—"I have no pleasure in the death of him that dieth, but had rather that he should turn unto me and live." God has done much for you. He sent you his Gospel. You are not born in a heathen land; he has given you the Book of Books; he has given you an enlightened conscience; and if you perish under the sound of the ministry, you perish more fearfully and terribly, than if you had perished anywhere else.

This doctrine is as much God's Word as the other. You ask me to reconcile the two. I answer, they do not want any reconcilement; I never tried to reconcile them to myself, because I could never see a discrepancy. If you begin to put fifty or sixty quibbles to me, I cannot give any answer. Both are true; no two truths can be inconsistent with each other; and what you have to do is to believe them both. With the first one, the saint has most to do. Let him praise the free and sovereign grace of God, and bless his name. With the second, the sinner has the most to do. O sinner, humble thyself under the mighty hand of God, when thou thinkest of how often he hath shown his love to thee, by bidding thee come to himself, and yet how often thou hast spurned his Word and refused his mercy, and turned a deaf ear to every invitation, and hast gone thy way to rebel against a God of love, and violate the commands of him that loved thee.

And now, how shall I conclude? My first exhortation shall be to Christian people. My dear friends, I beseech you do not in any way give yourselves up to any system of faith apart from the Word of God. The Bible, and the Bible alone, is the religion of Protestants: I am the successor of the great and venerated Dr. Gill, whose theology is almost universally received among the stronger Calvinistic churches; but although I venerate his memory, and believe his teachings, yet he is not my Rabbi. What you find in God's Word is for you to believe and to receive. Never be frightened at a doctrine; and above all, never be frightened at a name. Some one said to me the other day, that he thought the truth lay somewhere between the two extremes. He meant right, but I think he was wrong. I do not think the truth lies between the two extremes, but in them both. I believe the higher a man goes the better, when he is preaching the matter of salvation. The reason why a man is saved is grace, grace, grace; and you may go as high as you like there. But when you come to the question as to why men are damned, then the Arminian is far more right than the Antinomian. I care not for any denomination or party, I am as high as Huntingdon upon the matter of *salvation*, but question me about damnation, and you will get a very different answer. By the grace of God I ask no man's applause, I preach the Bible as I find it. Where we get wrong is where the Calvinist begins to meddle with the question of damnation, and interferes with the justice of God; or when the Arminian denies the doctrine of grace.

My second exhortation is,—Sinners, I beseech every one of you who are unconverted and ungodly, this morning to put away every form and fashion of excuse that the devil would have you make concerning your being unconverted. Remember, that all the teaching in the world can never excuse you for being enemies to God by wicked works. When we beseech you to be reconciled to him, it is because we know you will never be in your proper place until you are reconciled. God has made you; can it be right that you should disobey him? God feeds you every day: can it be right that you should still live in disobedience to him? Remember, when the heavens shall be on a blaze, when Christ shall come to judge the earth in righteousness and his people with equity, there will not be one excuse that you can make which will be valid at the last great day. If you should attempt to say, "Lord, I have never heard the word;" his answer would be, "Thou didst hear it; thou heardest it plainly." "But Lord, I had an evil will." "Out of thine own mouth will I condemn thee; thou hadst that evil will, and I condemn thee for it. This is the condemnation, that light is come into the world; and men love darkness rather than light, because their deeds are evil." "But Lord," some will say, "I was not predestinated." "What hadst thou to do with that? Thou didst do according to thine own will when thou didst rebel. Thou wouldest not come unto me, and now I destroy thee for ever. Thou hast broken my law—on thine own head be the guilt." If a sinner could say at the great day, "Lord, I could not be saved anyhow;" his torment in hell would be mitigated by that thought: but this shall be the very edge of the sword, and the very burning of the fire—"Ye knew your duty and ye did it not: ye trampled on everything that was holy; ye neglected the Saviour, and how shall ye escape if ye neglect so great salvation?"

Now, with regard to myself; you may some of you go away and say, that I was Antinomian in the first part of the sermon and Arminian at the end. I care not. I beg of you to search the Bible for yourselves. To the law and to the testimony; if I speak not according to this Word, it is because there is no light in me. I am willing to come to that test. Have nothing to do with me where I have nothing to do with Christ. Where I separate from the truth, cast my words away. But if what I say be God's teaching, I charge you, by him that sent me, give these things your thoughts, and turn unto the Lord with all your hearts.[7]

---

[7] Spurgeon, C. H. (1858). Sovereign Grace and Man's Responsibility. In *The New Park Street Pulpit Sermons* (Vol. 4, pp. 337–344). London; Glasgow: Passmore & Alabaster; James Paul; George John Stevenson; George Gallie.

THE FULNESS AND THE FILLING

A Sermon

PUBLISHED ON THURSDAY, MARCH 1ST, 1917.

DELIVERED BY

C. H. SPURGEON,

AT THE METROPOLITAN TABERNACLE, NEWINGTON.

"And of his fulness have all we received, and grace for grace."—John 1:16.

ONE Sabbath day I was staying in an Italian town on the other side of the Alps. Of course, the whole population was Romish. Two or three of us, therefore, being Protestants, held a little service for the worship of God in the simple manner that is our wont. After this, I went out for a walk. The weather being hot and sultry, I sought the outskirts of the town to get to as quiet and cool a spot as possible. Presently I came to an archway at the foot of a hill, where there was an announcement that any person who would climb the hill with proper intentions should receive the pardon of his sins and five days' indulgence. I thought I might as well have five days' indulgence as anybody else, and if it were of any advantage, to have it laid by in store. I cannot tell you all I saw as I went, first one way, and then another, up that hill. Suffice it to say that there was a series of little churches, through the windows of which you might look, as one in his boyish days looked through a peep-show. The whole scene and circumstance of the passion and death of Christ were thus modelled, beginning with his agony in the garden, where he was represented in a figure as large as life, with the drops of bloody sweat falling to the ground; the three disciples a stone's throw off, and the rest of the apostles outside the garden wall. Every feature looked as real as if one had been standing upon the spot. I scrutinised each group narrowly, and carefully read the Latin text which served as an index, till I reached the top of the hill, where I saw a garden, just like an English garden, and as I pushed open the door I faced these words, "Now there was a garden, and in the garden there was a new sepulchre." Walking down a path I came to a sepulchre; so I stooped down and looked in, as Peter had done. There, instead of seeing a picture of the corpse of Christ, I read in gilded letters these words—of course, in the Latin tongue—"He is not here, for he is risen; come, see the place where the Lord lay." Passing on, I came to a place where His ascension was represented. On the summit was a large church, into which I entered. No one was there, yet the place for me had a marvellous interest. High up in the ceiling there swung a rude representation of the Lord Jesus Christ, and round it were statues of the prophets, all with their fingers pointing up to him. There was Isaiah, with a scroll in his left hand, on which was written, "He was despised and rejected of men, a man of sorrows, and acquainted with grief." Further on stood Jeremiah, and on his scroll was written, "Behold and see if there was ever sorrow like unto my sorrow, which was done unto me." All round the church I read in great words, that were large enough to be seen, though they were blazoned on the top of the ceiling, "Moses and all the prophets spoke and wrote concerning him."

Now, though I cannot take you to see that remarkable sight, which I shall never forget, I would fain bring before your mind's eye something like it: Suppose that all the saints who lived from the days of Adam, down to the times when Malachi closed the Old Testament, and that all the saints who lived in Christ's time, and then on through the early ages of the Church in the days of Chrysostom, and Augustine, and all the holy men who afterwards gathered around the Reformers, and all who in every place have served God since then—suppose they all stood in one vast circle; to whom do you suppose they would every one point? To whom would they all bear witness? Why, with outstretched arm, every one of them would turn to the Lord Jesus Christ, and speak his praise. Could you then enquire into their individual history, you would find among them characters exceedingly diverse, though all remarkably beautiful; some renowned for courage, others for gentleness; some for patient endurance, others for diligent labour, and yet all inspired by a common faith; all of them aglow with fervent gratitude; all of them looking with steadfast gaze and love intense towards ONE from whom they had received every gift that profited them; and that One, Jesus Christ, the Son of God, the Saviour of men. The rule would admit of not a single exception. From each man in his own proper position, from every man in his own particular calling, from all the individuals severally in their own personal experience, the innumerable voices, distinct, but blending in chorus, would go up from earth to heaven, saying, "Of his fulness have all we received, and grace for grace." Then methinks from the excellent glory would come a response. The inhabitants of heaven would echo back the strain, "Of his fulness have all we, the glorified spirits, received, and grace for grace." This is the testimony of the Church militant, and of the Church triumphant; yea, it is the testimony of all who in every place and at every time have come and put their trust under the shadow of his wings.

Our text seems to suggest two thoughts—*the fulness* and *the filling*—upon each of which I will attempt to say a little, a very little. With so infinite a theme we can do no more than children do when they take up a little sea-water in a shell; their tiny scoop cannot embrace the ocean. I stand on the narrow edge of a vast expanse, and leave the boundless depths to your contemplation. *His fulness*! an inexhaustible reservoir. *Our filling*! an illimitable endowment. Beloved, the river of God, which is full of water, can well supply the little canals that are fed from such a fountain with grace for grace.

I. THE FULNESS I said. It is his fulness, the fulness of Jesus Christ, the Son of God. Oh! what a fulness he has! The fulness which *belongs to him personally*! Note this well; forget it not. Our Redeemer is essentially God. By nature he is divine. He has condescendingly taken upon himself our nature, and he is most truly and assuredly man. Very God! for to him belong all the attributes of Jehovah. Very man! for when he took our flesh and blood, he accepted the entire sympathies of our creatureship. In his complex nature he possesses fulness. In him dwelleth all the fulness of the Godhead bodily. He has the fulness of omnipotence, and all power is given unto him as Mediator in heaven and in earth. Omnipresence is his to perfection; "for where two or three are gathered together in my name, there am I (he said) in the midst of them." He has essential wisdom. Even when on earth, "he did not commit himself, because he knew all men, and needed not that any should testify of man, for he knew what was in man." In him is fulness of justice. The Father hath given all judgment unto the Son. "Shall not God judge the world in righteousness by that man whom he hath ordained, whereof he hath given assurance unto all men in that he hath raised him from the dead?" In him is fulness of mercy, for "through this man is preached unto you the forgiveness of sins." The attributes of God make up a perfect total. The unity, with all its uniqueness, is his. Divisions and sub-divisions are ours. The fractional parts of which we take account are but the breaking up of a great fact to our weak understanding. Think as you may, your thought cannot describe or compass God; for God is all that is good and blessed. And as is God, so is Christ. All the divine attributes are contained and represented in Christ Jesus in their fulness, not diminished by his humiliation, but resplendent by his triumph.

"In him dwelleth all the fulness of the Godhead." He is the express image of the Father's person, the brightness of his Father's glory; not mere glory, but the brightness of his Father's glory. What confidence this ought to inspire in our hearts! The fulness from which you and I derive the grace we receive is none other than the infinite fulness of God over all blessed for ever, whose name is Immanuel, God with us. *There was a fulness also in Christ in respect to his manhood*. Nothing was lacking to him that is involved in being by nature and constitution a perfect man. He was pure; he did not inherit any sin; his disposition did not tend towards any evil. Still, all that pertains to the original creatureship of man as created by God did Christ possess in the fulness of development. Hence, my brethren, there is in him at this moment a fulness of sympathy. He is not such a high priest as cannot be touched with a feeling of our infirmities, but he was tempted in all points like as we are, yet without sin. Do not suppose that Jesus is less human than you are yourselves; he is fully human. Do not imagine that he is less tender than you would be towards the weak and suffering; he is full of tenderness; his bowels melt with love. A mother has often a tenderness that we do not find in a father. Masculine strength and courage do not always blend with the gentle, sympathetic qualities of woman. Howbeit when God created man in his own image, male and female created he them. The virtues, if I may so say, of both sexes were combined in our Lord; the suavity as well as the staunchness—the feminine as well as the masculine of our common humanity. Human nature in its totality and completeness was fully possessed and thoroughly represented by him. The sympathetic nature which melts at the tear and smiles at the joy of others, was as truly his as the heroic nature that parleys not with fear, but acts with promptitude and suffers with fortitude, like a warrior in the hosts of the Lord. There is thus a fulness of humanity as well as a fulness of divinity in Christ Jesus, our Saviour—a fulness of perfection in his blessed person which may well fix your trust and rivet your admiration.

In our Lord, likewise, there is what I may venture to call, for lack of a better word, *an acquired fulness*. He has sojourned on earth, and rendered entire and undeviating obedience to the law of God, having taken upon himself the form of a servant, and by his righteousness earned wages; a fulness, an everlasting well-spring of merit. Throughout his whole life he honoured the divine law, and glorified God on the earth. In doing his Father's will, his action was so voluntary and so vicarious, that he has accumulated an inexhaustible fund of merit, which all of us who believe in his name may plead before the Father's throne. More especially did his death consummate the obedience, and constitute its sterling worth, its intrinsic virtue. His death, with all its surroundings—from the bloody sweat in the olive garden to the last cry, "Into thy hands I commit my spirit"—was sublime. All through the scourging and the splitting, the shame, the wounding, the crucifixion, the thirst, the desertion, and the death itself, he was working out an atonement for us;

> "Bearing, that we might never bear
> His Father's righteous ire."

And now with him risen from the dead, raised to the right hand of the Majesty on high, there is a fulness of prevalence in his intercession when he pleads his blood; a fulness of cleansing power when the Spirit applies the blood to the guilty conscience; a fulness of peace to the heart when his blood speaketh better things than that of Abel. In that fountain filled with blood drawn from Immanuel's veins there is a fulness that never can be exhausted by all the sin of man. He has finished the work which his Father gave him to do. Now the covenant is ratified with him that he shall see of the travail of his soul and shall be satisfied. In these respects we are convinced that there is an acquired as well as a personal fulness in our precious Lord.

No less hath he *a fulness of dignity, of high prerogative*. He is a Prophet. By him are all his people taught, warned, counselled, and encouraged with a blessed hope. He is a Priest, and by him they are cleansed from sin, and consecrated to God. Moreover, he is also a King, spreading the ægis of protection over all his liege subjects, and ordaining peace for them. Under his beneficent rule, they prosper. Thou good Shepherd! Thou great Shepherd of the sheep! there is no office or obligation that was necessary for our welfare, but thou hast taken it, and undertaken it in our behalf. Thou art to us all that we require, and all that we could desire. Join all the qualities involved in name or fame that commend themselves most closely to your heart, because they meet your necessities, or draw forth your sympathies, and you shall find that he comprises them all in liberal, lavish fulness. Nor hath his prerogative any limit. As a priest, who hath once offered a sacrifice of everlasting prevalence, his absolution or his benediction is final and irrevocable. As a prophet, his authority is unimpeachable; the authority with which he teaches allows of no appeal. As a king, he has right as well as might on his side. In the midst of Zion, willing subjects yield to his beneficent sway; in the outer world, reluctant rebels must submit themselves to his sceptre. He is no priest whose vain pretence has no valid prescript; he is no prophet whose teaching is uncertain in its tone, or limited in its range; he is no king whose prerogative is not sanctioned by his wisdom, and whose government awakens no fealty of love. But in the administration of all his offices, our Lord Jesus Christ shows a fulness of qualification, and gives a fulness of satisfaction. In such respects he has no rival; nor is there any room for a rival to arise.

And let me say here that the power with which our Lord exercises these offices may well command our devout confidence. Do you want to learn the truth? Oh! come to the prophet of Nazareth, and you shall find that there is a satiety of truth in his teaching such as was never found in heathen augur, or even to the same extent in Hebrew seer! Or do you want acceptance before God? Oh! then, come ye to the Priest who is not of the tribe of Levi, but a Priest after the order of Melchisedec, whose royalty confers dignity on his sacerdotal office! He can present your sacrifice with the much incense of his merit that is acceptable before the throne. Or do you want strength? Do you need one to fight your battles, to take hold of the shield and the buckler, and draw out the spear, and handle the bow? Behold, the Hero of Israel, whose exploits are told in your songs—Jesus, the King by right of conquest, as well as by right divine, hath a fulness of power and majesty with which no adversary can cope. He reigneth. His reign is the consolation of his people, the guarantee of their peace. These are bare outlines. Time would fail me to enumerate all his offices. They are very numerous; but, however numerous, Christ possesses them all. He enjoys the prerogatives peculiar to them all in the fullest degree. He possesses the power to exercise them all to the fullest extent.

But in Christ there is verily a blessed fulness *of every kind of perfection.* Whatsoever there may be that is lovely or of good repute is to be found in Christ. All that is virtuous or amiable in the character of men; all that is noble and illustrious in the endowments that Heaven bestows on the most privileged of creatures, our Lord possessed. It was said of Henry the Eighth that if all the likenesses of tyrants had been lost out of history, they might have been reproduced out of the one character of that monstrous tyrantking. So, if all the holy features of patriarchs and prophets, of saints and martyrs, that ever lived were blotted from the canvas of history, they all might be painted afresh from the one life of the Divine person of our ever-adorable Lord Jesus Christ. In him there was not only one perfection, but all perfections meet and blend to make up one matchless perfection. There was not one sweet alone in him, but in him all sweets combine in a perfect sweetness. John has love, Peter courage, Paul zeal—each saint has his own peculiarity, but in Christ all the qualities of goodness and grace converge. He exhibits them in the highest degree and the purest harmony. After such manner are they incorporated in him as to produce a character the like of which was never known before, nor ever shall be witnessed again.

And never forget that *a fulness of the Holy Spirit* abideth in Christ. The Lord gives not the Spirit by measure unto him. He hath the residue of the Spirit. His is the head upon which the anointing oil is fully poured. We, who are but as the skirts of his garments, are favoured with some droppings thereof, but the fulness of the anointing of the Spirit was bestowed upon Jesus Christ our Lord, and from him his members must receive the portion they enjoy.

His fulness! I linger on the word, for I revel in the meditation. Such a fulness as admits of no diminution, for it is *an abiding* fulness. What though all the saints of every age have come to Christ, and drawn their supplies from him, he is just as full as ever. Think not that those who first came drank of a copious fountain that has been partly drained by the myriads who have since slaked their thirst. The Apostles received of his fulness, and so do we; they without prejudice to us; we without prejudice to those who shall follow after us. When I came to Christ eighteen hundred years after the Apostles came, yet I received of the fulness at just the same rate as when Peter, John, or Paul received it. Should this dispensation last another thousand years, and some poor, trembling wretch should come to the foot of the cross to receive mercy, he will not receive Christ half full, but he shall receive of Christ's fulness, for it is an abiding fulness. It is never less than full; never can be more than full. In him there is an infinity of grace and truth. Such fulness is there in him at all times, under all your circumstances of trial, aye, and under all conditions of sin too. The fulness of Christ to supply will always exceed the faith of the believer to seek. And when you feel your emptiness more than you ever did before, then you will set the most store upon his abounding towards us in all wisdom and prudence. Considering, then, his abiding fulness, his inexhaustible fulness, his available fulness, I entreat you to avail yourself of this fulness now without demur, without delay. As there is *a fulness*, so there is:—

II. A FILLING.

This is to be our second part. I must speak of it with brevity. "Of his fulness have all we received." Surely, then, *all the saints were empty* before. You are empty, my brother, and so was Abraham, so was Paul. Grace, the free grace of God, has made all the difference between Peter and Judas, though the one repented and the other despaired; the one travelled the heavenly road, the other went down quickly to hell. They stood on equal footing in transgression, till grace made them to differ. What radical difference is there between one man and another from a legal point of view?

"All have sinned and come short of the glory of God." All alike have to come to Christ empty of merit, or they would never come at all. That was a pretty tale we heard the other day, and it points a right good moral. A worthy, consistent, industrious woman was married to a low, worthless, dissipated husband. Both of them, however, were alike ignorant of the gospel. They came together to the house of prayer; they heard together the tidings of mercy; they each believed, and each of them received the Saviour, and they both were saved the same way; they both found mercy on the same terms. To the rich, free, sovereign grace of God they vied with one another in ascribing the praise. That is a fact. It occurred last week. I do not know whether this makes it more convincing to you; but I might say, as Elihu said to Job, "Lo, all these things worketh God oftentimes with men, to bring back his soul from the pit, to be enlightened with the light of the living!"

Observe that the filling is universal. All the saints partake of it. "Of his fulness have *all we* received." There are manifold diversities of experience among the Lord's people, but in some things they share and share alike. Some saints do not undergo the stress of trial and tribulation that others pass through. Here, however, there is no partiality. They have, every one of them, received out of Christ's fulness. Not one of them could do without receiving it; not one of them could receive it from any other hand than that of the Divine Benefactor. They earned it not. They accepted it. They received it of Jesus Christ.

This is peculiar to the saints. While it says, "Of his fulness have all WE received," manifestly a certain body of people have become partakers of a privilege which it is no less evident that all men have not received. What thousands and tens of thousands there are who, when invited to the gospel feast, reject the call, "make a wretched choice, and rather starve than come." "All we!" that is, all of those who have believed. And who are "*we*," or what are "*we*," that such grace should be given to us in preference to anybody else? Ah! brethren, little cause enough have we for self-satisfaction! On the score of desert no choice had ever fallen on us We were the vilest, the least worthy, the least attractive, and, in some respects, the least hopeful! Oh! grace, it is thy wont into unlikeliest hearts to come, and it is the glory of love divine to find in darkest spots a home! "All we"; we who were once dead in trespasses and sins; we who were once lost like the prodigal son, lost like the wandering sheep, lost like the piece of money; we who needed seeking, needed finding, need saving; yet of his fulness have all we received. Recollect that the reception is peculiar to believers; it does not go beyond them.

Be it clear, however, that there is, and must be, *a personal reception in every case.* "Of his fulness have *all* we received." No one of us can receive it transmitted from another, but each one of us receives it directly from him. Your father's grace cannot save you. It was a wise speech of the wise virgins. When the foolish virgins said to them, "Give us of your oil," they replied, "Not so, lest there be not enough for us and you; go rather to them that sell, and buy for yourselves." Family piety involves responsibilities, but it cannot stand in the place of personal godliness. Dear hearer, you must go to Christ for yourself. All who ever were saved have done so, and you certainly will not be saved unless you are led to do the same. It is a personal filling. "Of his fulness have all we received."

The bounty is gratuitous. Notice the next words, "*and grace for grace.*" It is not said, "Of his fulness have we all purchased," nor "Of his fulness have we all earned a share"; but it is all passive. We have received. What does the vessel do to fit itself for the water that flows into it? Why, it does nothing. All its doing can fit it to receive is an undoing; that is to say, it empties itself to prepare itself to be filled. Oh! if any of you desire to find Jesus Christ, the doing must be in the way of undoing. You must be emptied to be filled. The preparation is a consciousness that you are not prepared. In such unpreparedness you are prepared for Christ. This is an enigma and a riddle. Those who think themselves prepared for him are not so, but those who know that they are not prepared are just the souls upon whom his grace will come. Poverty, not riches; blindness, not sight; emptiness, not fulness; sinfulness, not virtue—these are the things Christ looks for. He is come to seek and to save that which was lost; not that which had won victories; not that which was splendid in its own esteem, but that which was defeated, ruined, lost. If thou art lost, he comes to seek and to save such as thou art. Oh! thou who wast once lost, but now art found, bless his name that thou hast received of his fulness!

"*And grace for grace!*" What mean these words? We can only just touch them as a swallow with its wing touches the pool; we cannot pretend to enter into their depth. "Grace for grace." Does that mean that those who receive grace under the old dispensation were afterwards led to receive the grace of the new dispensation? Does it mean that we who have the grace of conviction, with the Holy Spirit as a spirit of bondage, shall receive by-and-bye the spirit of liberty, and get out of conviction, through conversion, into full pardon and enjoyment of peace with God? Is that the grace, when grace turns into glory, and we come before the throne does it mean grace by degrees; grace upon grace; a little grace to begin with, and more grace afterwards? "He giveth more grace"; grace following on grace, and, further on, superabounding grace, when grace turns into glory, and we come before the throne of grace for ever and ever. Does it mean that God leads us on step by step, adding to our spiritual wealth, initiating us first into simple things, and afterwards leading us into deeper matters? "Grace for grace."

Yes, it means that, but it means more. God gives *grace in preparation for further grace*—the grace of a broken heart—to make room for deep repentance and abhorrence of sin; the grace of hatred of sin to make way for the grace of holy and careful walking, humiliation, and faith in Jesus; the grace of careful walking to make room for the grace of close communion with Christ; the grace of close communion with the Lord Jesus Christ to make room for the grace of full conformity to his image; perhaps the grace of conformity to his image to make room for the higher grace of brighter views of himself, and still closer incomings into the very heart of the Lord Jesus. It is grace that helps us on in grace. When a beggar asks you for a penny, and you give him one, he does not ask you for a sixpence; or if you give him a shilling, he would not consider that an argument why you should give him a sovereign. But you may deal thus with God. If you have only got, as it were, an ounce of grace, that is a reason why you should then pray God for a great weight of grace, and afterwards for a far more exceeding and eternal weight of glory. Believe that he gives grace for grace; that is, grace that you may open your mouth for more grace. The grace you have expands your heart, and gives you capacity for receiving yet more grace. Do you not send your child to school to learn A B C? You may call that the grace of learning his alphabet. Yes, but it is preparatory to his learning to read the spelling-book. Well, but what does he learn to read the spelling-book for? Why, that is a preparation for something else. So one grace gives us a preparation for another grace, and thus as we have more grace we realise the blessedness of this divine filling out of his fulness.

Or, suppose we read the passage thus—*grace answerable to grace*—and even this will admit of two constructions. Let God give me grace to be a preacher; he will surely give me grace to discharge the office. Perhaps he has given you grace to teach in a Sabbath school, then you want a further supply of grace to enable you to be an efficient teacher. Peradventure you have the grace of resignation to suffer for Christ's sake, you will need the grace of patience to support you in the midst of pain or persecution. You are called to pray, and you yield yourself up to be a wrestler with God in prayer. This is a great grace. Oh! may you have grace answerable to that grace, that when you get with the angel by the brook Jabbok, you may take hold of his strength, plead his promise, his covenant, and his oath, and never let him go until he bless you. Thus, a halt and fainting Jacob comes off as a prevailing Israel. May we thus ever have grace answerable to grace. "Grace for grace" may imply grace received by us answerable to the grace that is in Christ. Oh! that we Christians had grace in some measure commensurate with the grace that is treasured up for us in him! All that is in him belongs to you. Then the degree of your daily supplies ought to be proportionate to his ample, unlimited wealth and fulness. A young heir to a large estate, though not of full age, generally gets an allowance made to him by the executors, or the trustees, or the Court of Chancery, suitable to the position he is presently to occupy. If he has £100,000 a year in prospect, he would hardly be limited to a penny a week, like a poor man's child. We cannot suppose that he would have a mean allowance made him such as would barely enable him to live in a humble cottage on the rich domain he is entitled to. Oh! no; thát would be a meagre pittance out of all proportion to his position. When I see one child of God always mourning, another always doubting, and yet another always scheming, I feel a kind of disappointment; I see they are living below their privileges. They do not seem to have grace in possession answerable to the grace they have in reversion. We always inculcate the propriety, on the part of all our people, of living within their incomes; but I will defy the child of God to live beyond his income in a spiritual sense. You that have but little spending money are like the elder brother in the parable. You say, "Thou never gavest me a kid that I might make merry with my friends"; and your Father replies, "Son, thou art ever with me; and all that I have is thine." If you do not have it, it is your own fault; it is all there, and is freely yours. You have but to ask, and you shall receive; to seek, and you shall find. Oh! could we once get grace in us at all like the grace that is in Christ, what Christians we should be! No longer starlight Christians and moonlight Christians, but sunlight believers, letting our light shine before the sons of men. Oh! to be among the three Mighties of our royal David! May each of us covet such a position as this, and God grant it to us for his love's sake!

"Grace for grace" obviously means *grace in abundance.* Like the waves of the sea, when one comes there is another close behind it. Before you can say that one is gone, there is another coming to fill its place. There they come. Who shall count them? In long succession, wave follows wave. So is God's grace. "Grace for grace." One grace has hardly come into your soul but what there is another one. You have heard the story of Rowland Hill having a hundred pounds entrusted to him for the benefit of a poor minister. He thought that if he sent him the hundred pounds, it would be too large a sum to give him all at once; he would scarcely know how to husband it, and perhaps he would not be so thankful for it as if he had it doled out in smaller amounts. So he sent him five pounds, and wrote in the letter, "More to follow." Letters did not come often in those days of ninepenny or eighteenpenny postage, but in about another week he forwarded another five pounds, and a note with it, "More to follow." After a short interval he did the like again, still saying, "More to follow." So it went on for ever so long, always with "More to follow," till the dear good man, I should think, must have been at his wits' end to know what could follow when so many good presents came to one who needed them so much. Now that is just how God has done with me, and I believe he is just doing the same with all of you who are his people. He has sent you a mercy, and when he has sent it, you might have seen, if you had looked at the envelope, that it was an earnest of further benefits and benefactions—"More to follow." The mercy you have received to-day has written upon it legibly, "More to follow," and that which will come to-morrow will have upon it, "More to follow." "Grace for grace." Oh! sing unto him a new song. Let him have fresh songs for fresh mercies, and as he multiplies the mercy, so do you multiply the praises you ascribe to his name.

"Grace for grace!" Does it not mean *grace from him to produce grace in us*? We receive from the fulness of Christ, of his grace, in order that it may be a living seed that shall produce grace in us as its natural fruit. The grace of gratitude should be produced in us by the grace of generosity from God. We ought to be gracious with a holy joyfulness for all his goodness. I hope we shall have the grace of patience under all sufferings, and the grace of zeal in all our labours. At a time like this, my brethren, when we are seeking the conversion of sinners with special efforts, may we have grace from Jesus that shall make all the graces fruitful and fragrant in us! So shall we be to the Saviour as a garden of olives and pomegranates, of lilies and sweet flowers, and may he take a delight in us! When Cyrus took the Greek Ambassador through his garden, he challenged him to admire its charms. The Spartan approved all he saw, but still his admiration was cool and critical. "This garden," said its master, "yields me more pleasure and satisfaction than you can imagine, or I can express." "And why?" asked the visitor. "Because," replied Cyrus, "I planted every tree in it myself. I planned all the paths, and all the flowers have I reared. No hand but mine has dug the soil, tended the plants, pruned the trees, or done aught beside but my own." His toil and his trouble thus endeared the place to the king. So, truly, Christ can say when he looks upon his people, "There is a fruitful bough there; I pruned that. He was sick, long laid aside from business, he feared his family would be starved; I was pruning him then; but I love the fruit that is on him because I know how it came there. That plant yonder which is blooming now and shedding such a sweet perfume of love, well do I recollect when it was drooping and ready to die. I came and watered it. She, timid disciple, would say, 'Blessed be the gentle hand that shed the dew and poured nourishment on my poor, parched, and withered root!' " Yes, the Saviour gives us "grace for grace" that we may produce grace. I leave the thought with you for meditation, and the issues for your edification, only praying that his Holy Spirit may work in you "grace for grace."

Oh! that all of you might receive grace from him. You will never get grace anywhere else. Go to him at once by faith, with humble prayer. Plenteous grace with him is found; all the grace you shall ever require between now and glory you shall find stored up in him. His grace is our benediction. Of it may you one and all partake! Amen.[8]

---

[8] Spurgeon, C. H. (1917). The Fulness and the Filling. In *The Metropolitan Tabernacle Pulpit Sermons* (Vol. 63, pp. 97–108). London: Passmore & Alabaster.

THE GLORIES OF FORGIVING GRACE

A Sermon

Delivered on Lord's-day Morning, August 29th, 1880, by

C. H. SPURGEON,

AT THE METROPOLITAN TABERNACLE, NEWINGTON.

"In whom we have redemption through his blood, the forgiveness of sins, according to the riches of his grace."—Ephesians 1:7.

Last Sunday morning the subject was redemption, "Ye are not your own: ye are bought with a price." The sequel to redemption is pardon: the text gives us that doctrine, for it tells us that redemption through the blood of Jesus involves the forgiveness of sins. Our subject at this time shall be the forgiveness of sin, the measure, mode, medium, and manifestation of it as set forth in the words before us. May the Holy Spirit sweetly open up to us the glories of our sin-forgiving God, and cause us to exult in the riches of his grace.

Beloved friends, no one can say that we have before us a theme which is unpractical, speculative, and fanciful; no one will be able to charge the preacher with discoursing upon a subject with which his hearers have little or nothing to do, or wandering into barren fancies which cannot affect their actual lives. It is true that some sermons are barely human, and might as well have been addressed to the inhabitants of Jupiter or Saturn as to ourselves; but such shall not be the case with our discourse. We have no hair-lines of metaphysical subtlety before us; our theme runs parallel with the beaten track of everyday life. Sin is, alas, too familiar with us. We have all committed it, the slime of the serpent has been upon us; we are affected by it still, as an adder in the path it biteth at our heels, and it will be our daily trial, like the fiery serpents in the wilderness, till we enter the promised rest. Sin as a thing of the past cannot be forgotten; was there ever a sorer bondage than that with which it made us serve with rigour? Sin as a matter of affliction for the present is not to be ignored:

was there ever a sterner fight than we have to wage against evil without and within? Sin as a danger still ahead must not be overlooked: were there ever rocks or quicksands more terrible to the mariner than temptations to sin which yet lie before us on our voyage to heaven? Sin is always around us. Whither shall we hasten to escape from its presence? If in holy communion we climb to Pisgah's top we stumble even in view of Canaan, and slip upon our high places; and if we descend into the lowest deeps, like David, till all God's waves and billows have gone over us, our despondency and unbelief cause us to sin amid our humiliations. Should I take the wings of the morning and fly unto the uttermost parts of the sea, unless I could escape from mine own self, even there would sin follow me, and its hand would smite me to my sore wounding. Nothing can be more practical than the doctrine which deals with sin and its removal, and no news can be more pleasant than the tidings of remission. Why, the very sound of that word, "Forgiveness of sins" is a joy for ever; no marriage bell hath more of music in its notes. To the guilty forgiveness is a tone of joy which their jaded ear is able to hear without strain. It ministereth refreshment to the weary heart. High joys and rare delights are apt to send forth raised notes which terrified consciences cannot endure; their very sweetness is sharp and distressing to the sorrowful, and their harmony causes a deeper discord in the broken heart: but forgiveness hath a soft, silver sound, mellow and tender, and when man's ear is stunned with the thunder and the terror of the wrath to come, then he is charmed to listen to its soothing melody. The gentle love-whispers of free grace and dying love, and pardons bought with blood, are as heaven's own sonnets to troubled souls.

It is my earnest desire, dear friends, that many this morning may come to believe in the joyful doctrine of the forgiveness of sins. It is an article in the creed, but I want it to be a substantive in your lives. Most men say that they believe it, but their belief is often nominal, and a nominal faith, like nominal wealth, only makes the absence of the reality the more deplorable. In two instances there is clearly no faith in forgiven sin; and the first is in the case of those who have never felt that they are sinful. How can he who does not believe in the existence of sin believe in the forgiveness of it? His whole confession on that matter belongs to the region of fiction. If sin is not a terrible fact to you, pardon will never be more than a notion.

A second class of persons who do not believe in forgiveness are those who know the guilt of sin but are not yet able to believe in the Lord Jesus for the remission of their transgressions. They need to be admonished as Luther was by the godly old monk. When he was greatly distressed under conviction of his guilt the aged man said, "Didst thou not say this morning in the creed, 'I believe in the forgiveness of sin'?" Luther, like many more, had repeated those words, but had never grasped their meaning. Oh, my dear hearers, do not be theoretical believers. You believe in sin, believe also in its pardon. Let the one be as much a truth as the other. You believe in the punishment of sin in the case of the impenitent, be equally sure of the pardon of sin to believers. You believe in the guilt of your own personal sin, believe also for yourself in the power of Jesus at this moment to blot out all your transgressions, and, lo, they shall vanish as a cloud which is driven before the north wind. Forgiveness in Christ Jesus accepted by faith is now to be enjoyed, and with it perfect rest and peace of heart. God grant it to you at this present moment: then shall my theme be marrow and fatness to you.

According to our text forgiveness of sins is a matter of grace, and yet it is connected with the price paid by our Redeemer. We spoke last Sunday morning of a price being paid, and here the text saith, "In whom we have redemption through his blood;" but the fact of Christ having paid a price and having satisfied justice does not remove the pardon of sin out of the region of pure grace. Because justice is satisfied we are not therefore to say that mercy is excluded. I cannot at this time go into the details to explain how the facts stand; but so it is according to the word of revelation, that, albeit the salvation of a sinner is conducted upon principles which are as just as his condemnation, yet at the same time the forgiveness of a sinner is an act of gratuitous favour on the part of God. As the giving of Jesus Christ, by whom justice is satisfied, was an act of free favour on the part of God, so the giving of the pardon which comes through Jesus Christ is in the same manner a matter of absolute grace, and by no means of debt or obligation. Do not, therefore, whenever you speak of our Lord's satisfaction which he made to justice, think that justice has eclipsed mercy; or, on the other hand, whenever you speak of the grace of God in pardoning sin, do not imagine that mercy has blinded the eyes of justice; for it is a part of the Christian faith that in the death of Christ justice shines out full-orbed like the sun at midday, while mercy is glorified after a like fashion. God is just, and yet the justifier of him that believeth; where sin abounded grace doth much more abound. Justice is not forgotten, but grace reigns through righteousness unto eternal life. Transgression, iniquity, and sin are put away by the All-merciful according to the riches of his grace.

Our text speaks of "the forgiveness of sins according to the riches of his grace," and from it we learn *the measure of forgiveness, the manner of it, and the manifestations of it*. O for heavenly light while we view this grand truth. Illuminate us, O thou Spirit of all grace!

I. From the text we learn THE MEASURE OF FORGIVENESS. Hear ye this, ye burdened souls, ye self-condemned spirits, ye that have shut yourselves out from hope of mercy—hear me earnestly, I pray you, that your souls may live. It may be while I am speaking to you your minds will be quieted, and you will find the key which will unlock every door in Doubting Castle, and you will be set at liberty from Giant Despair.

Observe, then, that the measure of forgiveness is the riches of God's grace, and this statement leads us to observe that *it is not the character or person of the offender which is the measure of mercy, but the character of the offended One*. Is there not rich consolation in this undoubted fact? The pardon to be hoped for is not to be measured by you and what you are, but by God and what he is. In matters of offence and forgiveness the rule almost always holds good, that pardon becomes likely or unlikely, easy or difficult, not so much according to the offence as according to the character of the person offended. One man will forgive a grievous wrong while another will not overlook a wry word. Take an instance from English history: John had most villainously treated his brother Richard in his absence. Was it likely that when he of the lion's heart came home he would pass over his brother's grievous offence? If you look at John, villain that he was, it was most unlikely that he should be forgiven; but then, if you consider the brave, high-souled Richard, the very flower of chivalry, you expect a generous deed. Base as John was he was likely to be forgiven, because Richard was so free of heart, and accordingly pardon was right royally given by the great-hearted monarch. Had John been only half as guilty, if his brother Richard had been like himself he would have made him lay his neck on the block. If John had been Richard and Richard had been John, no matter how small the offence, there would have been no likelihood of pardon at all. So is it in all matters of transgression and pardon. You must take the offence somewhat into account, it is true, but not one-half so much as the character of the person who has been offended. Suppose I were asked at this present time to reconcile two persons who are at enmity: if the one who evidently had been injured was one of certain brethren around me whose forgiving spirits I have long relied upon, I should feel my task to be easy, whatever the offence might have been: but I know some others about whom I should say, "I don't know. I am afraid I shall not get on the right side of them. I shall have to approach them very carefully; however small the offence, it will be hard to remove their anger." I know certain persons of old; they are quick-tempered and ready to be aggrieved for small reasons, and they are slow in burning out, having fine memories for an affront. It is hard to get a forgiving word out of such sour spirits. You see, the nature of a pardon materially depends upon the character of the pardoner. Let us establish this fact, and then see what light it throws upon the probability of pardon to any of you who are seeking it. With whom are you dealing? You have offended—who is he whom you have offended? Is it one whose anger is quickly aroused? No, the Lord is longsuffering, and exceedingly patient. Forty years long was he grieved with one generation; and many a time did he pity them and remove his wrath from them. Is he one who is hard to satisfy, and not easily persuaded to forgive? Nay, the choirs of the temple of old chanted as one of his sweetest praises, the oft-repeated words, "His mercy endureth for ever." Again and again they answered one to another, "His mercy endureth for ever." If the pardon were to be according to your character you would never be pardoned at all; if it were to be measured according to your offence you would never be forgiven; but since the probability of pardon lies in the character of God, then, O thou guilty one, thou self-condemned one, take heart of hope and come to thy Father's feet and say, "Father, forgive me, for I have sinned." Look into the face of God and see if he is not ready to forgive. Do you tell me that you dare not even think of the face of your offended God? Then I ask you to look into the face of Jesus Christ, for in his loving countenance shines all the brightness of the Father's glory. Is it possible for you to look at the Lord Jesus and doubt his willingness to forgive? He whose eyes wept over a guilty city, he whose hands were weary with incessantly doing good to those who despised him, he who gave his feet to the cruel nails for his adversaries, and who at last poured out the life-floods of his heart for those that mocked him, he must be willing to forgive! The measure of forgiveness, then, lies in the riches of divine grace, and this may encourage the chief of sinners to expect mercy.

Again, since the forgiveness of sins is "according to the riches of his grace," then *it is not according to our conceptions of God's mercy*, but according to that mercy itself, and the riches of it. We conceive hard things of God at times, we measure his corn with our bushel, we feel that he cannot pass by this and that crime, but that in certain points his grace may be vanquished by human wickedness. Our ideas of God's mercy are narrow, and we think him to be altogether such as we are. Listen, then: "My thoughts are not your thoughts, neither are my ways your ways, saith the Lord; for as the heavens are higher than the earth, so are my ways higher than your ways, and my thoughts than your thoughts." God's love is not to be measured by a mercer's yard, nor his mercy to be weighed in the balances of the merchant: he hath riches of grace surpassing all the wealth which the imagination could ascribe to him whose name is Love. When he gave his dear Son, his other self, that he might bleed and die, he gave us proof that there was no penury of love in the coffers of his heart. "He that spared not his own Son, but freely delivered him up for us all, how shall he not with him also freely give us all things?" The measure of mercy, then, is not our conception of God, but God as he really is; and who is he that can tell us how large is his love, how wide is his grace, how high is his goodness, how deep is his favour? I would have thee come, poor sinner, to God as to a deep abyss into which thy sins can be cast and never heard of more. I would have thee come to God in Christ as to one who is able with a glance of his eye to make thy sin dissolve like snow in the summer's sun, and vanish utterly, so that if it be searched for it shall not be found: yea, it shall not be, saith the Lord. Is there not a fountain in this truth overflowing with comfort to the most cast down one, whose bleeding heart is smarting under the lash of an angry conscience? I think if I had heard this truth plainly stated years ago I should not have remained so long in bondage, but I should have risen to my feet and have run to the Saviour and have found peace at once.

If, again, the measure of mercy is "according to the riches of his grace," then *no limit to pardon can be set by the amount of human sin which can be forgiven.* Sin is no trifle, and yet pardon is no impossibility. Nobody can measure the greatness of the guilt of a single sin: it is a world of iniquity. People talk of little sins, but there are no such things: the least rebellion against God is an intensely great evil. Yet there are degrees of sinning, and one offence may be greater than another, and one man's offences may be far more rank and crying than those of his neighbours. If it be possible that one of my hearers has committed all the grosser sins, has heaped them up, has raked the kennels for them, has committed crimes in a way scarcely to be spoken of, committed them again and again until the amount of his sins has become well-nigh incalculable, yet this does not render his forgiveness impossible. If there be one here who has gone to such an extreme of sin that he must set himself apart as being above all ordinary sinners, worthy of a special place in hell, worthy of a red-hot bolt from the right hand of the avenging God, yet pardon may be granted him. Hear me, O my friend: thou hast not gone beyond the power of God to pardon thee, for the measure of his pardon is "according to the riches of his grace." And he does not say that he stops short here or there by reason of excessive vileness on the transgressor's part. "All manner of sin and of blasphemy shall be forgiven unto men." There is a sin against the Holy Ghost which shall never be forgiven, but that is unpardonable only for this reason,—that where once it is committed the man never seeks forgiveness, nor desires it; that sin kills his conscience, for it is a sin which is unto death, and the sinner henceforth goes gaily down to destruction, never seeking forgiveness. If you seek mercy, be you who you may, you shall have it, if you will believe in Christ Jesus. If all the sins of all mankind were heaped upon you, if you sought mercy by confession of sin and faith in Christ, you should not be denied, but your sin should be blotted out, "according to the riches of his grace."

Another comfortable conclusion follows from this, that *no limit is set to the time in which a man has sinned*, so as to bound the reach of grace by the lapse of years. Our text does not say that there is forgiveness of sins according to such and such a time of life, but "according to the riches of his grace." It is a blessed thing to come to God when you are young, a thing to sing of throughout the rest of your existence. Happy day when my young heart first leaped at the sound of the Saviour's name! But oh, if grey hairs are covering your head, and years have ploughed their furrows on your brow, think not the forgiveness of sin to be impossible to you. What though your remaining days are so few that a little child may write them, and the last of them will soon flicker away into darkness, yet if you will come and put your trust in Jesus, your transgressions shall vanish, and your soul shall be even as a new born child; for Christ makes all things new. "According to the riches of his grace": this reaches the oldest man, this brings hope of mercy to the most aged woman. I would to God I could speak familiarly with all unconverted persons who are getting into years, and tell them not to stand back from Jesus through any fear that the past has sealed their doom, for there is forgiveness and plenteous redemption. Still the gate of mercy stands wide open, and if you are the oldest sinner that ever came to Christ, then you will be one of the special wonders of heaven; you will be one that they will gaze upon with astonishment in glory, and point you out with pleasure, saying, "Here is the oldest sinner that was born again." I think you are more likely to be received than anybody, "according to the riches of his grace."

Let me draw another inference. If pardon be "according to the riches of his grace," *it is not according to the bitterness of the sorrow which has been felt by the sinner*. There is a notion abroad that we must pass through a period of keen remorse before we can expect to be accepted with God. "Yes," says one, "I do not wonder that such a person was pardoned, since for years he was ready to destroy himself in his despair; he scarcely slept, he forgot to eat bread, he went about wringing his hands in agony." Beware of doting after this fashion. There must be sorrow for sin in every true believer, and there will be; but the best form of sorrow for sin generally follows forgiveness, and does not precede it. I never hated sin so much as when I knew that God had forgiven me. With all my soul do I sometimes sing to myself the choice lines of Mr. Monsell:

> "My sins, my sins, my Saviour!
>   How sad on thee they fall,
> Seen through thy gentle patience,
>   I tenfold feel them all.
>
> "I know they are forgiven,
>   But still their pain to me
> Is all the grief and anguish
>   They laid, my Lord, on thee.
>
> "My sins, my sins, my Saviour!
>   Their guilt I never knew
> Till, with thee, in the desert
>   I near thy passion drew;
>
> "Till with thee in the garden
>   I heard thy pleading prayer,
> And saw the sweat-drops bloody
>   That told thy sorrow there."

"But," saith one, "I am so afraid that I can never be forgiven." You have no right to entertain such a fear, for that is giving God the lie. "But I dare not trust Christ." My hearer, mind what you say on that score, for it is a tender point. You ought not to dare to doubt Christ, but there is no daring in trusting him. When God sets forth his dear Son to be a propitiation for sin, it is not humility, it is wicked pride that makes anyone say, "I dare not trust him." Who are you to raise a question about trusting Jesus, the faithful and true? It is black presumption to refuse your confidence to God who cannot lie. The Lord himself bids you come and trust his Son; do you refuse his command? Will you sooner perish than do the Lord Jesus the justice to trust him? "Ah, but surely," saith one, "I knew a person who was months and years in distress about his sin." I know such a person now. I know one who was five years an unbelieving seeker, but he was a fool for being so. There was no reason why he should have been in the dark so long, for the sun had arisen; his eyes were blindfolded by his own folly. If he had believed in Jesus Christ right off he might have had the forgiveness of sin at once. Half of that which is put down in biographies as the work of the Spirit is the work of the devil, and the result of unbelief. John Bunyan gives a long story in "Grace Abounding," and I am thankful that he does; but he never meant that we were to imitate him in his unbelief and hard thoughts of God. Those hideous doubts and horrible fears were not the work of the Spirit of God; they were the work of John Bunyan's vivid imagination and the devil together: they had nothing to do with the pardon of his sin except that they hindered him from finding it month after month. Your business, poor guilty sinner, is to believe that mercy is dealt out by God to sinners, not according to their despair and remorse, but "according to the riches of his grace." Where has God commanded us to despair? Doth he not command us to believe? Where hath he ever commanded remorse? Doth he not bid us hope in his mercy? We are to come to Jesus just as we are, and trust him, and we shall be forgiven all trespasses in a moment by our loving, waiting Father. "He that believeth in him is justified from all things, from which he could not be justified by the law of Moses." "He that believeth in him hath everlasting life."

And so let me say that the measure of God's forgiveness is *not even the strength of a man's faith*. The measure of God's forgiveness is "according to the riches of his grace." You, dear soul, are to come and trust in what Jesus Christ did when he bled away his life for sinners, and then your pardon shall be measured out to you, not according to the greatness and strength of your confidence, but according to the immeasurable mercy of the heart of God. You may have faith but as a grain of mustard seed, your faith may only dare to touch the garment's hem of the great Saviour, you may get no further than to say, "He hath said, 'Him that cometh to me I will in no wise cast out,' and I do come to him: if I perish, I will perish trusting him," and yet that faith will save you. I would your faith were stronger; I believe it will be so before long: but if it be only as the green blade which timidly springeth up from the soil in the cold spring and is almost afraid of the biting wind, if there be but life in it, if it live alone upon Christ Jesus, it will suffice for salvation. Jesus saith to the weak believer as well as to the strong saint, "thy faith hath saved thee; go in peace." Thy sins which are many are all forgiven thee if thou believest in Jesus; for the measure of thy forgiveness is not thy faith, nor thy tears of repentance, nor thy bitter regrets, nor thy sin, nor thy conception of God's goodness, nor thy character, either past or present or future; but the forgiveness which is granted from the Lord is "according to the riches of his grace." I feel half envious of men who can speak with the tongue of eloquence, for this theme deserves better speech than mine, and yet if I had the tongues of angels I could not set forth to you one half of the comfort which is to be found in this charming subject. My bare and unadorned style may not ill beseem the matchless beauty of the grace which stands before you in its own native loveliness. The God of heaven and earth who hateth sin nevertheless loveth sinners: he hath given his dear Son to die for them, and upon their accepting his Son as their hope and trust he passeth by their transgression, iniquity, and sin, not according to the feeble measure of their conceptions, but "according to the riches of his grace." Glory to God in the highest, on earth peace, goodwill towards men! Thanks be unto God for such amazing grace.

II. In the second place, I am going to spend a little time, as God may help me, in speaking upon THE MANNER OF FORGIVENESS. The manner of forgiveness is "according to the riches of his grace." Then I see in the mode and manner of forgiveness, first of all, *absolute freeness*, "According to the riches of his free favour," for that is the meaning of the word "Grace." God forgives none because of payment made by them in any form. If we could bring him mountains of gold and silver, they would be nothing worth to him: if we bring him tears in rivers or alms in alps, or resolves, vows, and promises in countless numbers, all will amount to nothing as a bribe of grace. Forgiveness, like love, is unpurchasable by us. God's pardons are absolutely free. He forgives because he chooses to forgive, out of sheer pity to the sinner, out of clear, unmixed compassion, but with no adulteration of anything like bribe or price. Forgiveness is absolutely free. Then why should not *you* have it? Oh, you who have said, "It will never come to me,"—why not to you? "Oh," you have said, "I am not prepared." Why should it not come to you though you are unprepared? Is preparedness a sort of price? Since it comes freely, why not to you? "But I have scarcely thought of it: I dropped in here this morning merely to spend an hour;"—and why not spend that hour in singing of free grace and pardoning love? Why not let this be the first hour of your true life—the hour in which you begin to live unto God? Pardon is absolutely free: "Whosoever will, let him take of the water of life freely."

"According to the riches of his grace": this hints *a royal ease*. When you and I give away money to the poor, we have to pause, and see how much is left in our purse; we have to calculate our incomes to see whether we may not be spending too much in charity; but those who have great riches can give and not calculate: even so God when he grants forgiveness gives it "according to the riches of his grace." He never has to think whether he will have grace enough left: he will be none the richer if he withholds it, none the poorer if he bestows it. There is a magnificent ease about the benefactions of God: he scatters the largesse of his mercy right and left with unstinted liberality. The Roman conquerors, traversing the Via Sacra in triumph, were accustomed to scatter gold and silver with both hands as they rode along, and the eager crowd gathered up the shower of gifts. Our Lord, when he ascended on high and led captivity captive, scattered gifts among men with royal splendour and munificence. So does God pardon sinners as if it were every-day work with him: his goodness flashes on all sides as water from a fountain in full play, or as light and heat from the noonday sun. You have not to extract forgiveness from a palm fast closed: God is more pleased to pardon than we are to be pardoned. When the prodigal son laid his head in his father's bosom, and his father kissed him, who had the most joy, think you, the son or the father? I know the prodigal's heart overflowed with gladness, but then the father's heart was more capacious, and when he said, "This my son was dead, and is alive again; was lost, and is found," there was an incalculable depth of delight in the expression. It was the father who called for music and dancing, feasting and merriment: I fear the son was hardly so demonstrative in his delight. O poor weary seekers, hear ye this inspired word and be glad—"He delighteth in mercy." Come home: come home, poor wanderer! It is harder work to you to come home than for your Father to receive you. It is more trouble for you to ask for mercy than for God to give it you; it is harder work for you to believe that he can save than it is for him to do it. To him mercy is pleasant work, the cunning art of his right-hand, which he never can forget. Oh, come and receive the mercy which the Lord gives lavishly, according to the wealth of his goodness.

"According to the riches of his grace": that means *unquestionable fulness*. The man who is forgiven of the Lord is not half forgiven, but altogether absolved. There is a theology which teaches that when a man believes in Jesus Christ he is pardoned up to a point, but in future he may get into arrears again, and if he does not see to it he may again be accused, and summoned before the judgment-seat. This is not our theology. We believe in him who said, "I give unto my sheep eternal life; and they shall never perish, neither shall any pluck them out of my hand." I believe that when Jesus Christ died for his people he did not make atonement for half their sins, but for all of them; and in that day when he said, "It is finished," there was a virtual wiping out of all the score of all his redeemed from the book of God's remembrance. Hence his salvation is complete, and those who have it are altogether delivered from the ruin which sin involves. If you come to Christ he will grant you deep, full, living, substantial pardon, such pardon as will put you among God's children, such pardon that God will have no back reckonings with you, no calling of you to account at some future time; such pardon that you shall be as much accepted as if you had never sinned, and God shall love you as though your whole life had been spent in his fear. The blood of Jesus makes us whiter than snow, and absolute innocence cannot be more white than that. There shall be no sin left against you to be in the future quoted to your dismay. Thus saith the Lord, "In those days and in that time, the iniquity of Israel shall be sought for, and there shall be none: and the sins of Judah, and they shall not be found; for I will pardon them whom I reserve." Such a mode of pardon is "according to the riches of his grace."

Again, the text implies, *irreversible certainty.* "According to the riches of his grace." For God to pardon and then afterwards to condemn would not be "according to the riches of his grace." If Her Majesty were to issue a free pardon for a criminal, and then afterwards hang him, it would be poor work: it would not be according to the riches of her favour certainly; and if you and I get pardon through Jesus Christ, we can no more be lost than God can become poor in love. Believe in Christ Jesus, and get a pardon for thy transgressions under the sign manual of Jehovah, and thou art clear for ever. "There is, therefore, now no condemnation to them that are in Christ Jesus." "As far as the east is from the west, so far hath he removed our transgressions from us;" and how far is that? It is an infinite distance, and from an infinite distance our sins can never be brought back. They are gone; they are blotted out; drowned like the Egyptians in the Red Sea: their faces we shall never see again for ever. That pardon must be irreversible which is given "according to the riches of his grace."

Once more, it suggests *unfailing renewal.* It is "forgiveness of sins according to the riches of his grace." It does not mean forgiveness up to a certain point, and then if you sin again no more forgiveness; but daily forgiveness for daily sin, a fresh spring rising for fresh thirst. Joseph Hart sings—

> "This fountain from guilt, not only makes pure,
>   And gives, soon as felt, infallible cure;
> But if guilt removèd, return, and remain,
>   Its power may be provèd again and again."

We may come to Christ as freely to-day as we did thirty years ago, and find ourselves washed white again: we may come again with all the accumulated wanderings and backslidings of our past years, and just believing as we did at first, we shall find our soul again set at its first liberty and admitted into its first joy. God grant us to know all this in our own souls. I wish I could speak as I can sometimes think, or think as the word of God allows me to think. O blessed thought, that you and I, condemned and lost and ruined by our guilt, should only need to look to Christ on the cross and in a moment should receive pardon, "according to the riches of his grace"; all for nothing, all freely given, not given as a sham, but as a reality; real pardon for real sin, abiding pardon, everlasting pardon, a pardon which retrieves all our loss, and adds a charm which unfallen spirits cannot know. O the splendour of God! Where does it flame forth so overpoweringly as in pardoning grace! Is not this the glory of God at its full, that he passeth by transgression and remembers not the iniquity of his people?

III. Our last word is to be upon THE MANIFESTATION OF THIS PARDON. "In whom we have redemption through his blood, the forgiveness of sins, according to the riches of his grace." Here we see that *forgiveness of sin comes to us entirely through Jesus Christ our Saviour*, and if we go to Jesus Christ, fixing our eyes especially upon his atoning sacrifice, we have pardon by virtue of his blood. I see nothing here about any human priest: Christ is priest enough for us. I see nothing about absolution by man. No: "In him we have redemption through his blood, the forgiveness of sins." It must be a very dangerous thing to be hoping for pardon because you have confessed to a mere man; whatever manipulations may have been performed upon his shaven head, it must be a very risky thing to have your salvation depend upon whether or not he was properly ordained by a priest of higher rank. We escape all such perils by going to the fountain-head, even to Christ himself, the one Mediator between God and man. According to God's command we trust Jesus and receive pardon, not in word only, but in spirit and in truth. There is no hazard in faith in Jesus, for all those who have tried it will tell you how blessed the result has been in their own cases. Pardon by any other means is impossible, but by Jesus Christ it is certain. Everything else fails, but faith in Christ never fails. Only trust him, only trust him, you are pardoned, pardoned at once through his most precious blood.

The text says, "We *have*" it, and I want to lay stress on that for just a minute. "*We have redemption, the forgiveness of sins.*" We *have* it. As many as believe in Christ are pardoned. Why, then, should we go to Church and say that we are "miserable sinners?" Believers are not miserable sinners; they are full often happy in a sense of full remission. If our sins are blotted out, why do we speak to God as if his anger still remained? Shall we lie unto God? We are indeed miserable sinners if we assume a misery which we have no reason to feel. We are miserable sinners for not believing God and pretending that we do. Is there no difference between a believer and an unbeliever, so that the self-same words will suit both one and the other, and they may kneel down side by side and alike call themselves "miserable sinners"? Then what has the gospel done for believers? What is the use of the sprinkled blood? There is all the difference in the world between a believer and an unbeliever. The unbeliever hath the wrath of God abiding on him; but as for the believer, his sin is forgiven him for Christ's name sake, and let him know it and declare it. "Am I not, then, daily to confess sin?" Yes, daily as you commit it, but not under the garb of misery, as though you were an unpardoned criminal. Are you not a beloved child? Confess sin with the certainty that you are forgiven, and that still the sentence of forgiveness runs on and includes these present and future sins as well as all that are past. You are to humbly sue for continued mercy, but you are not to pray as if you were at enmity with God and miserable under a sense of his wrath. Far better is the spirit which sings "O God, I will praise thee, for though thou wast angry with me, thine anger is turned away, and thou comfortest me." That is the way to talk. If you believe, you should speak in that fashion. No longer is the weight and burden of sin lying on your conscience and heart: your load is lifted; you are forgiven. If your child has been offending you, and you are angry with him, he feels ill at ease in your presence. At last you say, "My boy, it is all gone now; do not offend again. You are quite forgiven; come here, and let me kiss you." Does he reply, "Father, I am afraid"? If so it is evident that he does not understand that you have forgiven him: and even if he receives your kiss, but still remains unhappy in your presence, it is clear that he does not believe in you or in the sincerity of your forgiveness. As soon as the light dawns on his mind "Father has quite put all my fault away," then he is merry in his play and easy in his conversation with you. Now, be with God like a child at home. Do not act towards him as if still he frowned upon you. He smiles. Do not pray to him as if you dreaded him, and thought he would smite you. He cannot smite you: he has smitten Christ instead of you. Your debt has been paid, and can never be demanded of you. Christ nailed the receipted bill to his cross in the face of heaven and earth and hell.

Eternal justice cannot charge you now with sins which were, once for all, charged on your great Substitute, and borne by him. God is not unrighteous first to punish Christ and then to punish those for whom Christ died; to take the payment first from Christ and afterwards from you; from the Surety, and then from the debtor. No, no. Rest then in perfect peace. "Forgiveness according to the riches of his grace" is yours by faith, yours at this moment, and you may know it. You that have believed in Christ ought to know that you are accepted in Christ, for you are so accepted, and it is a pity not to have the joy of it.

I want you to feel the love which rises out of pardoned sin. You must love him who has removed all your iniquities. I want you to feel the zeal which finds fuel in the forgiveness in sin. Bring your alabaster box, and pour the ointment upon his head who has forgiven you so freely. There are no workers like pardoned men; there are no givers like pardoned men and women; there are no lovers like pardoned men and women: there are no singers like pardoned men and women: there are no saints before the throne, no courtiers at the right hand of the eternal Sovereign like those who have washed their robes and made them white in the blood of the Lamb. Come, then, ye guilty, and receive forgiveness in Christ! Come, ye vilest of the vile, the door is set open for you, and a loving heart invites you through these lips. I am full of hope that you will come. You must come. Love will constrain you to believe in my Lord. Oh, may the Holy Spirit compel you *now* to come to the Saviour, and to be cleansed from all sin. When you have obtained mercy hasten to tell others of the boundless mercy of the God of love, and of the riches of his grace displayed in forgiving you all trespasses. God bless you for Christ's sake. Amen.

PORTION OF SCRIPTURE READ BEFORE SERMON—Ephesians 1.

HYMNS FROM "OUR OWN HYMN BOOK"—241, 231, 51.[9]

---

[9] Spurgeon, C. H. (1880). The Glories of Forgiving Grace. In *The Metropolitan Tabernacle Pulpit Sermons* (Vol. 26, pp. 481–492). London: Passmore & Alabaster.

THE GREATEST WONDER OF GRACE

A Sermon

Published on Thursday, October 23rd, 1913.

Delivered by

C. H. SPURGEON,

At the Metropolitan Tabernacle, Newington.

"And I was left."—Ezekiel 9:8.

SALVATION never shines so brightly to any man's eyes as when it comes to himself. Then is grace illustrious indeed when we can see it working with divine power upon ourselves. To our apprehension, our own case is ever the most desperate, and mercy shown to us is the most extraordinary. We see others perish, and wonder that the same doom has not befallen ourselves. The horror of the ruin which we dreaded, and our intense delight at the certainty of safety in Christ unite with our personal sense of unworthiness to make us cry in amazement, "And I was left."

Ezekiel, in vision, saw the slaughtermen smiting right and left at the bidding of divine justice, and as he stood unharmed among the heaps of the slain, he exclaimed with surprise, "I was left." It may be, the day will come when we, too, shall cry with solemn joy, "And I, too, by sovereign grace, am spared while others perish." Special grace will cause us to marvel. Emphatically will it be so at the last dread day.

Read the story of the gross idolatry of the people of Jerusalem, as recorded in the eighth chapter of Ezekiel's prophecy, and you will not wonder at the judgment with which the Lord at length overthrew the city. Let us set our hearts to consider how the Lord dealt with the guilty people. "Six men came from the way of the higher gate, which lieth toward the north, and every man with a slaughter weapon in his hand." The destruction wrought by these executioners was swift and terrible, and it was typical of other solemn visitations. All through history the observing eye notices lines of justice, red marks upon the page where the Judge of all the earth has at last seen it needful to decree a terrible visitation upon a guilty people. All these past displays of divine vengeance point at a coming judgment even more complete and overwhelming. The past is prophetic of the future. A day is surely coming when the Lord Jesus, who came once to save, will descend a second time to judge. Despised mercy has always been succeeded by deserved wrath, and so must it be in the end of all things. "But who may abide the day of his coming? or who shall stand when he appeareth?" When sinners are smitten, who will be left? He shall lift the balances of justice, and make bare the sword of execution. When his avenging angels shall gather the vintage of the earth, who among us shall exclaim in wondering gratitude, "And I was left"? Such an one will be a wonder of grace indeed; worthy to take rank with those marvels of grace of whom we have spoken in many former discourses in this place. To each one of you, I put this enquiry, will you be an instance of sparing grace, and cry, "And I was left"?

We will use the wonderfully descriptive vision of this chapter that we may with holy fear behold *the character of the doom* from which grace delivers us, and then we will dwell upon the exclamation of our text, "I was left," considering it as the joyful utterance of *the persons who are privileged to escape the destruction;* and lastly, *the emotions which the escaped feel.*

By the help of the Holy Spirit, let us then solemnly consider:—

I. THE TERRIBLE DOOM from which the prophet in vision saw himself preserved, regarding it as a figure of the judgment which is yet to come upon all the world.

Observe, first, that it was a *just* punishment inflicted upon those who had been often warned; a punishment which they wilfully brought upon themselves. God had said that if they set up idols he would destroy them, for he would not endure such an insult to his Godhead. He had often pleaded with them, not with words only, but with severe providences, for their land had been laid desolate, their city had been besieged, and their kings had been carried away captive; but they were bent on backsliding to the worship of their idol gods.

Therefore, when the sword of the Lord was drawn from its scabbard, it was no novel punishment, no freak of vengeance, no unexpected execution. So, in the close of life, and at the end of the world, when judgment comes on men, it will be just and according to the solemn warnings of the word of God. When I read the terrible things which are written in God's book in reference to future punishment, especially the awful things which Jesus spoke concerning the place where their worm dieth not, and their fire is not quenched, I am greatly pressed in spirit. Some there be who sit in judgment upon the great Judge, and condemn the punishment which he inflicts as too severe. As for myself, I cannot measure the power of God's anger; but let it burn as it may, I am sure that it will be just. No needless pang will be inflicted upon a single one of God's creatures: even those who are doomed for ever will endure no more than justice absolutely requires, no more than they themselves would admit to be the due reward of their sins, if their consciences would judge aright. Mark you, this is the very hell of hell that men will know that they are justly suffering. To endure a tyrant's wrath would be a small thing compared with suffering what one has brought upon himself by wilful wanton choice of wrong. Sin and suffering are indissolubly bound together in the constitution of nature; it cannot be otherwise, nor ought it to be. It is right that evil should be punished. Those who were punished in Jerusalem could not turn upon the executioners and say, "We do not deserve this doom"; but every cruel wound of the Chaldean sword, and every fierce crash of the Babylonian battle-axe fell on men who in their consciences knew that they were only reaping what they themselves had sown. Brethren, what wonders of grace shall we be if, from a judgment which we have so richly deserved, we shall be rescued at the last!

Let us notice very carefully that this slaughter was *preceded by a separation* which removed from among the people those who were distinct in character. Before the slaughtermen proceeded to their stern task, a man appeared among them clothed in linen with a writer's inkhorn by his side, who marked all those who in their hearts were grieved at the evil done in the city. Until these were marked, the destroyers did not commence their work. Whenever the Lord lays bare his arm for war he first gathers his saints into a place of safety. He did not destroy the world by the flood till Noah and his family were safe in the ark. He would not suffer a single firedrop to fall on Sodom till Lot had escaped to Zoar. He carefully preserves his own; nor flood, nor flame, nor pestilence, nor famine shall do them ill. We read in the Revelation that the angel said, "Hurt not the earth, neither the sea, nor the trees, till we have sealed the servants of our God in their foreheads." Vengeance must sheath her sword, till love has housed its darlings. When Christ cometh to destroy the earth, he will first catch away his people. Ere the elements shall melt with fervent heat, and the pillars of the universe shall rock and reel beneath the weight of wrathful deity, he will have caught up his elect into the air, so that they shall be ever with the Lord. When he cometh he shall divide the nations as a shepherd divideth his sheep from the goats; no sheep of his shall be destroyed: he shall without fail take the tares from among the wheat, but not one single ear of wheat shall be in danger. O that we may be among the selected ones, and prove his power to keep us in the day of wrath. May each one of us say, amid the wreck of matter and the crash of worlds, "And I was left." Dear friend, are you marked in the forehead, think you? If at this moment my voice were drowned by the trumpet of resurrection, would you be amongst those who would awake to safety and glory? Would you be able to say, "The multitude perished around me, but I was left"? It will be so if you hate the sins by which you are surrounded, and if you have received the mark of the blood of Jesus upon your souls; if not, you will not escape, for there is no other door of salvation but his saving name. God grant us grace to belong to that chosen number who wear the covenant seal, the mark of him who counteth up the people.

Next, this judgment was placed *in the Mediator's hands*. I want you to notice this. Observe that, according to the chapter, there was no slaughter done, except where the man with the writer's inkhorn led the way. So, again, we read in the tenth chapter, that "One cherub stretched forth his hand from between the cherubims unto the fire that was between the cherubims, and took thereof and put it into the hands of him that was clothed with linen; who took it, and went out," and cast it over the city. See you this. God's glory of old shone forth between the cherubim, that is to say, over the place of propitiation and atonement, and as long as that glow of light remained, no judgment fell on Jerusalem, for God in Christ condemns not. But by-and-by "the glory of the God of Israel was gone up from the cherub, whereupon he was, to the threshold of the house," and then judgment was near to come. When God no longer deals with men in Christ, his wrath burns like fire, and he commissions the ambassador of mercy to be the messenger of wrath. The very man who marked with his pen the saved ones threw burning coals upon the city, and led the way for the destruction of the sinful. What does this teach but this, "The Father judgeth no man, but hath committed all judgment unto the Son"? I know of no truth more dreadful to meditate upon. Think of it, ye careless ones: the very Christ who died on Calvary is he by whom you will be sentenced. God will judge the world by this man Christ Jesus: he it is that will come in the clouds of heaven, and before him shall be gathered all nations; and when those who have despised him shall look upon his face, they will be terrified beyond conception. Not the lightnings, not the thunders, not the dreadful sound of the last tremendous trump shall so alarm them as that face of injured love. Then will they cry to the mountains and hills to hide them from the face of him that sitteth upon the throne. Why, it is the face of him that wept for sinners, the face which scoffers stained with bloody drops extracted by the thorny crown, the face of the incarnate God, who, in infinite mercy, came to save mankind! But because they have despised him, because they would not be saved, because they preferred their own lusts to infinite love, and would persist in rejecting God's best proof of kindness, therefore will they say, "Hide us from the face," for the sight of that face shall be to them more accusing, and more condemning, than all else besides. How dreadful is this truth! The more you consider it, the more will it fill your soul with terror! Would to God it might drive you to fly to Jesus, for then you will behold him with joy in that day.

This destruction, we are told, *began at the sanctuary*. Suppose the Lord were to visit London in his anger, where would he begin to smite? "Oh," somebody says, "of course, the destroying angel would go down to the low music-halls and dancing-rooms, or he would sweep out the back slums and the drink palaces, the jails and places where women of ill-life do congregate." Turn to the Scripture which surrounds our text.

The Lord says, "Begin at my sanctuary." Begin at the churches, begin at the chapels, begin at the church members, begin at the ministers, begin at the bishops, begin at those who are teachers of the gospel. Begin at the chief and front of the religious world, begin at the high professors who are looked up to as examples. What does Peter say? "The time is come that judgment must begin at the house of God: and if it first begin at us, what shall the end be of them that obey not the gospel of God? And if the righteous scarcely be saved, where shall the ungodly and the sinner appear?"

The first thing the slaughtermen did was to slay the ancient men which were before the temple, even the seventy elders of the people, for they were secret idolaters. You may be sure that the sword which did not spare the chief men and fathers made but short work with the baser sort. Elders of our churches, ministers of Christ, judgment will begin with us; we must not expect to find more lenient treatment than others at the last great assize; nay, rather, if there shall be a specially careful testing of sincerity, it will be for us who have taken upon ourselves to lead others to the Saviour. For this cause let us see well to it that we be not deceived or deceivers, for we shall surely be detected in that day. To play the hypocrite is to play the fool. Will a man deceive his Maker, or delude the Most High? It cannot be. You church members, all of you, should look well to it, for judgment will begin with you. God's fire is in Zion, and his furnace in Jerusalem. In the olden time the people fled to churches and holy places for sanctuary; but how vain will this be when the Lord's avengers shall come forth, since there the havoc will begin! How fiercely shall the sword sweep through the hosts of carnal professors, the men who called themselves servants of God, while they were slaves of the devil; who drank of the cup of the Lord, but were drunken with the wine of their own lusts; who could lie, and cheat, and commit fornication, and yet dared to approach the sacred table of the Lord? What cutting and hewing will there be among the base-born professors of our churches! It were better for such men that they had never been born, or being born, that their lot had fallen amid heathen ignorance, so that they might have been unable to add sin to sin by lying unto the living God. "Begin at my sanctuary." The word is terrible to all those who have a name to live and are dead. God grant that in such testing times, when many fail, we may survive every ordeal and, through grace, exclaim in the end, "And I was left."

After the executioners had begun at the sanctuary, it is to be observed that they *did not spare any, except those upon whom was the mark*. Old and young, men and women, priests and people, all were slain who had not the sacred sign; and so in the last tremendous day all sinners who have not fled to Christ will perish. Our dear babes that died in infancy we believe to be all washed in the blood of Jesus, and all saved; but for the rest of mankind who have lived to years of responsibility, there will be only one of two things—they must either be saved, because they had faith in Christ, or else the full weight of divine wrath must fall upon them. Either the mark of Christ's pen, or of Christ's sword, must be upon every one. There will be no sparing of one man because he was rich, nor of another because he was learned, nor of a third because he was eloquent, nor of a fourth because he was held in high esteem. Those who are marked with the blood of Christ are safe! Without that mark all are lost! This is the one separating sign—do you wear it? Or will you die in your sins? Bow down at once before the feet of Jesus, and beseech him to mark you as his own, that so you may be one of those who will joyfully cry, "And I was left." Now, secondly, I have to call your very particular attention to:—

II. THE PERSONS WHO ESCAPED, who could each say, "And I was left." We are told that those were marked for mercy who did "sigh and cry for the abominations that were done in the midst thereof." Now, we must be very particular about this. It is no word of mine, remember: it is God's word, and therefore I beg you to hear and weigh it for yourselves. We do not read that the devouring sword passed by those quiet people who never did anybody any harm: no mention is made of such an exemption. Neither does the record say that the Lord saved those professors who were judicious, and maintained a fair name and repute until death. No; the only people that were saved were those who were exercised in heart, and that heart-work was of a painful kind: they sighed and cried because of abounding sin. They saw it, protested against it, avoided it, and, last of all, wept over it continually. Where testimony failed, it remained for them to mourn; retiring from public labours, they sat them down and sighed their hearts away because of the evils which they could not cure; and when they felt that sighing alone would do no good, they took to crying in prayer to God that he would come and put an end to the dreadful ills which brooded over the land. I would not say a hard thing, but I wonder, if I were able to read the secret lives of professors of religion, whether I should find that they all sigh and cry over the sins of others? Are the tenth of them thus engaged? I am afraid that it does not cause some people much anxiety when they see sin rampant around them. They say that they are sorry, but it never frets them much, or causes them as much trouble as would come of a lost sixpence or a cut finger. Did you ever feel as if your heart would break over an ungodly son? I do not believe that you are a Christian man if you have such a son, and have not felt an agony on his behalf. Did you ever feel as if you could lay down your life to save that daughter of yours? I cannot believe that you are a Christian woman if you have not sometimes come to that. When you have gone through the street and heard an oath, has not your blood chilled in you? has not horror taken hold upon you because of the wicked? There cannot be much grace in you if that has not been the case. If you can go up and down in the world fully at ease because you are prospering in business, and things go smoothly with you, if you forget the woe of this city's sin and poverty, and the yet greater woe which cometh upon it, how dwelleth the love of God in you? The saving mark is only set on those who sigh and cry, and if you are heartless and indifferent, there is no such mark on you. "Are we to be always miserable?" asks one. Far from it. There are many other things to make us rejoice, but if the sad state of our fellow-men does not cause us to sigh and cry, then we have not the grace of God in us. "Well," says one, "but every man must look to himself." That is the language of Cain— "Am I my brother's keeper?" That kind of talk is in keeping with the spirit of the wicked one and his seed, but the heir of heaven abhors such language. The genuine Christian loves his race, and therefore he longs to see it made holy and happy. He cannot bear to see men sinning, and so dishonouring God and ruining themselves. If we really love the Lord, we shall sometimes lie awake at night sighing to think how his name is blasphemed, and how little progress his gospel makes.

We shall groan to think that men should despise the glorious God who made them, and who daily loads them with benefits. It sometimes lies upon my heart like a huge mountain, which crushes my spirit, to think that Jesus should be rejected, and that in this land of Bibles, where Latimer lit a candle which shall never be put out, the old madness is returning, and many are again bowing before the images of jealousy which the priests have set up. Yes, we have priests among us again. You can see them in their long and ugly garments in every street. And women have begun to confess to them! Shame! Shame! I marvel that the crimson blush does not mantle the cheek of every one who dares to ask or answer the questions appointed for the confessional, and yet the questions are asked, and modesty is outraged, and the multitudes tamely look on. My countrymen are going back to Rome. Their fathers' noble blood was shed for God, and none was left for the veins of their sons. In vain the conflicts of the years gone by! In vain a Cromwell's mighty arm, and the purging of the land! In vain the Puritans driven from their pulpits and witnessing in poverty and persecution! England must needs go back again to wear the fetters forged by papal Rome. My God, prevent it! Prevent it if it cost the lives of thousands of us, for we would be glad to die to save our country from so dire a curse. If you never sigh and cry because of the spread of Ritualism, I do not understand you. What stuff are you made of? "Oh, but my business goes on exceedingly well." Yes, and so does mine when souls are saved, but when they are led away into error, my business cannot prosper, but I have loss upon loss. I am happy enough when I think Christ's kingdom comes; but nothing beneath the sky can give me solid satisfaction if my Lord's work is at a standstill. I would to God we were all so taken up with the glory of God that the wickedness of mankind would grieve us to the heart.

But it was not their mourning which saved those who escaped—it was the mark which they all received which preserved them from destruction. We must all bear the mark of Jesus Christ. What is that? It is the mark of faith in the atoning blood. That sets apart the chosen of the Lord, and that alone. If you have that mark—and you have it not unless you sigh and cry over the sins of others—then in that last day no sword of justice can come near you. Did you read that word, "But come not nigh any man upon whom is the mark." Come not even near the marked ones lest they be afraid. The grace-marked man is safe, even from the near approach of ill. Christ bled for him, and therefore he cannot must not, die. Let him alone, ye bearers of the destroying weapons. Just as the angel of death, when he flew through the land of Egypt, was forbidden to touch a house where the blood of the lamb was on the lintel and the two side posts, so is it sure that avenging justice cannot touch the man who is in Christ Jesus. Who is he that condemneth since Christ has died? Have you, then, the blood mark? Yes, or no. Do not refuse to question yourself upon this point. Do not take it for granted, lest you be deceived. Believe me, your all hangs upon it. If you are not registered by the man clothed in linen, you will not be able to say, "And I was left."

This brings me to this last point which I desire to speak of. What were:—

III. THE PROPHET'S EMOTIONS WHEN HE SAID, "AND I WAS LEFT"?

He saw men falling right and left, and *he* himself stood like a lone rock amidst a sea of blood; and he cried in wonder, "And I was left."

"Let us hear what he further says—"I fell on my face." He lay *prostrate with humility*. Have you a hope that you are saved? Fall on your face, then! See the hell from which you are delivered, and bow before the Lord. Why are you to be saved more than anyone else? Certainly not because of any merit in you. It is due to the sovereign grace of God alone. Fall on your face and own your indebtedness.

> "Why was I made to hear thy voice,
>   And enter while there's room,
> When thousands make a wretched choice,
>   And rather starve than come?"

"And I was left."

If a man has been a drunkard, and has at length been led to flee to Christ, when he says, "And I was left," he will feel the hot tears rising to his eyes, for many other drinkers have died in delirium. One who has been a public sinner, when she is saved, will not be able to think of it without astonishment. Indeed, each saved man is a marvel to himself.

Nobody here wonders more at divine grace in his salvation than I do myself. Why was I chosen, and called, and saved? I cannot make it out, and I never shall; but I will always praise, and bless, and magnify my Lord for casting an eye of love upon me. Will you not do the same, beloved, if you feel that you by grace are left? Will you not fall on your face and bless the mercy which makes you to differ?

What did the prophet do next? Finding that he was left he *began to pray for others*. "Ah, Lord," said he, "wilt thou destroy all the residue of Israel?" Intercession is an instinct of the renewed heart. When the believer find that he is safe, he must pray for his fellow-men. Though the prophet's prayer was too late, yet, blessed be God, ours will not be. We shall be heard. Pray, then, for perishing men. Ask God, who has spared you, to spare those who are like you. Somebody has said, there will be three great wonders in heaven, first, to see so many there whom we never expected to meet in glory; secondly, to miss so many of whom we felt sure that they must be safe; and thirdly, the greatest wonder of all will be to find ourselves there. I am sure that everyone who has a hope of being in glory feels it to be a marvel; and he resolves, "If I am saved, I will sing the loudest of them all, for I shall owe most to the abounding mercy of God."

Let me ask a few questions, and I have done. The first—and let each man ask it of himself—shall I be left when the ungodly are slain? Answer it now to yourselves. Men, women, children, will you be spared in that last great day? Are you in Christ? Have you a good hope in him? Do not lie unto yourselves. You will be weighed in the balances; will you be found wanting or not? "Shall I be left?" Let that question burn into your souls.

Next, will my relatives be saved? My wife, my husband, my children, my brother, my sister, my father, my mother—will these all be saved? Happy are we who can say, "Yes, we believe they will," as some of us can joyfully hope. But if you have to say, "No, I fear that my boy is unconverted, or that my father is unsaved," then do not rest till you have wrestled with God for their salvation. Good woman, if you are obliged to say, "I fear my husband is unconverted," join me in prayer. Bow your heads at once and cry unto your God, "Lord, save our children! Lord, save our parents! Lord, save our husbands and wives, our brothers and sisters; and let the whole of our families meet in heaven, unbroken circles, for thy name's sake!"

May God hear that prayer if it has come from the lips of sincerity! I could not endure the thought of missing one of my boys in heaven: I hope I shall see them both there, and therefore I am in deep sympathy with any of you who have not seen your households brought to Christ. O for grace to pray earnestly and labour zealously for the salvation of your whole households.

The next earnest enquiry is, if you and your relatives are saved, how about your neighbours, your fellow-workmen, your companions in business? "Oh," say you, "many of them are scoffers. A good many of them are still in the gall of bitterness." A sorrowful fact, but have you spoken to them? It is wonderful what a kind word will do. Have you tried it? Did you every try to speak to that person who meets you every morning as you go to work? Suppose he should be lost! Oh, it will be a bitter feeling for you to think that he went down to the pit without your making an effort to bring him to God. Do not let it be so. "But we must not be too pushing," says one. I do not know about that. If you saw poor people in a burning house, nobody would blame you for being officious if you helped to save them. When a man is sinking in the river, if you jump in and pull him out, nobody will say, "You were rude and intrusive, for you were never introduced to him!" This world has been lost, and it must be saved; and we must not mind manners in saving it. We must get a grip of sinking sinners somehow, even if it be by the hair of their heads, ere they sink, for if they sink they are lost for ever. They will forgive us very soon for any roughness that we use; but we shall not forgive ourselves if, for want of a little energy, we permit them to die without a knowledge of the truth.

Oh, beloved friends, if you are left while others perish, I beseech you, by the mercies of God, by the bowels of compassion which are in Christ Jesus, by the bleeding wounds of the dying Son of God, do love your fellow-men, and sigh and cry about them if you cannot bring them to Christ. If you cannot save them, you can weep over them. If you cannot give them a drop of cold water in hell, you can give them your heart's tears while yet they are in this body.

But are you in very deed reconciled to God yourselves? Reader, are you cured of the awful disease of sin? Are you marked with the blood-red sign of trust in the atoning blood? Do you believe in the Lord Jesus Christ? If not, the Lord have mercy upon you! May you have sense enough to have mercy upon yourself. May the Spirit of God instruct you to that end. Amen.[10]

---

[10] Spurgeon, C. H. (1913). The Greatest Wonder of Grace. In *The Metropolitan Tabernacle Pulpit Sermons* (Vol. 59, pp. 505–514). London: Passmore & Alabaster.

THE SHANK-BONE SERMON; OR, TRUE BELIEVERS AND THEIR HELPERS

A Sermon

Intended for Reading on Lord's-day, April 13th, 1890, delivered by

C. H. SPURGEON,

at the Metropolitan Tabernacle, Newington,

On Lord's-day Evening, March 23*rd,* 1890

"Who, when he was come, helped them much which had believed through grace."—Acts 18:27.

Apollos is not Paul, and Paul is not Apollos. To blend the two in one would be to spoil each one of the two, without producing a good third. It is a great mercy that we have Paul, and Apollos, and Cephas, and other varieties of preachers; for not only is variety charming, but it is necessary. It is not everybody that can be profited by Paul; for it requires a great deal of fixed attention to follow him, and many hearers cannot concentrate their thoughts for long. It is not everybody that can be profited by Apollos, for fine speech is thrown away on simple souls. It is written, "Then shall the lambs feed after their manner"; and assuredly each one of them has a peculiar manner of feeding. Some of God's people are edified by one minister, and some by another: it is not mere whim, but it arises out of conformation of character, and habit of mind. Let Paul be Paul, and edify the Pauline class; and let Apollos be Apollos, and instruct those of his own sort. For my part, I would try to profit by either Paul, Apollos, Cephas, John, or James; but, alas! I do not know where to go to hear them. I am happy in hoping that their successors are still with us, each one with his peculiar style of things. I am not going to compare them with each other; but I would commend each one, and thank God, by whose grace he is what he is. It would be a very bad day's work, if we could do it, to reduce Paul to Apollos, or to bring Apollos to the style of Paul. In the body there are different members, and all members have not the same office; and in the church of God there are different ministries, and all ministries do not work after like manner, though they all work towards the selfsame end. If, my dear friend, God gives you grace to bring sinners to Christ, and to plant churches, be thankful that you can imitate Paul; and if you cannot do that, but can help those who are already converted, be thankful for such a gift, and imitate Apollos. Let not the man who plants envy the man who waters; and let not the man who waters boast over the man who simply plants and goes his way; for Paul has his place, and is honoured of his Master as a planter; and Apollos has his place, and shall not lack his reward as a waterer.

You see that the Holy Spirit has been pleased, by the pen of Luke, to give to Paul's travels and labours a very large proportion of the Book of the Acts of the Apostles; this passage from the twenty-fourth to the twenty-eighth verse is an episode—a corner marked off to be a record of Apollos. What Apollos did afterwards we do not know. He may have been a very great evangelist; he certainly was an exceedingly useful brother. But, dear friends, I find no complaint from Apollos, because, being mentioned in the sacred despatches, he has so small a space allotted him. He does not sulk because he has only four or five verses, while Paul is described at great length. If you and I should work for Christ, and never be mentioned in the records of earth at all, let us not be sorry: *there is most peace to those who are least talked about.* God, who is a Sovereign, dispenses according to his will, and it may be that one working brother will have all his story told, and his life will make a useful biography, instructing and stimulating many for generations. Be it so. Another brother, equally earnest and fervent, may never have his life written: there may only remain in the traditions of the church one or two anecdotes about him, helpful and good; but let him not mind his obscurity, his real usefulness may be none the less. Our record is on high. If the chronicles of earth be faulty, the registers of heaven are perfect. Many a man who has been forgotten here shall be remembered there; and I wot that in heaven it will give no saint the least trouble that he was not honoured among men. What if no monument was set up, yet all true work is immortal. The diligent workman will be perfectly contented when his Master says to him, "Well done, good and faithful servant." The echo of those words shall be heaven to him. Sweeter than all the harps of angels shall be the voice of his Lord's approval. Go on, Apollos! Work on, though there be little said about you, and do not envy Paul, with whose name the halls of the church are ringing. He did not seek himself any more than you did, and his content in the published record lies only in the fact that it honours his Lord.

But now, to come close to the text, I want you to notice these words—"When he was come, he helped them much which had believed through grace." Apollos, following Paul at Corinth, did useful service by confirming those who had already believed in the Lord Jesus. Our first head is—*true believers have believed through grace*; secondly, *such believers need help*; and, thirdly, *it is a worthy work in which to engage*—to help those who have believed through grace. May the Holy Spirit use many of us in this hallowed service! May we ourselves be helped through grace at this time!

I. First, then, THOSE WHO HAVE TRULY BELIEVED HAVE BELIEVED THROUGH GRACE. I suppose Luke felt it necessary to insert those words, "through grace." Nobody in his day doubted the fact that salvation is wrought in men by the grace of God; but the Holy Spirit foresaw that many, in after days, would conceal or obscure this truth, and therefore he moved the evangelist to notify it very plainly. We have it under hand and seal from the Holy Ghost that those who believed in the Lord Jesus believed through grace. Surely, grace is to the front in all good things. And here let me say, *it is grace that gives us the gospel which we believe.*

> "Grace first contrived the way
> To save rebellious man;
> And all the steps that grace display
> Which drew the wondrous plan."

It was grace that chose the people whom God would save, and gave them over to the Lord Jesus. It was grace that gave Jesus Christ to stand in their room, and place, and stead, and bear for them that which was due to the justice of God on account of their sin. It was grace which led the Saviour to undertake and carry through the work of substitution. Grace wrote the first letter of the gospel: grace will write the last letter of it. Salvation is all of grace from first to last. I would to God that all preachers and hearers knew the meaning of that word "grace," and did not confuse it and mix it up with human endeavours and creature merits; for, indeed, "it is not of him that willeth, nor of him that runneth, but of God that sheweth mercy." If it be of grace, it is no more of works, otherwise grace is no more grace; and if it be of works, it is not of grace, otherwise work is no more work. "By grace are ye saved through faith; and that not of yourselves: it is the gift of God." Grace signifies free, undeserved favour; and as it comes from God to us, it is sovereign grace which is moved only by the good pleasure of Jehovah's will. Grace is the active movement of the divine will to produce the results which have been graciously determined on. Grace makes a distinction between man and man, and it must have all the glory of what it does. Grace is exercised according to the will of God, and not according to the will of man, for the Lord hath said it—"I will have mercy on whom I will have mercy, and I will have compassion on whom I will have compassion." Grace sat in the council chamber of eternity and devised the scheme of mercy, the plan of redemption, the method of peace through the blood, the whole dispensation of salvation by grace through faith in Christ Jesus.

I say, then, that while grace gives us the gospel to believe, *grace also gives us to believe the gospel*. We are personally to believe the gospel, and so only can we be saved. But if I came before you to-night, and had nothing further to say than "Believe the gospel, and you shall be saved," the message would add to your solemn responsibility, and yet it would not save you; for you would not believe, but would continue in your sins. Man left to himself is an unbeliever, and an unbeliever he will remain. To meet the deep depravity of our nature, and its settled unbelief, he who gave the gospel to be believed, also gives the faith that believes the gospel. This is a wonder of grace; but then in the realm of grace everything is wonderful. We are so set on mischief, so proud, so vain-glorious, so unbelieving, that we never do come to receive the gospel, except through the operation of the grace of God upon our consciences and wills. The faith which comes to God first came from God. I remember, when I believed in Christ, and took him to be my trust, and was saved: I believed, and thus I entered into life and peace. It was not till some time after that I saw the reason why I had believed. I said to myself, "How is it that I have believed in Christ, while others who have attended the same gospel ministry, and have enjoyed the same advantages, have not believed in him?" The enquiry was not, "Why did *they* refuse to believe?" I saw at once that their unbelief was their own fault and folly, and that the blame must be laid at their door, for they wilfully refused the Saviour; but this was not the question: I was not judging *them*, but I was examining myself, and enquiring why I had believed in the Lord Jesus. I saw that if I had believed, it was not to be set down to my personal credit. I could not take to myself any honour because of it. My believing, when they did not believe, did not spring from any betterness of nature on my part. God forbid that I should dream such a thing! It did not spring from any natural excellence of my will. There was a submissive will in me; but a something from above made that will submissive, and that something lay at the back of everything. Then I understood that it was God's grace that had made me to differ; and I gave to God, there and then, the glory of my faith, and the credit of my choice of Christ. I have never met with any Christian man, whatever his doctrinal views, but he has been willing to give to God the glory of his conversion. He has ascribed it to the working of the Holy Spirit, and not to himself; and he has joined with me in praising God for it. Though the brother may cavil at the doctrine of distinguishing grace in the gross, yet, in his own case in particular, he has been willing to confess that not only did grace give him a gospel to believe, but grace gave him to believe the gospel. We come; but God draws. We come to God because he draws us. We came to believe in Christ because his Spirit enlightened and persuaded us, and brought us into the happy state of salvation by faith in Christ.

Furthermore, I wish to add that *such believing is a sure evidence of grace*. If thou believest in the Lord Jesus Christ with all thine heart, thou hast the grace of God in thee. There is no surer proof of it than this. Where there is faith there is grace: the one is the inseparable fruit of the other. "He that believeth on him hath everlasting life." "He that believeth on him is not condemned." These are not sentences of mine. I am quoting Holy Scripture to you; and the Scripture cannot be broken. "Therefore being justified by faith, we have peace with God." It is the believing that brings us into this condition of peace with God. I care not what works thou shalt bring me, be they never so many; if thou dost not bring with thee faith, which is the chief of all works, thou hast brought me nothing. If thou believest in Jesus Christ, whom God has sent, thou hast the one sure and certain evidence of grace. If thou believest in Christ alone, and art resting thy salvation upon his finished righteousness, thou hast the clearest evidence that the grace of God is in thy heart. Wilt thou not search and see whether thou hast real faith in the Lord Jesus? Make sure work on this point. If thou believest not, thou art condemned already.

And what is more, if thou believest through grace, *that grace which made thee believe is the best guarantee that thou shalt keep on believing*. Faith which is born of self will die of self; but that which is the child of grace will live for ever. If thou hast begun to believe of thyself thou wilt leave off of thyself; but if God's grace began thy believing, God's grace will continue thy believing, and thou wilt abide in this faith wherein thou standest even to the end. This gives me great comfort whenever I think of it; for I desire certainty for days to come. If the faith whereby I have laid hold on Christ to be my Saviour be altogether wrought in me by the Holy Ghost, through grace, then I defy the devil to take away that which he never gave, or to crush that which Jehovah himself created in me. I defy my free-will to fling away what it never brought to me. What God has given, created, introduced, and established in the heart he will maintain there. "Every plant, which my heavenly Father hath not planted, shall be rooted up"; but what he hath planted none shall root up; for it is written, "I the Lord do keep it; I will water it every moment: lest any hurt it, I will keep it night and day."

The men of Corinth to whom Apollos came had believed *through grace*. Beloved, there is a sweet ring about this description. They "had believed," and their faith secured their souls; but they "had believed through grace," and that secured their faith. "Through grace" is the hall-mark upon the precious metal of believing. There is no such thing as true believing where grace is not present. We believe: it is an act of our own mind. But we believe through grace: it is the result of God's grace working upon our mind. We both will and do, because God worketh in us to will and to do. We believe, because the Holy Spirit leads us to trust in the Lord Jesus. So much upon the first point. May grace work in us true believing! O my hearers, how I wish that you were all such believers!

II. Now for the second consideration. SUCH BELIEVERS NEED HELP. I know they do, because we are told in the text that Apollos "helped them much which had believed through grace"; and his work was not a superfluous one, or it would not have been mentioned here with commendation. In what respects do those who have grace need help? In what ways can true believers be helped?

Many believers need help in *further instruction*. Young Christians cannot be supposed to know much when they first come to Christ; but they come to be disciples, that is to say, learners. They know the three R's—Ruin, Redemption, and Regeneration; and that is by no means a small part of spiritual education. But they do not know even these elementary truths so fully as they might know them, and even about these things they will be the better for more teaching. Oftentimes they need somebody to open up passages of Scripture, to expound to them the analogy of faith, and to help them to compare spiritual things with spiritual. Beloved, you may be a great help to new converts if you will teach them "the way of God more perfectly." Oh, that ministries were more instructive! Alas, it seems often as if the preacher skimmed the surface, and did not care to enter into the treasure-house of doctrine, and open up the deep things of God. If public ministry falls short, private Christians must try to make up for it. We want the people instructed, for ignorance is the mother of superstition and scepticism. The uninstructed are easily carried away with novelties and delusions. Those who are established in the faith, and know what they believe, generally stand fast. Had the teaching from the pulpit been more clear and decisive during the past twenty years we should not now be living in an age of uncertainty.

Many who have believed through grace also need help by way of *consolation*. You would be astonished if you knew the large number of believers in Christ who are tempted to doubt, despondency, and distress of mind. In the present congregation there are a number of persons depressed in spirit, who can hardly look up, who will judge, when I am speaking, that I am referring to them; and I must confess that I am thinking of them, and do very often think about them, and long to see them come forth from their present gloom. It is a great joy to me if I can help them at all by describing my own experience of down-casting and up-lifting. These bruised and broken ones need binding up. Brothers, if you are like Barnabas, "sons of consolation," be not slack in your blessed service! O ye spiritual men, trained in the school of sorrow, put forth your best endeavours to minister to minds diseased. Pour in the oil and wine of the gospel wherever there is a wound gaping and bleeding. A word fitly spoken, a promise seasonably quoted, may help much those who have believed through grace.

Apollos helped them much, also, by *defending them against opponents*. We find that "he mightily convinced the Jews"; and in doing this he screened believing Gentiles from many a rude assault. He disputed with all his might, and with great fervour of spirit, against those who tried to subvert the faith of the Christians. Nowadays the Christian had need go fully armoured, for arrows fly thick as sleet in a storm. Objections are always being raised; doubts are always being insinuated. It is hard for a man to keep his feet amidst the present torrents of unbelief that sweep down our streets. You that can stand fast should help those who cannot. Ye that are strong ought to bear the infirmities of the weak in the matter of doubt. Give tremblers a word to confirm them in "the faith once delivered to the saints." Older Christians can do much in this direction by mentioning their own experience of the certainty of divine truth. Tell the young people how God has helped you in the day of trial. Tell them how he has answered your prayers. Tell them what joy and peace you have had in dark times by trusting in God. Tell them, I pray you, the way by which the Lord has led you; and when you do this they will not be so likely to be staggered and cast down by every caviller who may assault them. "He helped them much which had believed through grace." Elderly Christians can do very much of this by baffling the adversary with those blessed facts of their own lives, which even to sceptics are stubborn things.

And we can also help those who have believed through grace by *giving them a word of direction*. They frequently do not know what to do. They come to the end of their wits and their knowledge; and then the Christian who, by reason of use, has had his senses exercised, may be of great service to the bewildered. We are commissioned by the Lord to be eyes to the blind, and feet to the lame, and guides to wanderers. It is the lot of some of us to be employed by the King to conduct trains of pilgrims to the celestial city; and full often we have to put ourselves in front of the women and the children to fight with Giant Grim or Giant Despair. For their sakes we enter the lists with lions, dragons, and other monsters. The journey of the weaker ones to heaven is a personally-conducted tour, and the Lord of the way employs us to be their guardians. All that have spiritual strength should carry out the commission which is implied in the very possession of that strength. You should help the weak, and give a brotherly word of advice to the inexperienced. O beloved, do we lay ourselves out for this—those of us who have been long the people of God—as we ought to do? Do you not think that there is a tendency among many to despise the weak and leave them to themselves. How are they to grow wiser and more instructed if they have no better society than their own? Do I hear an older one say, "Oh, that young lad, what does he know? What can he do towards my edification?" This is a very selfish question; let it not be heard among you. "I never got much out of the church," said one to me; and he was somewhat surprised when I replied, "I never joined the church to get anything out of it." "What did you join it for?" "Why, to do all I could for all who are in it." This wretched self-seeking poisons everything it touches. A certain lady went out with a number of Christian friends, and being very easily displeased, she was soon complaining, and turning to a friend she asked him if he enjoyed himself. "No," said he, "I did not come here to enjoy *myself*, I came here to enjoy other people." There is a great deal in that. If you live for yourself, your object is mean and unsatisfactory. In fact if you live to yourself, you will die; but if you will learn to live to help the feeble, and guide the doubtful, and to be a Great-Heart for King Jesus, you will live abundantly, for God will bless you.

Dear friends, the bulk of Christians, when first converted, *need leaders*. They need somebody to show them the way, and to go before them; I would to God that many here present who have been taught of

God, if they do not become preachers and ministers, may, nevertheless, by their conduct and conversation vie with Apollos in this blessed work of helping much those who have believed through grace. By word and by example may the Holy Spirit teach you how to be convoys to the little ships which are now making the voyage of life.

III. So I come to the third observation, which is this: IT IS A WORTHY WORK IN WHICH TO ENGAGE. Helping those who have believed through grace is a work worthy of the highest talent and the greatest experience. I want to impress upon many of my instructed brethren and sisters that they should engage in it at once, and keep at it continually. We are going to have a great number of converts in this place. We have been praying for them, and we are sure to have them, for the Lord hears prayer, and blesses his own truth. I want you to get ready to receive the new converts and nurse them for Christ. Whenever children are expected, somebody is warned of it, and a skilled person is in readiness to cherish the weaklings. God will not send his babes to a church that is not prepared to nurse them; and I want to stir you up to be ready to help much those who shall believe through grace. I claim this assistance of you, and I feel sure that you will cheerfully render it, even as Apollos thus aided Paul.

First, *because you have been helped*, I claim it. Apollos became a helper because he had himself been helped. He began to preach, and he preached all that he knew; but his knowledge was very defective. What he said was good—very good; but it was not fully the gospel; for he had only learned of John the Baptist, and had not yet been taught the doctrine of Jesus. Apollos teaches very eloquently; but still there is a lack about his teaching. He has not yet reached the full chord; he does not sound out the blessed music of the gospel to perfection. Aquila and Priscilla ask him into their tent warehouse, and they say to him, "Dear friend, do you notice, you went just so far, but you should have gone a little farther. You spoke about the Lamb of God; but you did not tell them that Jesus was the Lamb of God, and that he had died to take away sin." Apollos replied, "I pray you, tell me all about it." And when they further informed him of the death, and the resurrection, and the ascension of the Lord Jesus, and of the coming of the Holy Ghost, Apollos said, "Thank you. Thank you. Now I have grand truths to preach, and my message will be more full and gracious than it has been. I shall go forth to the synagogue to-morrow to tell them about the Messiah who has truly come, and I shall speak with greater freedom concerning him." Apollos had been helped, and therefore Apollos was bound to help other people. Do you not think, you Christian people, that you owe something to the church of God as well as to the Christ of God? You were converted; was it not by a pastor's preaching, or by a teacher's instruction in the school, or by a book that had been written by a Christian man? Will you not repay the church of God that which you owe to her instrumentality? If you have been helped as well as converted, you are especially bound to lay yourself out to help others. When a person who has been very despondent, comes out into comfort, he should look out for desponding spirits, and use his own experience as a cordial to the fainting. I do not think that I ever feel so much at home in any work as when I am trying to encourage a heart which is on the verge of despair, for I have been in that plight myself. It is a high honour to nurse our Lord's wounded children. It is a great gift to have learned by experience how to sympathize. "Ah!" I say to them, "I have been where you are!" They look at me, and their eyes say, "No, surely, you never felt as we do." I therefore go further, and say, "If you feel worse than I did, I pity you indeed; for I could say with Job, 'My soul chooseth strangling rather than life.' I could readily enough have laid violent hands upon myself, to escape from my misery of spirit." In talking to those who are in that wretched condition, I find myself at home. He who has been in the dark dungeon knows the way to the bread and the water. If you have passed through depression of mind, and the Lord has appeared to your comfort, lay yourself out to help others who are where you used to be. If you are in prison, and you get out, do not enjoy your own liberty alone, but hasten to set free another captive. Are your chains broken? Then be a chain-breaker in the Lord's name. A sailor, who had long been a prisoner in France, gained his liberty. He went into Seven Dials, bought a cage full of birds, and when he had paid for them, he opened the cage, and let them all fly. People cried with wonder, "What did you buy them for?" "Oh," he said, "I bought them to let them fly. I know what it is to be a prisoner myself, and I cannot bear that birds should be shut up in a cage." Go to those who are what you were—caged birds—and let them fly by telling them of Jesus, and the ransom price. Seek out poor, bound sinners, and proclaim freedom to them. Proclaim liberty at the market-cross in the name of Christ.

I speak to some here who have *a measure of natural ability for this work*. May be, you resemble Apollos, because Apollos was an eloquent man. "Ah!" says one, "I am not eloquent." I do not know that. There may be a difference of opinion as to what eloquence is. Eloquence is speaking out from the heart. I will tell you what I call eloquence in a child: it is the whole child working itself up to gain its wish and have its way. There is a pretty thing that the child wants. He is very little, but he tries to speak about it, and does his best to express his longings. He points to what he wants, and clutches at it, and cries after it. Still he does not succeed, and then he works himself up into an agony of desire. The boy cries all over—every bit of him pleads, demands, strives. Every hair of his head is pleading for what he wants. He not only cries with his eyes and with his tongue, but he cries with his fingers and his hair. He thinks of nothing but the one thing on which his little heart is set. I call that eloquence. There is, in the Vatican, the famous group of the Laocoon: I stood one day looking at it. You remember how the father and his sons are twisted about with venomous snakes, and they are writhing in agony as the deadly folds enclose them. As I stood looking at the priceless group, a gentleman said to me, "Mr. Spurgeon, look at that eloquent great-toe." Well, yes, I had looked at that great toe. It was like a live thing, though only marble. I had not called it "eloquent" till he gave me the word; but certainly it was eloquent, though silent. It spake of anguish and deadly pain. When a man speaks in earnest, he is eloquent even though he may be slow of speech. His whole nature is stirred as he pleads with sinners for the Lord Jesus; and this makes him eloquent. O my brothers, you know not what you can do till you get at it with your whole souls. But if you happen to have the gift of fluent speech, I pray you use it in helping those who have believed through grace. "I have not the gift of speech," says one. Well, dear brother, have you tried? have you tried? Many a man has great powers of speech, but he has been too bashful to develop them. Shall I put it in Saxon? He has been too much of a coward to find out his own capacity. If he could but have got rid of his fear under the impulse of a strong affection for others, he could have spoken; and, by degrees, he would have spoken well. We want more young men in this church to go forth and preach the gospel. What are you at, you dumb dogs? How will you answer for it if your Lord is robbed through your sinful silence? All our organizations are in want of speaking men, and of earnest, loving, Christian women, who can plead with souls. I believe that there is much more of gift lying idle than we have ever suspected. I charge you, place your talent in the Lord's treasury at once, lest its rust should witness against you.

But if you have not a great measure of gift, never mind about that. I do not know but what Apollos did mischief through being too gifted, and too ready of speech. When he went to Corinth, he could speak better than Paul; and, after a while, he weaned the fickle ones from the apostle, to his grief. Apollos did not do this intentionally—it was not his fault; but some of them said, "Listen to Apollos! Is he not a splendid speaker? Did you ever hear such eloquence? Paul cannot talk in that way." One said, "I like Paul, for he is so deep; but yet he is neither a polished scholar, nor an elegant speaker like Apollos. He has never been to the college at Alexandria; he has never been polished by Egyptian philosophy. Apollos is the man for me." One cried, "I am of Paul"; and another, "I am of Apollos"; and another, "I am of Cephas"; while a few even said, "I am of Christ"—as if Christ could head a party within his own church. This led to a grievous dividing into parties and wretched following of men. When he saw it, Paul told them they were carnal, and mere babes in Christ. Talent and education may stand in the way of a believer, and may not help him. But in your infirmity there is no such danger, wherefore get to work despite your weakness. If you can only stutter, go and stutter the gospel; and it is the gospel that God will bless, not your stuttering nor your orating. If you can only write a letter in the simplest words about Jesus, go and do it; and the simplicity with which you write, while it looks like a weakness, may really be a source of strength, fitting it the better for God to use it.

If we have a measure of natural ability, be it great or small, let us use it; but if we have not that ability, we may *acquire one form of capacity in which Apollos abounded*. He was mighty in the Scriptures.

Now, we can all study our Bibles. If we believe in Jesus in our hearts we ought to have the Bible at our fingers' ends; and, if so, we shall help many by our instructive talk. The good Bible student has lips like a springing well. When the word of God dwells in a man richly his speech drops fatness. Those who speak Scripture sow seed; and it is living and growing seed—seed whose harvest is salvation. It is God's Word, not our comment on God's Word, that saves men. Keep on quoting God's inspired truth, and be yourself inspired by it, so as to explain it by your own experience, and in that way you will help much them that have believed through grace.

But, dear friends, in addition to this, you will not do much unless you are like Apollos, *fervent in the spirit*. Notice that twenty-fifth verse—"fervent in the spirit." He was a burning man: a man on fire. He burned his way by his zeal. He was not content to speak calmly and coolly, but he threw his soul into his preaching. That is half the battle. I do not know whether it is not three-quarters of it. "Fervent in the spirit." If you are full of fire, and full of life, and full of heart, you will be a blessing to others. "How can I get warmth of heart?" says one. Live in the presence of God. I cannot give you any other prescription. Let the Lord shine upon you as the Sun of Righteousness, and you will be fervent: all other methods are mere speculations, and will fail. The famous naturalist, Buffon, had once a large number of the wise men of the Academy of France in his grounds. They were all philosophers; and you know what a philosopher is. If you do not know, you should meet one; and I do not think that your appreciation of the sect will be increased. However, these were all philosophers, great men walking in a great man's gardens—all great together. In the grounds there was a glass globe, and when one of these profound philosophers touched this glass globe on the shady side, he found that it was very, very warm, while on the side that was exposed to the sun it was comparatively cool. Herein was a marvellous thing. He called his brother philosophers around him, and I picture them as they gave out their various theories why this glass globe was hotter on the side away from the sun than on the side which was bearing the full blaze of noonday. One had a theory of reflection, another of refraction, another of absorption: I cannot give you all their words, for they were wonderful words, and wonderful theories, and they discussed, and discussed, and discussed, till Buffon, not quite satisfied with the philosophical conclusions which they had reached, called the gardener, and said, "Gardener, can you tell me why this side of the globe, away from the sun, is hotter than the other side upon which the sun is shining?" "Yes, sir," said the gardener, "Just now I turned the globe round, because it was getting too hot on one side." This did not uphold the new philosophical theories, but it maintained an old-fashioned doctrine— namely, that the sun gives heat. You may depend upon it that the only answer to the question why a man is fervent in spirit is, that he keeps his heart near his Lord. You need not enter upon any philosophical disquisitions as to how to maintain fervour and enthusiasm, and all that. That is the most fervent heart which enjoys most of the light of God, and there is the end of the whole matter. If you live in the light of God's countenance, you will be fervent; and if you turn away from him you will grow cool. God give us to be fervent in spirit!

But now notice one thing more. Apollos greatly helped these people because *he preached Christ to them*. "For he mightily convinced the Jews, and that publicly, shewing by the scriptures that Jesus was Christ." If we are going to help those who have believed in Christ, our conversation with them must be full of Christ. Nothing will really feed the soul but Jesus. His flesh is meat indeed. His blood is drink indeed. All else is froth, or wind. Reading yesterday, in "Israel my Glory," a book by Mr. Wilkinson, who is the director of the Jewish mission at Mildmay, I saw a statement there which was quite new to me. He is speaking of the Jewish passover at the present day. Now, you know what the passover was according to the law of Moses—how a lamb was killed, and the blood was sprinkled on the lintel and the two sideposts, while the flesh was roasted and eaten. The Jews at this day observe the passover; but they observe it in a way which is according to the Rabbis, and not according to Moses. On the table there are passover cakes, lettuce, chervil, and parsley, as the bitter herbs. This I understand, but what is this Charoseth—a mixture of lime and mortar? And whence come the egg and the salt water? Moses knows nothing of eggs and mortar. What is there, do you suppose, besides? "Oh," say you, "the Paschal Lamb." No, no; they have left that out. What is there at the Jewish passover at the present time instead of the lamb? A shank-bone! A shank-bone, mark you—with no meat upon it! Only a shank-bone! The blood is gone, and in place of it is an egg. The Lamb is gone, and instead thereof is a shank-bone. "Ah, me! How can they thus make void the law of God?" This I said involuntarily; but very soon I remembered that I could not blame the Jews, for they are only imitating the Christians. Go and hear many who pretend to preach the gospel. Where is the Lamb, the Sacrifice, to be fed upon? Where is the sprinkled blood? Why, they are ashamed to speak of "the blood." They think the very word is vulgar. But what do they give us? A bone! A bone! A bone that no dog would care for—a bone of modern thought put in the place of the Lamb, who ought to be fed upon by all the living Israel of God. I thank Mr. Wilkinson for such a simile. I smile to think of my Israelitish friends sitting down to the table with their shank-bone, and calling it the passover; but they are quite as near the mark as my Christian friends sitting down to their divinity, out of which the great doctrine of the atonement has been taken, and calling it the Christian faith. There is no food for bodies in the shank-bone, nor any food for souls in the modern theology; but in Christ crucified there is every help that a soul can want. Are you burdened with sin? He bore it on the tree. Are you afraid that sin will conquer you? You shall overcome by the blood of the Lamb. Trust in the atoning sacrifice alone and entirely, and you shall enter into a peace and joy which shall be the strength of your soul in future conflicts with evil.

I need not say more; but I would press upon my dear friends who know the Lord to go "help them much that have believed through grace." As for those who have not yet believed in Jesus, may they now come and trust him! The moment that you trust him you are saved. "Look unto me," saith he, "and be ye saved, all the ends of the earth." Look at once! Look and live!

> "There is life in a look at the Crucified One."

The Lord, by his grace, constrain and enable you to give that look, and to him be glory for ever and ever! Amen.

PORTION OF SCRIPTURE READ BEFORE SERMON—Acts 18.

HYMNS FROM "OUR OWN HYMN BOOK"—414, 483, 781.[11]

---

[11] Spurgeon, C. H. (1890). The Shank-Bone Sermon; or, True Believers and Their Helpers. In *The Metropolitan Tabernacle Pulpit Sermons* (Vol. 36, pp. 193–204). London: Passmore & Alabaster.

GRACE FOR GRACE

A Sermon

Delivered on Lord's-day Morning, May 19th, 1889, by

C. H. SPURGEON,

at the Metropolitan Tabernacle, Newington.

"Now we have received, not the spirit of the world, but the spirit which is of God; that we might know the things that are freely given to us of God."—1 Corinthians 2:12.

The course of our fallen race has been a succession of failures. Whenever there has been an apparent rise, it has been followed by a real fall. Into ever-increasing darkness the human mind seems resolved to plunge itself in its struggles after a false light. When men have been fools, they have danced in a delirium of sin; when they have been sober, they have given themselves up to a phantom wisdom of their own, which has revealed their folly more than ever. It is a sad story, the story of mankind! Read it in the light of God's Word, and it will bring tears from your very heart.

The only hope for man was that God should interpose; and he has interposed, as though he began a new creation, or wrought a resurrection out of the kingdom of death. God has come into human history, and here the bright lights begin. Where God is at work in grace, abounding sin is conquered, hope begins, and good becomes perceptible. This better state is always markedly the effect of a break in the natural course of things, a supernatural product which would never have been seen in this poor world had it been let alone. See yonder avalanche rushing down the steep mountain-side; such is humanity left to itself. Lo, God in Christ Jesus throws himself in the way; he so interposes as to be crushed beneath the descending rocks. But, beloved, he rises from the dreadful burial; he stops the avalanche in its terrible career; he hurls back the tremendous mass, and changes the whole aspect of history. In this divine interposition, of which the

Bible gives us the best record, to which, I trust, our experience has added a happy appendix, we behold and adore the almighty grace of God.

In the interposition of omnipotent grace, we note that the Lord so works as to preserve his own glory. He takes care that no flesh shall glory in his presence. He might have used the power of the great, but he has not; he might have instructed man by man's own wisdom, but he has not; he might have declared his gospel with the excellency of human speech, but he has not. He has taken for his tools, not the armour of a king, but the sling of a shepherd; and he has placed his treasure of truth, not in the golden vase of talent, but in the earthen vessels of lowly minds. He has not made men speak for him under the spell of genius, but as they have been moved by his Holy Spirit. The Lord of hosts will save men, but he will not give men a yard of space for boasting; he will grant them a salvation, which shall humble them in the dust and lead them to know that he is God, and beside him there is none else. "The Lord of hosts hath purposed it, to stain the pride of all glory, and to bring into contempt all the honourable of the earth." God's gracious interposition reveals his sovereignty, his wisdom, his power, his love, his grace; but it reveals nothing in men which can admit a boastful thought.

The Lord our God has worked in a way parallel with his central interposition, which is seen at the cross, where Jesus unveiled Jehovah's way of revealing power in weakness. It is in such a connection that Paul says, "I determined not to know anything among you, save Jesus Christ, and him crucified." He knew that there was nothing else to know. The plan of the cross is to conquer death by death, to remove sin by the endurance of the penalty, to work mightily by suffering terribly, to glorify himself by shame. The gibbet whereon Christ died was the abyss of reproach and the climax of suffering; but it was also the focus of God's interposing grace. He there glorified himself in connection, not with honour and power, but with shame and death. The great self-sacrifice of God is the great victory of grace. Beloved, it is most sweet to think that all the ways of God to men are in harmony with this way of the cross, and that the cross is the pattern of the Lord's constant method of accomplishing his designs of grace rather by weakness than by strength, by suffering rather than by the splendour of his majesty.

Let me also add, that this way which God has taken, by which he saves men and glorifies himself, is entirely suitable to the condition of those whom he saves. If salvation had been by human excellence I could never have been saved. If the plan of salvation had required that in which a man might rightly glory, how could it have come to sinners without strength or goodness? Such a gospel would have been no gospel to us, for it would have been far out of our reach. God's plans are workable plans, suitable to the weakness of our fallen race. In Christ he comes to the wounded man where he is, and does not ask him, in his fainting condition, to come a certain part of the way. Grace does not begin half-way down the alphabet, but it is the Alpha of our hope.

It is my delightful task, though in much weakness, to set forth the exceeding freeness of the grace of God, and thus to set before you an open door, that you who have never entered may boldly do so; and that you who have already entered may sit within, and sing to the praise of the glory of his grace, wherein he hath made you "accepted in the Beloved." My text speaks of the gifts of God freely given to us, and of the way by which we may receive them, and come to know their excellence and value: in all these three things it shows us that everything is of grace—it is given of grace, it is received through grace, it is understood by grace. "Grace reigns," and grace alone.

This morning I shall speak, first, of *the things which are freely given* to us of God; secondly, of *the power to receive them, which is also given*, since it is spoken of as "received"; and, thirdly, of *the knowledge of them, which is also given through the Spirit*. When we have set forth these three things we shall have ranged through a wide domain of sovereign grace.

I. First, then, THE THINGS OF GOD ARE FREELY GIVEN.

All the blessings of salvation are a gift. All the inheritance of the covenant is a gift. All that which comes by our Lord Jesus to save and sanctify men is a gift. A gift is not a return for purchase-money. We are not asked, in any sense, to bring a price to God wherewith to purchase pardon, justification, or eternal life. Where the notion of purchase is for an instant hinted at, it is only to show more plainly how free is the blessing: "Come, buy wine and milk without money and without price." God freely gives his grace, expecting nothing in return, but that we do as freely receive as he does freely bestow; and even that free reception is a part of the gift which he bestows upon us. Be not feeling in your purse: money is useless as to purchasing salvation. Be not searching in your character, or in your resolutions, to find some little recommendation: neither the coins of the merchant nor of the self-righteous are current here. The free grace of God would be insulted by being put up to auction, or set forth to sale. "The gift of God is eternal life through Jesus Christ our Lord."

It is a gift, and not a prize. There are heavenly prizes to be run for, to be fought for, and to be obtained by divine help. There is a recompense of reward to which we are to look, and a crown for which we are to strive; but the grace that forgives sin, and works faith, is no prize for exertion, but a gift to those without strength. "It is not of him that willeth, nor of him that runneth, but of God that showeth mercy." Jehovah will have mercy on whom he will have mercy, and he will have compassion on whom he will have compassion, according to the good pleasure of his own will. Salvation is not granted to men as the result of anything they are, or do, or resolve to be, but it is the undeserved gift of heaven. If it were of works, it would not be of grace; but it is of faith, that it might be of grace alone.

The blessings of salvation are freely *given* us of God, therefore they are not a loan, handed to us for a time, and to be one day recalled. Our heavenly heritage is not held on lease, upon terms of annual payment: it is an unencumbered freehold to every man that hath by faith put his foot upon it. To give a thing and take a thing is for little children in their play; and even among them it is the subject of ridicule. But the gifts and calling of God are without repentance on his part. When he has given it, the deed is done outright, and can never be reversed. O believer, if thy sin be blotted out, it can never be written in again! God has declared, that he has forgiven our transgressions; and then he adds, "Their sins and their iniquities will I remember no more." There is no playing fast and loose in connection with the everlasting love of God and its glorious acts; if thou hast God, thou hast him by an eternal holding, of which none can deprive thee. "This God is our God for ever and ever." The better part which Jesus gives to his beloved shall not be taken away from us. The things of God are all of them free gifts, with no legal condition appended to them which would make their tenure one of payment rather than of absolute gift. We may not say that the blessings of salvation, such as pardon, justification, and eternal life, are gifts with an "if" in the core of them, rendering them uncertain. No, the gift of God is not temporary life, but "eternal life."

We will dwell for a minute upon the fact that saving blessings are the gifts *of God*. Some despise the work of salvation, and the blessings which accompany it; but, surely, they know not what they despise. Every part of salvation, from its Alpha to its Omega, is to the highest degree precious, for it is of God. It is the gift of the heavenly King, the gift of the Almighty Sovereign, whose hand makes the gift priceless. If the Lord himself has given thee this or that blessing, thou shouldst prize the gift as coming from such a hand! That which thy father gave thee, preserve; for there is a sanctity in the gift of love. That which thy choice friend has given thee, wear it, and for his sake value it as the token of friendship. But that which thy God has given thee, prize above all things else; his touch hath perfumed it with unutterable fragrance. Value every part of the work of grace because it came from God and leads to God. God's gifts are always worthy of the giver. God gives not trinkets and counterfeits; his gifts are solid gold and lasting treasure. The gifts of divine grace have a quality of divinity about them: they are all God-like. The Lord gives upon a God-like style. His grace is like the rest of his nature. How art thou blest if thou art divinely pardoned and divinely justified! "It is God that justifieth." Who is he that condemneth?" Jehovah is thy strength and thy song, he also hath become thy salvation.

I like to think of every blessing of grace that I have received as coming from God; because each mercy then becomes prophetic of more. God is unchangeable, and therefore what he has given he will give again. "Still there's more to follow," is a popular way of putting a great truth. The stream which has begun to flow will never cease flowing. The more the Lord gives, the more we may expect. Every blessing is not only in itself a mercy, but it is a note of hand for more mercies. When we get the most of God's mercy that we can hold, we are by its greatness enlarged to receive still more. Realization begets expectation, and expectation increases realization. Each mercy as it comes makes room for another larger than itself, even as the narrow end of the wedge opens the way for its wider portion. Every mercy bears a thousand mercies in its bowels. John Bunyan said that God's flowers bloom double: not only do they bloom double, but they bloom sevenfold; and out of every one of those flowers there comes a seed which will yield seventy times seven. Therefore, be encouraged. The least of the things which are freely given to us of God draws behind it an endless chain of more than golden links of love. The seed of salvation, glory, and eternal life, is small as a grain of mustard seed; but he that hath it hath received what neither earth nor heaven can fully contain. What a mercy is a single mercy! I cannot talk to you about the gifts of God; you must think over the subject. That which comes from God's own hand should be much on our mind.

I am going to dwell for a minute or two upon that word "freely": "The things that are *freely given* to us of God." Hearken, ye that have never found grace yet; and sing while you listen, you that have found it, and are now enjoying it. "Freely given." "Well," say you, "the word 'given' is enough to express the meaning, is it not?" Yes, it would be enough, if men were willing to understand; but the additional word "freely" is meant to make the meaning doubly plain. When we say "grace," there is no need to say *free* grace, is there? Yet there are some people who will be conveniently deaf, if they can. We wish to speak so that they not only can understand us, but cannot misunderstand, if they try. The text is very expressive—"Freely given to us of God."

How is salvation "freely given"? It comes from God *without compulsion*. If a man is stopped on the road with, "Your money or your life," he gives his money; but it is not *freely* given. Now, none can force mercy from God; blessed be his name, there is no need to think of such a thing. God gives freely, that is, even *without persuasion*. God was never persuaded to be gracious. He is ready to pardon, and his grace persuades us to accept mercy. Our praying does not turn the heart of God to love us, but proves that we are turning to love him. It is because he is gracious that he sets us praying. You have not, poor sinner, to convert an unwilling God to be willing to forgive: the conversion is in *your* will, not in *his* will: "He delighteth in mercy." He persuades Japhet to dwell in the tents of Shem, but Japhet does not need to persuade Jehovah to receive him. The fountain of divine love pours forth its streams of grace at all seasons without pressure. There is no need to tread the grapes of mercy to force forth their cheering juice. The paths of the Lord drop fatness, distilling spontaneously as the dew and the rain.

Yea, the grace of God is so free in its gifts that they come *without suggestion*. A man may be generous at heart, and yet he may need a hint to put it into his mind to relieve the needy. Mention a charity to him, and inform him that it is in need, and his guineas are forthcoming; but he needs a prompter. No one has prompted the grace of God. No one ever suggested any deed of bounty to God; out of his own heart the thought has come of itself. The gifts of his grace were in his eternal purpose from of old, and there of his own good pleasure. He freely instructs us how to pray for those gifts which he has of old purposed to bestow. Our prayer does not instruct the Lord; it only shows that he has, in a measure, instructed us. He gives freely in the sense of absolute spontaneousness.

He also gives *without grudging*. We have known men say, "Well, I suppose I must give something; but these claims come terribly often; my purse is always being drawn upon; but I suppose I cannot get out of it without a subscription." He gives as if he were parting with his blood. His fingers tremble and linger long over the shilling, which has to be extracted as forcibly as if it were a tooth. One wonders that the Queen's image is left upon it when it has been held with such pressure. But the Lord gives out of the greatness of his heart, without so much as a trace of unwillingness. Even when the boon was his own Son, he *freely* delivered him up. There is never a grudge in the Lord's mind towards those who draw upon him the most largely and the most frequently. "He upbraideth not." Many who give take the opportunity to upbraid, saying, "I do not think you ought to have been in this plight. You must have been wasteful, and not so industrious as you ought to have been, or you would not be drawing upon me," and so on, until they have taken full compensation for their shilling out of the poor creature, who feels bound to endure the chastisement. God giveth liberally, and adds no sorrow therewith to those who humbly seek wisdom at his hands. Oh, the splendour of the generosity of God! He is ready to save—waiting to deliver. It delights him to bestow his goodness. The cost was paid long ago on Calvary's tree, and that is over. Since the great sacrifice has been presented, all the blessings of grace are freely given to us of God, with a willingness which shows that his heart goes with them.

Once more: you know that we use the word "freely" in the sense of *bountifully*. We say of such and such a person, "His banquet was spread with a free hand," or we say, "He helps his poor neighbours very freely"; that is to say, his gifts are without stint. The benefits bestowed by some are like the provisions of a workhouse, weighed out by ounces; but free grace does not limit itself by calculations, nor bound the applicant by estimates. As a free-handed housekeeper makes liberal provision, so does the Lord provide more than need demands. The mere crumbs from the Lord's table would suffice to feed multitudes. The Lord giveth not his Spirit by narrow measure: we are not straitened in him. Come along with you, you needy saint or sinner; the more you can take in the better pleased will the Lord be with you; and if, sitting at his table, you feel as if you could eat all that is upon it, hesitate not to make the trial, for you shall be heartily welcome. Your capacity will fail long before the provision. The Lord desires you to open your mouth wide, and he will fill it: it is easier for him to give than for you to open your mouth. He encourages and requests you to bring large petitions with you when you come before his mercy-seat. Come and receive "the things that are freely given to us of God."

I do not know whether I have made my intent quite so plain as I wanted to do; but this I would set before you—God gives his grace *freely*, in the most emphatic sense. His sovereign grace is of himself: "It is not of him that willeth, nor of him that runneth, but of God that showeth mercy." He is not compelled to be gracious by the force of our importunity, but he often gives to those who have never asked of him, as it is written: "I am found of those who sought me not." He calls by his divine power those who aforetime were unwilling to come to him; even as in the case of Saul of Tarsus, who received light and grace when he was in the act of persecuting the saints. God gives his grace as freely as the sun, which, as soon as it rises from its chambers in the east, "sows the earth with orient pearl." See how freely it visits the tiny flower, which holds up its cup to have it filled with sunshine! How it peers into the glade of the forest, where, by the brook, the fern loves the shade. Whether the lark flies up to meet it, or the mole burrows in the earth to escape its light, the sun shines all the same. It fills the heavens and floods the earth with the brilliance which it is its nature to diffuse. The Lord comes by promise to those who seek him; but he comes also in sovereign grace to those who seek him not. He is coming this morning to some of you who look not for him; for he is like the dew, which waiteth not for man, neither tarrieth for the sons of man. You came from the country, and you said that you would go and hear Spurgeon this morning; but you did not know that the Lord was about to save you. Give yourself up to the writ of grace, of which I am the officer this morning. Surrender your hearts to almighty love; and when you do so, you will perceive many of "the things that are freely given to us of God."

Now, let us talk about what these things are. *They are altogether immeasurable*, these "things that are freely given to us of God." Shall I tell you what they are in one word? GOD. God gives us God. *God the Father gives himself* to the unworthy sons of men. He becomes their Father and their friend. He gives them his wisdom, his power, his love, his immutability. He gives himself to men to be their possession for ever. In adoption he gives his fatherhood, and grants them sonship, so that they may cry, "Our Father, which art in heaven." He gives them pardon and acceptance. He grants them answers to their prayers in ten thousand ways. He gives them his Providence to guide and lead them. He gives them all they need for this life, and then he gives them an inheritance with himself for ever in the world to come. He who gave us Jesus, with him also freely gives us all things.

Beloved, *the Son of God also gives himself*. "He loved me, and gave himself for me." "He his own self bare our sins in his own body on the tree." Jesus gives his people his blood to wash out their sins, his righteousness to cover them with beauty, his intercession to plead their cause, and his enthronement to secure their victory. He gives his loving care to prepare a place for them in the sky; he gives his resurrection to bring them up from the grave, and his union with them to preserve them through the perils of life. We are married to himself, and so he freely gives his heart's love to us. Even his crown, his throne, and his heaven he freely gives to his chosen. Oh, what a gift of grace this is that is freely given to us of God! "God so loved the world, that he gave his only-begotten Son." He is God's unspeakable gift. Nobody can speak it, for nobody can compass it within the range of thought.

The Holy Spirit also freely gives himself to us. He is the "free Spirit," and never freer than when he gives himself to enlighten, quicken, convert, comfort, and sanctify his people. He leads to repentance and to faith. He conducts to knowledge and holiness; he preserves and perfectly conforms us to the image of Christ. Thus see a summary of the things which are freely given to us of God, the Father, the Son, and the Holy Ghost.

All things are yours, the free gifts of God. Now if Paul, when he was writing as an apostle, spoke of these things, not as what he had won or deserved, but as free gifts to him, you and I, poor sinners that we are, may well be glad to accept these priceless boons on the same terms. We are happy to think that these benisons are laid at our door, with nothing to pay and nothing to do but simply to accept them as the "things that are freely given to us of God." I have used simple language, but my theme is sublime. The Lord bless it!

II. Our second head is: THE POWER TO RECEIVE THESE GIFTS IS ALSO FREELY GIVEN. Some of you are saying, "I see very clearly that salvation is the gift of God, but how can I get it? How can I apprehend these blessings, and make them my own?" Dear friend, the text says, "We have received the spirit which is of God." The power with which we receive these gifts, which God freely gives, is the power of the Holy Ghost; and this, also, we do not purchase or deserve, but we freely receive it.

The power to grasp Christ does not lie in our nature in its own strength or goodness. Our state is that of death, and death cannot grasp life. God the Holy Spirit must breathe life into us before we can rise from the grave of our natural depravity, and lay hold upon Christ, who is our life. It is not in unrenewed human nature even to see the kingdom of God, much less to enter it. "The natural man receiveth not the things of the Spirit of God."

The power to receive the things of God lieth not in high gifts or attainments. We may not think that a Homer, or a Socrates, or a Plato would be able to obtain the things of God more readily than common men. Genius is no help towards grace. Indeed, great talent and great learning often miss the way where lowliness travels with ease. Do not sit down and say, "I am a poor stupid, and cannot be taught of God." Or, "I am a humble countryman, or a poor woman keeping house for others; I cannot know these precious things." It is not so. Read the words of Paul in the first chapter of this epistle: "Ye see your calling, brethren, how that not many wise men after the flesh, not many mighty, not many noble, are called." The power to receive the blessings of God does not lie in talent at all, but it lies in the Spirit of God. You think that if you had a long hand you could reach the grace of God. No, but if you have a withered hand, that grace can reach you. You suppose that if you had a clear eye you could see the Lord; ay, but if you have no eye but a blind one, the Lord can open it, and give you sight. Grace is not tied to the rare gifts of genius, nor to the precious acquirements of experience, nor to the high attainments of learning. No young child may say, "I cannot receive the things of God, for I am too young." Out of the mouth of babes and sucklings he hath perfected praise. Persons who have had a long and instructive experience are often as far from grace as if they had never suffered anything. Persons who have taken degrees at the university may be still as ignorant as Hottentots concerning heavenly things. The power to receive is still of the Holy Spirit, and the Holy Spirit does not find good in us, but brings it to us. "Well," says one, "but surely we must pass through a period of great anguish and distress before we can receive the things of God." Very often men do suffer greatly from a sense of guilt, and the fear of punishment before they lay hold on Christ; but they do not lay hold on Christ by this experience. The wounded man is not restored by his pains, the famishing man is not fed by his hunger. The power to lay hold on Christ is a spiritual power, which must be given from above; it lies not concealed within, but is implanted by the Lord from without. No process of discipline, or education, or evolution, can enable a man to lay hold on the things of God. He must be born again from above, and his heart must be opened to receive the grace of God. A man can receive nothing unless it be given him to receive it, and that gift is the Holy Spirit.

The receptive power is *not bestowed by human excitement*, nor by the oratorical power of the preacher to whom the man listens. Possibly some have thought, "If I could hear So-and-so preach, I should then be able to believe." Put that thought away: you will believe in Jesus Christ when the Holy Spirit leads you to see how worthy your Saviour is of your confidence. You will never believe in him if you are looking to yourself for the power to believe, rather than to the truth itself, and to that Spirit who can make the truth clear to you, and work in you to will and to do of God's good pleasure. Come, then, dear hearts, you that feel so dull and dead, and so strengthless that you cannot do anything, remember right confidently that the Holy Spirit can enable you to receive all the gifts of God. May he at this time bless the truth to you, and you will feel the soft, sweet influence of repentance, melting you to tears on account of sin: you will feel a something telling you that in Christ there is just what you want, and you will feel a resolve forming in your heart, "I will have it if it may be had." Then you will come to a solemn decision for the present hour, "I will have it *now*. I will even now rest in Jesus, who died for the ungodly. Once for all I will turn my eyes to the cross, and look to him that did hang upon it, and trust my soul's weight on him." That is how the work is done. You may not know at the time that the moving power is the Spirit of God, but no one else works us to this thing but the Holy Ghost. We do not see the Spirit, nor hear his voice, nor recognize his person at the time, but being emptied of self, and led to accept the things that are freely given to us of God, we are spiritually enriched, and then we perceive that it was all of grace by the free gift of the Spirit of God.

One thing I should like to say before leaving this point: remember there are two spirits: there is the Spirit of God and the spirit of the world. This last is everywhere active, and believers feel it to be their foe: it worketh evil, and only evil. Only the Spirit of God can save you: the spirit of the world will ruin all who yield to it. I warn you against the spirit of this age—the spirit of the world. Do not lay yourselves under the influence of the spirit of the world; for even if you are truly saved, its pestilential influence will injure you. Are you seeking salvation? Keep clear of the spirit of the world as much as possible; and you will have no easy task, for its contagion will be found in men professing religion, but cunningly undermining it; and in books which pretend to reverence our Lord while they betray him. The religious world is more dangerous by far than the sensual world; it wears the sheepskin, but it has all the fierceness of the wolf. You cannot expect the Spirit of God to bless you if you yield to the spirit of the world. Do not meddle with that which is doubtful. There are works of fiction nowadays in abundance whose tendency is polluting: the world is drenched with them; avoid them as you would a bath of vitriol. If you would find eternal life, go where the Spirit of God works: search the Scriptures, and hear the truth through which the Spirit of God usually operates; and associate with those in whom the Spirit of God dwells. Hear that preaching which comes from God, for that alone will lead you to him. You can soon tell what sort the preaching is. I do not think you need stay ten minutes before you will find out whether it is according to the spirit of the world, or is in the power of the Spirit of God. Those two opposite spirits are waging a fierce battle at this hour; and, I grieve to say it, many who profess godliness are tainted with the spirit of the world. Take you good heed that you follow the right Spirit, for in so doing you will find the things which are freely given us of God, and with them glory, and immortality, and eternal life.

Now, I have done what I wanted to do, if I have made you feel how free salvation is. I would have you know that not only are the gifts of grace most free, but that the very hand with which we take the gift is nerved to do so by God's grace. Undeserved bounty bestows not only the money, but the purse in which we carry it home. God gives not only the blessing to the heart, but the heart to receive the blessing. Hallelujah!

III. My last head is this: THE KNOWLEDGE OF THESE GIFTS IS FREELY GIVEN.

This is so in the lowest and most ordinary sense, since a knowledge of the things freely given of God is communicated to our minds by the revelation contained in the inspired Scriptures. These sacred writings are open to all, and all are invited to search them. Read the Word of God, and you will know in the letter what are the free gifts of God to men. But this form of knowledge suffices not: we cannot savingly know the things of God by mere reading, neither can they be taught to us by a book. The head learns by nature, but the heart must learn by grace. The way to know the things of God is for that which is written in the Word of God to be also written upon the heart by the same Spirit who wrote in the book. I heard about repentance, but I never knew repentance until I repented; I heard of faith, but I never knew faith until I believed; I heard of pardon, but I never knew pardon until I was washed in the blood of the Lamb; I read about justification by faith, but I was never justified till, by faith, I received the Lord Jesus to be my righteousness. Appropriation by faith gives an apprehension by the understanding: experimental enjoyment creates true acquaintance. Beloved, go to the Holy Spirit, and ask him to enable you to take the things which God freely gives, and when you possess them, you will "know" them.

If still you desire to know more of the infinite preciousness of the gifts of God, it is a wise ambition; and it will be fully and freely satisfied by the Holy Spirit. Resort to him, for he is the great Teacher; there is no instructor like him. His knowledge surpasses all other, for he knows the mind of God. No man can communicate to you what he does not know, and no man knows the mind of God but the Spirit of God. The Holy Ghost knows the infinite and the unsearchable; and therefore he is able to teach you what you cannot learn elsewhere. The mind and meaning of God in every gift of grace the Spirit can unfold to you. There is no being taught effectually except you are taught of the Spirit of God. All other teaching is superficial, and therefore temporary and vain; but the Holy Spirit speaks to the soul, and writes the lines of truth on the fleshy tablets of the heart, so that they can never be erased. If you would know the things freely given us of God, the Holy Spirit must lead you into the inner secret of the sacred treasure-house.

By the same divine aid you must be enabled to feed upon these choice things, and have a full enjoyment of them. The things of God, as I have said before, are best known by a personal enjoyment of them. Who can know meat and drink except by living upon them? When you can feed upon a Scripture, when you can suck out the marrow of a doctrine, when you can extract the juice from a divine promise, when you are made fat and flourishing by inspired teaching, then hath the Lord made you freely to know the blessings of his covenant. Oh, that the Holy Spirit may be to you as the seven-branched lamp gladdening your eyes with his light, and as the loaves of the shewbread nourishing your heart, and then may he lead you within the veil, and make you to see the mercy-seat, and all the glory of the Lord your God! Oh, to realize that blessing, "All thy children shall be taught of the Lord"! May we be taught by actual enjoyment and heavenly communion, so that we may come into holy familiarity with the choice things that are freely given to us of God. I do not know that I want to hear any lecture on bread; I know all that I want to know about that form of food, because I eat it every day; even so, we need little talk about covenant blessings, because they are the continual portion of our souls, our strength in every stage of our heavenward pilgrimage, and our song in anticipation of the eternal rest.

My dear brothers and sisters, go to this high-school of heaven. The terms are, "nothing to pay," though the education is beyond all other. Blessed school, wherein sinners are made saints, and saints are made to grow into the likeness of Jesus. Everything is as free in this university as in the first dame-school of humble faith, where the sinner learns repentance, and ventures to trust his Saviour. Eternal life is the gift of God, in its first breathing; and it is still the gift of God in its highest development. When you stand before the throne of the Most High, you will stand there through grace alone. All along, from sin's pit to heaven's gate, without a break, the whole road is paved with grace. We do not begin with grace, and then go on to trust in works: we do not at first receive freely, and then afterwards have to live upon a hard-earned wage. No; still, still, still he worketh in us to will and to do, and we lovingly work under his divine guidance, as we are strengthened by his divine power. Grace lays the foundation-stone, and

> "Grace all the work shall crown,
>   Through everlasting days;

> It lays in heaven the topmost stone,
> And well deserves the praise."

What of all this? Listen to me for a very few minutes more.

I speak to those of you who know the things that are freely given to you of God. Learn from these things to *be humble*. If you know anything, you have been taught it. If you possess anything, it has been given you. You are a charity child. The clothes on your back are furnished by the Lord's favour. The bread in your mouth is the provision of his love. A proud saint is a contradiction in terms. "What hast thou which thou hast not received?"

In the next place, *be generous*. I cannot believe in a stingy saint. Here again there is a flat contradiction in terms. All things are freely given you, are you going to be mean over them? "Freely ye have received, freely give." He who turns over the coin in his pocket, to make it as small as ever he can before he gives it, is a poor creature. He gets the smallest change on Saturday, that he may give it on Sunday. He is a saint, is he? Let those believe in his saintship who can. The child of God should be free-hearted. He should give himself away, because Jesus gave himself for us. You should be of large heart, for you serve a large-hearted Christ, who has given you all things freely to enjoy.

Next, *be ready to impart what you know*. If the Spirit of God has made you to know the things freely given of God, try to tell somebody else. Don't act as if you had a patent, or a monopoly, and wanted grace to be a secret. You have not the gift of God yourself if you have no desire that others should have it. The first instinct of a converted man is to try to convert others. If you have no wish to bring others to heaven, you are not going there yourself.

Try and impart this knowledge in the way in which you received it. You received it by the Holy Spirit; then go and teach it, not in the words which man's wisdom teacheth, but in the power of the Spirit of God. Last night I felt so unwell that I thought I should not be able to preach to-day; but I cheered myself with this reflection—if you cannot give wealth of illustration, if you can display no beauty of style, never mind, you can tell out the soul-saving truth in plain words, and God will own it. Holy Spirit, bless my feeble words this morning! Thou canst do it, and thou shalt have all the praise. Go to your Sunday-school class this afternoon, dear friend, and say, "Lord, put words into my mouth, and teach me, that I may teach others. Enable me to labour, not in the power of my knowledge, eloquence, or experience, but under the guidance of thy Spirit." Better five words in the Spirit than a long oration in your own power.

Lastly, if the Lord has given us all these things freely, *let us praise him*. I did not mind hearing our brother over there cry out "Amen." He may do it again, if he likes. Sometimes it is well to let the living water of praise to God burst the pipes, and flood the streets. What a dumb set we are! The Lord has to pull hard at the rope before our bell speaks at all. Let us praise him for what he has done for us, and make this vow this morning:

> "I will praise him in life, I will praise him in death,
> And praise him as long as he lendeth me breath;
> And say, when the death-dew lies cold on my brow,
> 'If ever I loved thee, my Jesus, 'tis now.' "

The Lord himself bless you all, according to the riches of his grace. Amen.

PORTIONS OF SCRIPTURE READ BEFORE SERMON—1 Cor. 1:18-31; 2.

HYMNS FROM "OUR OWN HYMN BOOK"—386, 491, 236.[12]

---

[12] Spurgeon, C. H. (1889). Grace for Grace. In *The Metropolitan Tabernacle Pulpit Sermons* (Vol. 35, pp. 289–300). London: Passmore & Alabaster.

REAL GRACE FOR REAL NEED

A Sermon

Delivered on Sunday Morning, September 5th, 1869, by

C. H. SPURGEON,

AT THE METROPOLITAN TABERNACLE, NEWINGTON.

"He healed them that had need of healing."—Luke 9:11.

"He healed them that had need of healing," that is to say, on this gracious occasion no single case came before him which baffled him. However rampant might be the disease, however extreme the condition of the patient's malady, Jesus wrought an instantaneous cure. And truly to this very hour no spiritual sickness has defeated the great Physician. No sick souls have ever been carried away from his feet to perish hopelessly, because their need outreached his power. Satan's worst is soon undone by Jesus' best. The Son of God in no solitary instance has been foiled, still in the goings forth of his mercy he has "healed them that had need of healing."

The text also indicates that our Lord continued unweariedly to heal all the multitudes that came. From morning till night, as fast as the various patients presented themselves, he wrought their cure. There was an eye to be opened here, hearing to be given there, a lame man to be made to leap, a withered limb to be outstretched, there was leprosy to be cleansed, dropsy to be dried, fever, epilepsy, madness, and all manner of maladies to be subdued, but Jesus paused not, virtue continued still to flow to heal "them that had need of healing." Though they had been countless as the sands, his love, like the sea, should have touched them all. His restoring power was by no means exhausted, the oil only ceased to flow when there was not another vessel to fill; but had the needy continued still to come even to this day, our Master would still have multiplied his miracles of mercy. In spiritual sicknesses, the great Healer of our sin-sick nature has by no means declined in power. He is far from being exhausted by the number of applicants who have come to him. We do well to sing—

> "Thy precious blood
> Shall never lose its power,
> Till all the ransomed church of God
> Be saved to sin no more."

If this present world should continue through a century of thousands of years, yet no sinner shall apply to Jesus for pardon, and find that his cleansing efficacy has ceased; so long as sin shall pollute this earth, the Saviour shall remain to purify those who believe in him.

But the text seemed particularly to me, as it flashed upon my mind, to indicate this further truth, that as the Redeemer was neither baffled by any one disease, nor drained of his healing virtue by the multitude, so the diseases which he healed were intense, the cures which he wrought were memorable. They were not feigned sicknesses which were brought before him, nor counterfeit miseries, else his cures also had been shams, and he himself had been a mock Saviour. Those whom he healed had deep, true, undoubted, urgent need of healing; they were not pretended patients, with sores which they had manufactured for the occasion, or sentimental sufferers with griefs imagined but not existent; but he wrought health for persons who were well known to be cruelly diseased, in whom the mischief was no dream, the misery no fiction; and consequently the cures which he wrought were no fictions either, but they were evident, permanent, and true. Fancied ills he left to others; he healed those that had need of healing. Sentimental grievances may be left to jangling philosophers and hair-splitting rabbis—Jesus deals with actual evils whose cure is urgent. Of all men who ever lived, the Prophet of Nazareth was the most practical; doing nothing for show, nothing for mere custom, but everything to work solid good and efface real evil. Not a motion of his finger has he for feigned or fancied grievance, but all his power goeth forth to those who have true need of healing.

We shall take this thought, this morning, and dwell upon it. It seems to us to be full of comfort. May God grant it may bring into light and liberty some who have long been bound.

I. Our first head, this morning, shall be that THOSE WHOM CHRIST HAS SAVED WILL ALL CONFESS THAT THEY HAD NEED OF SAVING.

Out of the whole multitude who have believed in Jesus, there is not one to whom his salvation has been a superfluity. I will be spokesman for them, this morning, according to my ability—they will all confess that what they have received was what they greatly wanted, that the salvation which Jesus has given them was a salvation without which they would have perished everlastingly. For first, beloved, all the saved saints confess that they had need of healing through *their natural depravity*. There is a sad bias in us all towards sin. Whoever may dispute concerning original sin as a universal fact, all the saints confess it as a particular evil in their own case. We are compelled to own that David's confession must be ours, "Behold, I was shapen in iniquity; and in sin did my mother conceive me." Our nature was vitiated at its fountain head. When at any time we were put upon right courses by the stress of moral suasion, or by the urgency of fear, yet still our heart laboured to follow its own devices against wind and tide. Even as the bowl from the player's hand, however straightly it runs for awhile, before long begins to curve according to the bias, even so under all circumstances we tend towards evil. To our nature to do evil is easy, to do good is difficult. We loved darkness naturally rather than light. Uphill work it was to serve God, but as swiftly as a stone hurled down from a crag pursues its downward course, so readily did we follow the way of rebellion. Our sin was of the heart, not of the surface, "The leprosy was deep within." Our tendency to evil did not spring from imitation—for we had set before us, some of us, the noblest of Christian examples, but the prompting to evil was within, the taint was in our vital blood. Now there was need of healing here, since the disease had corrupted our essential being, and rendered us hopelessly unclean. To our heart's centre there was urgent need of healing.

But, beloved, many of us have been led to feel that in addition to ordinary original sin, evil tendencies had in the case of some of us assumed peculiar shapes and dreadful forms of *besetting and constitutional sin*. I will appeal to certain of my brethren here, whether they had not a natural tendency to a quick temper, an anger soon excited, and exceedingly mad when once aroused? In others, there was a strong disposition to pride. Even now, with the grace of God in them, it costs them much to keep their heads in their proper places. Alas! in how many others the animal passions are forceful and eager like hungry lions roaring for their prey, and nothing but grace can keep them in check! Ah! there are some of us who may do well to imagine what we should have been if grace had not interposed; we are bold in spirit, eager in desire, intent in purpose, stubborn in will, energetic and ardent, and had we been set on mischief, nothing could have restrained us in our headlong course. Grace leads us in glad captivity, but apart from this, we had been sinners before the Lord exceedingly. All providences that might have thwarted us would but have incited us to more vehement endeavours to pursue our wicked and wilful way; grace has conquered, but what if we had been left alone? A Scotch gentleman was observed to look very intently upon the face of Rowland Hill: the good old man asked him, "And what are you looking in my face at?" The observer replied, "I have been studying the lines of your face." "And what do you make out of them?" said Rowland. "Why I make out," said he, "that if the grace of God had not changed your heart you would have been a great rascal." "Ah!" said Rowland, "you have made out the truth indeed." Many of us have to confess humbly that in us there was pressing need of healing, for if healing had not come, we should not only have been sinful as others, but should probably have taken the lead in iniquity, and been carried away by the wild sweep of inward passion to the utmost excess of riot.

Brethren, this need of healing will be confessed by the saints in this further respect, that there was not only in us a tendency to sin, but *we had grievously sinned* in act and deed before conversion. I know it is very customary with those who are seeking Christ, to imagine that the saints of God whom they respect and esteem could never have sinned before conversion as they themselves have done. They cannot imagine that the man who is now rejoicing in Christ was once as hardened in sin as themselves. Yet in truth we were even as you. When the apostle mentioned the greatest of sinners, he added, "Such were some of us: but we are washed, but we are sanctified." O dear seeker, do not believe as Satan tells you, that those who are washed were never as black as you; we were just as vile. It were a shame for us to confess in public all our transgressions and iniquities before we knew pardoning mercy of the Lord, but it will suffice us to say that the remembrance of them lays us in the very dust, so that we should not dare to lift up our head were it not that we have an advocate with the Father, Jesus Christ the righteous. There is not a saint in heaven but what had sinned enough to damn him to the lowest hell if he had not been saved by one who knew he had need of saving. Where had Peter been? As bad as Judas certainly if sovereign grace had not prevented. Where had John been, even loving John? Cursing and blaspheming the very Christ upon whose bosom he laid his head, if it had not been that converting love stepped in and made him in the fulness of time to become a child of God. There would have been no difference between the best and the worst of men if divine favour had not wrought some better thing in the godly. And let this always be treasured up as a hopeful circumstance to you who would be saved, that in the matter of actual sin there was a deep and real need of healing in the saints who are healed. No, sirs, our sins were not mere fiction, our repentances were not fanatical sentiment. Southey, when he writes upon the repentance of John Bunyan, and his terrible accusations of himself, cannot refrain from thinking him a little beside himself, and morbid in his feelings. The good man is candid and honest, and wants to make something out of it, but he cannot see in young Bunyan any cause for such outcries against himself. Had Southey been able to look upon sin in that same vivid but truthful light which had shone upon the young tinker's soul, he would have seen the least sin to be exceeding sinful, and would have felt that exaggeration in horror against sin is not possible. To sin against light, against conscience, against the Holy Ghost, is to sin with a vengeance. No degree of outward moral purity can comfort a heart which is once made aware of its inward defilement, and of the actual sinfulness of what man calls a trifle. Our actual sins would have been draughts of poison to our souls if the divine antidote had not been given; there was, indeed, great need of healing.

Further, let me say there was need of healing in our case because, in addition to having sinned, we wilfully continued in it. In the very teeth of divine mercy, in despite of conscience and of the invitations of the gospel, we persevered in our sinful courses. Do I not remember how often I was invited to come to Christ, and even felt the gentle drawings of his cords of love? but I started back like a bullock unaccustomed to the yoke! Do I not recollect how God's law ploughed me again and again? and yet in those very furrows the cursed darnel and thistle of my sins dared to spring up! How often have I stood and wept, and trembled, but have procrastinated, and so have gone my way to dry those eyes and look again into the face of sin without alarm! Yes, there was need of healing in that heart which the cross of Christ could not affect, which the terrors of hell could not subdue, which the loving invitations of a mother could not persuade to holiness, and that even the warnings of sickness and the fear of death could not bend to the will of God. Some of you were long years before you yielded to the power of divine grace. You will sorrowfully acknowledge, this morning, that in your obstinate will there was need of healing, for had not that healing come, it is as certain as that you are here to-day pilgrims on the way to heaven, that you would have continued to pursue the road to hell. There was need of healing, for the disease was not one that would have died out of itself; it would never have come to a head and then have lost its power. It was a disease that would have spread until it defiled you beyond bearing, and until the righteous God would have said, "Put it away with the unclean for ever and ever, for within the courts of heaven it can never dwell." O praise your God, this morning, you that are saved, for you had solemn need of saving. The longer I live the more I feel the need of daily salvation. I have need of my great Master's healing hand every hour. If the Lord do not carry on the work which he has begun, it will surely fail. If he does not continue to repress and destroy in us our carnal inclinations, they will get the better of us even now. If the Holy Spirit does not fan with his living breath that spark of grace which lives within us, it will certainly be quenched with the waterfloods of temptation. If there were no other proof of our need of healing than our experience since conversion, we should have more than enough. If ever I get to heaven, I will praise God more loudly than any of you, for I shall owe more to the grace that will bring me there. But I suppose the like feeling is in every man that is conscious of the sin that dwelleth in him, and trembleth at his own want of strength. God will carry on his work, he will not take away his hand from you, nor suffer you to perish; but in the fact that if he did so withdraw, the best of you would be cast away, and ere tomorrow would be apostates from the faith, you have proof that you have need of healing. You will have need of healing all along until you come to die. Even when just about to enter into the joy of your Lord, when the last sin is under your foot, and your sanctification is all but perfect, when you have almost destroyed by his grace the last indwelling lust, even then you will have need of healing. He must be the Omega who was the Alpha, or you never can finish. He must carry on even to its close the work which in his tenderness he has commenced, or else it will be incomplete to your eternal overthrow.

So, then, it is established beyond a doubt, and I speak as the witness of ten thousand of God's servants, that those who are saved were such as had need of saving. The Son of Man came to seek and to save us when we were lost, emphatically lost. He has healed us, but it has not been of a finger-ache or a flea-bite disease; he has healed us of a disease most deadly, that was damnable. Blessed be his name, while we are forced to speak depreciatingly of ourselves, in that very proportion we can speak gloriously of him. We had need of healing, and he has given us just the healing that our spirits needed.

II. Having, as it were, cast up my earthworks round about the soul that I desire to win for Jesus, I shall now come point blank to the attack. You, dear hearers, you unsaved hearers, YOU ALSO HAVE NEED OF SAVING.

I am not going to talk to you, this morning, about your feeling your need of Christ. I know that you make that quite a favourite question and a fond excuse for unbelief; so we shall not speak of your sense of that need, but what is far more vast a subject, namely, your need itself. You unsaved souls, you have great need of saving. You have need of saving, because *you are inclined to evil*. You have lately been, in a measure, desirous to find eternal life, you are not now so callous as you once were, conscience is awakened, and you are seeking more or less earnestly after Christ; but still with all this your natural inclinations are towards evil. Your goodness will soon pass away like the dew of the morning, but your love to sin is graven, as with a diamond, into your heart of stone. The strong self-will within your soul is set on mischief still. You will not come unto Christ that you may have life. Perhaps you have never thought of your natural corruption, and above all, have never been humbled by it; but it is there notwithstanding your forgetfulness of it. You are a fallen, degenerate creature. You are not a pure spirit, whose judgment is accurately balanced; you judge unrighteous judgment. You are not a creature with a free will that is equally inclinable either to good or evil, according as it may seem most beneficial to yourself. Your overpowering tendency now is towards that which is evil. Your mind puts bitter for sweet and sweet for bitter, darkness for light and light for darkness; and your nature, like an evil tree, brings forth evil fruit. You perhaps have never perceived this, but the very fact that you have not perceived it, only proves that you have the greater need of healing, since the disease has become so thorough as to have made you insensible of its own existence. When there is no pain in the limb, then is it certainly in greater risk of mortification; and while your natural depravity causes you no pain whatever, and you are even inclined to deny it and take no shame to yourself concerning it, the more urgent is the need that the Holy Ghost should convince you of sin, and that the Lord Jesus Christ should come and deliver you from it. Ah, poor sinner, what a ruin you are at best! Alas! for human dignity, with its lofty pinnacles of morality and turrets of excellency. What theatrical pasteboard! What sand-built rubbish all appears when seen in the blaze of divine light! Vain are your filmings of your deadly sore; your heart is in itself vile and deceitful above all things, and desperately wicked. You may wash the platter as you may, you may make the outside of the cup as clean as you will, but your inward parts are very wickedness. The imaginations of the thoughts of your hearts are evil, only evil, and that continually. "Ye must be born again;" your nature is too depraved for mending. You must be created anew in Christ Jesus. You have need of healing indeed.

In addition to this, dear hearer, thou art day by day proving thy need of healing by *thine actual sin*. I cannot publicly rehearse thy particular and personal sins, but this I know, the charge may be legitimately brought against every unconverted person here, that you are daily living in sin. Take down the ten commandments and read them through. I will but remind you of one, and beg you to examine yourself upon it, "Thou shalt love the Lord thy God with all thy heart, and with all thy soul, and with all thy mind, and with all thy strength." Are you keeping that? Why, you live as if there were no God, you know you do; and day after day, and even month after month, you never do anything to manifest love towards God. You have some love towards your relatives, but no passion like that is kindled in your spirit towards your God; you have no love at all, and yet the precept is, "Thou shalt love him with all thy heart." Why, that one command is lodging charges against thee at the bar of God every day. Indeed, the whole ten thou art constantly breaking, there is not one that thou dost keep. These sins of thine are speeding as messengers up to the record office in heaven, and there thou shalt find written down every idle word, every sinful thought, and every guilty action of thy whole life. How wilt thou bear to hear of all these in the latter days, when thy body shall have arisen from the grave at the archangel's trumpet? How wilt thou bear to hear the book read out that shall rehearse thy sins? At the very thought thereof thy bones may be dissolved within thee: sins against a righteous God, sins against his people, sins against his day, sins against his book, sins against your bodies, sins against your souls, sins of every kind, sins unseen of human eye, sins unknown to any but yourself and your God, all read and all proclaimed with trumpet voice while men and angels hear. You have need of healing, for you are scarlet, you are crimson, you are double-dyed with your iniquities. O that you did but know this! O that you did but feel this! You have need of healing, and yet dark as the thought is, it gives me comfort, and it ought to give you comfort, to remember the text—Jesus healed those that had need of healing; and if you are such, why should he not heal you? Your many sins only prove that you have need of healing, and the desperate depravity of your heart only proves still more that you are such as Jesus came to heal. He healed those that had need of healing; he healed just such as you are.

Further, I think I hear some of you confess *that you do not feel this as you ought*. Now I was about to bring this to you as a proof that you have need of healing. When a man does wrong, and yet will not confess it, how wrong he must be! or when, having confessed it, he feels not the proper shame; or feeling for awhile the proper shame, he yet returns to the same evil like the dog to his vomit, how deep must the evil be in his moral nature, how trebly diseased must he be, inasmuch as he does not feel sin to be sin at all! When a man has done wrong and knows it, and stands with bitter repentance to confess the evil, why, you think hopefully of him; after all there are good points about the man; there is a vitality in him that will throw out the disease; but when the villain, having perpetrated a grave and causeless offence, does not for a moment acknowledge that he has done amiss, but continues calmly to perpetrate the offence again; ah, then, where is there any good in him? Is he not thoroughly bad? Now, such are you. If you were at all right with God you would fall at your Father's feet, and never rise until you were forgiven, your tears would flow day and night until you had the assurance of pardon. But since your heart seems to yourself to be made of hell-hardened steel, and to be like the nether millstone, that feels not at all, why, then there is the more need of healing, and you seem to me this morning the very man I am after, the very man that Christ came to save, for he came not to call the righteous but sinners to repentance, not to save those who had no need of healing, but to heal just such as you whose need is desperate indeed.

As if to prove your own need of healing, you are this morning, according to your own statement, *unable to pray*. You have been trying to pray of late, and wished you could. You put yourself upon your knees, but your heart does not talk with God; a horrible dread comes over you, or else frivolous and vain thoughts distract you. "Oh," you have said, "I would give a thousand pounds for one tear of repentance; I would be ready to pluck out my eyes if I could but call upon God as the poor publican did, with 'God be merciful to me a sinner.' I thought it the easiest thing in the world once to pray, but now I find that a true prayer is beyond my power." O soul, you have need of healing indeed, possessed with a dumb devil, and all your other devils to boot, and unable to cry out for mercy; yours is a sad case. You have need of healing, and I cannot help repeating my text to you, "He healed them that had need of healing," why should he not heal you?

Ah, but you tell me your feelings, your desires after good things, are very often damped. Perhaps this morning you are sincerely in earnest, but to-morrow you may be just as careless as ever. The other day you went into your chamber and did wrestle with God, but a temptation came across your path, and you were as thoughtless about divine things as if you had never been aroused to a sense of their value. Ah! this shows what a need you have of healing. You are vile indeed when you dare to trifle with eternity, to sport with death and judgment, and to be at ease while in danger of hell—your heart indeed has need of healing; and though I grieve that you should be in such a plight, yet do I rejoice that I am able to add, "He healed those that had need of healing."

Though you know your case to be so bad, yet at times you set up a kind of self-repentance, and try to justify yourself in the sight of God. You say, "I have repented, or tried to do so; I have prayed, or tried to pray; I have done all I can to be saved, and God will not save me; that is to say, you throw the blame of your damnation upon God, and make out yourself to be righteous in his sight. You know this to be wrong. If you are not saved, it is because you will not believe in Jesus. There is the only hitch and the only difficulty. Your damnation is not of God, but of yourself; it is necessitated by your own wilful wickedness in not believing in Christ; but inasmuch as you are so wicked as to dare to excuse yourself, you have great need of healing, urgent need of saving. But, then, the minute that you have thus excused yourself, you rush to the opposite extreme; you declare that you have sinned past hope, that you deserve to be now in hell, and that God can never forgive you. You deny the mercy of God, you deny the power of Christ to forgive you and cleanse you; you fly in the face of God's word, and you make him out to be a liar. When he tells you that if you trust Jesus you shall find peace, you tell him it is not possible there can be any peace to you; when he reminds you that he never rejected one, you insinuate that he will reject you; you thus insult the divine majesty by denying the truthfulness and honesty of God. You have need of healing when you thus allow wicked despair to get the mastery of you; you are far gone, very far gone; but, oh! I rejoice to know that you are still among such as Jesus was wont to heal. He came to heal those that had need of healing, and you cannot deny you are one of those. Why, Satan himself will not have the impudence to tell you that you have no need of healing. O that you would but cast yourself into the Saviour's arms—not trying to make yourself out to be good, but acknowledging all that I have laid to your charge, and then, trusting as a sinner to that dear Lamb of God that taketh away the sin of the world.

Remember, dear hearer, thou hast need of healing, for except thou be healed of these sins, and of all these wicked tendencies and thoughts of thine, as sure as thou art a living man thou wilt be cast into hell. O my dear friend, I know of no truth that ever causes me such pain to preach as this, not that sinners will be damned, awful truth as that is, but that *awakened* sinners will be damned unless they believe in Jesus. You must not make a Christ out of your tears, you must not hope to find safety in your bitter thoughts and cruel despairs. Except ye believe ye shall never be established. Except ye come to Christ, ye may be convinced of sin, of righteousness, and judgment too, but those convictions will only be preludes to your destruction. My dear hearer, dost thou know what thou art this morning? Thou callest thyself a seeker, but until thou art a finder thou art an enemy to God, and God is angry with thee every day. Let but one drop of thy blood go wrong this morning, let but thy beating pulse be suspended, and where art thou? Why, in hell, despite those tears, despite those cries, for if thou wilt not believe in Jesus, there is no purgatory for thee, no place where afterwards thou mayst find space for repentance, and seek the Christ whom thou dost to-day disregard. I have no alternative for you, however tender and broken-hearted you may be, but this one, believe and live, refuse to believe, and you must perish, for your broken-heartedness, and tears, and professed contrition, can never stand in the place of Christ. You must have faith in Jesus, or you must die eternally.

I shall press on very briefly to the next point, but I pray God to make these words of use to you before you forget them. I am endeavouring to speak simply, personally, and pointedly. He knoweth how my soul yearneth over those who are here, that they may this morning find life in Jesus. O may he grant the desire of my soul, and bring them to himself now.

III. Our third point is to thee, O needy sinner. JESUS CAN SAVE THEE.

I need not enter into what thy case is. Remember, Jesus has saved a parallel case to yours. Yours may seem to yourself to be exceedingly odd, but somewhere or other in the New Testament you will find one as singular as yours. You tell me that you are full of so much wickedness. Did not he cast seven devils out of Magdalen? Yes, but your wickedness seems to be greater than even seven devils. Did not he drive a whole legion of devils out of the demoniac of Gadara? You tell me that you cannot pray, but he healed one possessed of a dumb devil; you feel hardened and insensible, but he cast out a deaf devil. You tell me you cannot believe; neither could that man with the withered arm stretch out his arm, but he did do it when Jesus bade him. You tell me you are dead in sin, but Jesus made even the dead live. Your case cannot be so bad but it has been matched, and Christ has conquered the like of it. O poor soul, if thou dost but come to him, thou shalt not find thyself one half the singularity that thou dost suppose, for another has been saved just like thyself.

Remember again, Christ can save you, for there is not a record in the world, nor has there ever been handed down to us by tradition a single case in which Jesus has failed. If I could meet anywhere in my wanderings a soul that had cast itself on Christ alone, and yet had received no pardon; if there could be found in hell a solitary spirit that relied upon the precious blood and found no salvation, then the gospel might well be laid by in the dark, and no longer gloried in; but as that has not been, and never shall be, sinner, thou shalt not make the first exception. If thou comest to Christ—and to come to him is but to trust him wholly and simply—thou canst not perish, for he has said, "Him that cometh to me I will in no wise cast out." Will he prove a liar? Wilt thou dare to think so? O come thou, for he cannot cast thee out. Bethink thee for a moment, sinner, and this may comfort thee, he whom I preach to thee as the healer of thy soul is God. What can be impossible with God? What sin cannot he forgive who is God over all? If thy transgressions were to be dealt with by an angel, they might surpass all Gabriel's power, but it is Immanuel, God with us, who is come to save. Though thou wert between the jaws of hell, so long as the pit had not shut her mouth upon thee, he could save thee. Doubt not, where thou hast to deal with Deity, nothing is impossible, or even difficult.

Moreover, thou canst not doubt his will. Hast thou ever heard of him—he that was God and became man? He was gentle as a woman—

> "His heart is made of tenderness,
> His bowels melt with love."

It was not in him to be harsh. When the woman taken in adultery, in the very fact, was brought to him, what did he say? "Neither do I condemn thee: go, and sin no more." It was said of him, "This man receiveth sinners, and eateth with them," and he is not changed now that he reigns above; he is just as willing to receive sinners now as when he was here below.

Once more, dost thou still doubt? Remember what he has done to save sinners. My time fails me, else would I ask thee to go with me to Gethsemane and view him covered with the sweat of blood; I would ask thee to stand with me in Pilate's hall when Pilate cries "*Ecce Homo;*" to see the Saviour as his shoulders are crimsoned with streams of gore for sinners who were his enemies; I would ask thee then to stand beneath the cross and view the hands, and feet, and side, all pouring forth his life-blood. These are the drops that take our sins away; these are the griefs of him who took our guilt that our guilt might be forgiven. Can Jesus the Son of God suffer like this, and yet there be no power in his blood to cleanse? What, was the atonement a fiction? Was the death of the eternal Son of God a thing without effect? There must be power enough there to take away sin. Come and wash, come and wash, ye vile and black, come and wash, and ye shall find instant cleansing the moment that by faith you touch his purifying blood.

Lastly, Jesus demands of you, sinner, this morning, your trust. He deserves it, let him have it. You have need of healing; he came to heal those that have need of healing; he can heal you. What is to be done in order that you may be healed this morning, that all your sins may be forgiven and yourself saved? All that is to be done is to leave off your own doing, and let him do for you; leave off looking to yourself, or looking to others, and just come and cast yourself on him. You know Dr. Watts's lines:—

> "A guilty, weak, and helpless worm,
>   On Christ's kind arm I fall;
> He is my strength and righteousness,
>   My Jesus and my all."

"Oh," say you, "but I cannot believe." Cannot believe! Then do you know what you are doing? You are making him a liar. If you tell a man, "I cannot believe you," that is only another way of saying, "You are a liar." Oh, you will not dare to say that of Christ. No, my friend, I take you by the hand and say another word—*you must believe him*. He is God, dare you doubt him? He died for sinners. Can you doubt the power of his blood? He has promised. Will you insult him by mistrusting his word? "Oh! no," you say, "I feel I must believe, I must trust him; but suppose that trust of mine should not be of the right kind? Suppose it should be a natural trust?" Ah! my friend, a humble trust in Jesus is a thing that never grew in natural ground. For a poor soul to come and trust in Christ, always is the fruit of the Spirit. You need not raise a question about that. Never did the devil, never did mere nature empty a man of himself and bring him to Jesus. Do not be anxious on that point. "But," says one, "the Spirit must lead me to believe him!" Yes, but you cannot see the Spirit; his work is a secret and a mystery. What you have to do is to believe in Jesus; there he stands, God and yet a suffering man, making atonement, and he tells you if you trust him you shall be saved. You must trust him; you cannot doubt him. Why should you? What has he done that you should doubt him?

> "O believe the record true,
> God to you his Son has given."

And if you trust him, you need not raise the question as to where your faith came from. It must have come from the Holy Spirit who is not seen in his workings, for he worketh where he listeth. You see the fruit of his work, and that is enough for you. Dost thou believe that Jesus is the Christ? If so, thou art born of God. If thou hast cast thyself, sink or swim, on him, then art thou saved. We read in the papers this week, how a man was saved from being shot. He had been condemned in a Spanish court, but being an American citizen and also of English birth, the consuls of the two countries interposed, and declared that the Spanish authorities had no power to put him to death, and what did they do to secure his life? They wrapped him up in their flags, they covered him with the Stars and Stripes and the Union Jack, and defied the executioners. "Now fire a shot if you dare, for if you do you defy the nations represented by those flags, and you will bring the powers of those two great nations upon you." There stood the man, and before him the soldiery, and though a shot might soon have ended his life, yet he was as invulnerable as though in coat of triple steel. Even so Jesus Christ has taken my poor guilty soul ever since I believed in him, and has wrapped around me the blood-red flag of his atoning sacrifice, and before God can destroy me or any other soul that is wrapped in the atonement, he must insult his Son and dishonour this sacrifice, and that he never will do, blessed be his name. May the Lord save each one of you. May he do it now, and his shall be the glory. Amen and Amen.

PORTION OF SCRIPTURE READ BEFORE SERMON—Luke 7:1–30.[13]

---

[13] Spurgeon, C. H. (1869). Real Grace for Real Need. In *The Metropolitan Tabernacle Pulpit Sermons* (Vol. 15, pp. 493–504). London: Passmore & Alabaster.

GRACE ABOUNDING OVER ABOUNDING SIN

A Sermon

Delivered on Lord's-day Morning, March 4th, 1888, by

C. H. SPURGEON,

at the Metropolitan Tabernacle, Newington

"Moreover the law entered, that the offence might abound. But where sin abounded, grace did much more abound."—Romans 5:20.

THE first sentence will serve as a preface; the second sentence will be the actual text.

"Moreover the law entered, that the offence might abound." Man was a sinner before the law of Ten Commandments had been given. He was a sinner through the offence of his first father, Adam; and he was, also, practically a sinner by his own personal offence; for he rebelled against the light of nature, and the inner light of conscience. Men, from Adam downward, transgressed against that memory of better days which had been handed down from father to son, and had never been quite forgotten. Man everywhere, whether he knew anything about the law of Moses or not, was alienated from his God. The Word of God contains this truthful estimate of our race: "They are all gone out of the way, they are together become unprofitable; there is none that doeth good, no, not one."

The law was given, however, according to the text, "that the offence might abound." Such was the effect of the law. It did not hinder sin, nor provide a remedy for it; but its actual effect was that the offence abounded. How so?

It was so, first, because it revealed the offence. Men did not in every instance clearly discern what was sin; but when the law came, it pointed out to man that this evil, which he thought little of, was an abomination in the sight of God. Man's nature and character was like a dark dungeon which knew no ray of light. Yonder prisoner does not perceive the horrible filthiness and corruption of the place wherein he is immured, so long as he is in darkness. When a lamp is brought, or a window is opened and the light of day comes in, he finds out to his dismay the hideous condition of his den. He spies loathsome creatures upon the walls, and marks how others burrow out of sight because the light annoys them. He may, perhaps, have guessed that all was not as it should be, but he had not imagined the abundance of the evils. The light has entered, and the offence abounds. Law does not make us sinful, but it displays our sinfulness. In the presence of the perfect standard we see our shortcomings. The law of God is the looking-glass in which a man sees the spots upon his face. It does not wash you— you cannot wash in a looking-glass; but it prompts you to seek the cleansing water. The design of the law is the revealing of our many offences, that, thereby, we may be driven out of self-righteousness to the Lord Jesus, in whom we have redemption through his blood, the forgiveness of sin.

The law causes the offence to abound by making an offender to stand without excuse. Before he knew the law perfectly, his sin was not so wilful. While he did but faintly know the commands, he could, as it were, but faintly break them; but as soon as he distinctly knows what is right, and what is wrong, then every cloak is taken away from him. Sin becomes exceeding sinful when it is committed against light and knowledge. Is it not so with some of you? Are you not forced to admit that you commit many sins in one, now that you have been made to know the law, and yet wilfully offend against it, by omission or commission? He who knows his Master's will and does it not, will be beaten with many stripes, because he is guilty of abounding offences. The law enters to strip us of every cloak of justification, and so to drive us to seek the robe of Christ's righteousness.

Next, I think the law makes the offence to abound by causing sin to be, more evidently, a presumptuous rebellion against the great Lawgiver. To sin in the front of Sinai, with its wonderful display of divine majesty, is to sin indeed. To rebel against a law promulgated with sound of trumpet, and thunders, and pomp of God, is to sin with a high hand and a defiant heart. When thou hast heard the Ten Commands, when thou knowest the law of the kingdom, when thy

Maker's will is plainly set before thee, then to transgress is to transgress with an insolence of pride which will admit of no excuse.

Once more: the entrance of the law makes the offence to abound in this sense, that the rebellious will of man rises up in opposition to it. Because God commands, man refuses; and because he forbids, man desires. There are some men who might not have sinned in a particular direction if the commandment had not forbidden it. The light of the law, instead of being a warning to them to avoid evil, seems to point out to them the way in which they can most offend. Oh, how deep is the depravity of human nature! The law itself provokes it to rebel. Men long to enter, because trespassers are warned to keep away. Their minds are so at enmity against God, that they delight in that which is forbidden, not so much because they find any particular pleasure in the thing itself, but because it shows their independence and their freedom from the restraints of God. This vicious self-will is in all of us by nature; for the carnal mind is enmity against God; and therefore the law, though in itself holy and just and good, provokes us to do evil. We are like lime, and the law is as cold water, which is in itself of a cooling nature; yet, no sooner does the water of the law get at the lime of our nature, than a heat of sin is generated: thus, "the law entered, that the offence might abound."

Why, then, did God send the law? Is it not an evil thing that the offence should abound? In itself it may seem so to be; but God dealeth with us as physicians sometimes deal with their patients. A disease, which will be fatal if it spends itself within the patient, must be brought to the surface: the physician therefore prescribes a medicine which displays the evil. The evil was all within, but it did not abound as to its visible effects; it is needful that it should do so, that it may be cured. The law is the medicine which throws out the depravity of man, makes him see it in his actions, and even provokes him to display it. The evil is in man, like rabbits in yonder brushwood: the law sets alight to the cover, and the hidden creatures are seen. The law stirs the mud at the bottom of the pool, and proves how foul the waters are. The law compels the man to see that sin dwelleth in him, and that it is a powerful tyrant over his nature. All this is with a view to his cure. God be thanked when the law so works as to take off the sinner from all confidence in himself! To make the leper confess that he is incurable is going a great way towards compelling him to go to that Divine Saviour, who alone is able to heal him. This is the object and end of the law towards men whom God will save.

Consider for a moment. You may take it as an axiom, a thing self-evident, that there can be no grace where there is no guilt: there can be no mercy where there is no sin. There can be justice, there can be benevolence; but there cannot be mercy unless there is criminality. If you are not a sinner God cannot have mercy upon you. If you have never sinned God cannot display pardoning grace towards you, for there is nothing to pardon. It were a misuse of words to talk of forgiving a man who has done no wrong, or to speak of bestowing undeserved favour upon a person who deserves reward. It would be an insult to innocence to offer it mercy. You must, therefore, have sin or you cannot have grace—that is clear.

Next, consider that there will be no seeking after grace where there is no sense of sin. We may preach till we are hoarse, but you good people, who have never broken the law, and are not guilty of anything wrong, will never care for our message of mercy. You are such kind people that, out of compliment to religion, you say, "Yes, we are sinners. We are all sinners." But you know in your heart of hearts you do not mean it. You will never ask for grace; for you have no sense of shame or guilt. None of you will seek mercy, till first you have pleaded guilty to the indictment which the law of God presents against you. Oh, that you felt your sins! Oh, that you knew your need of forgiveness! for then you would see yourselves to be in such a condition that only the free, rich, sovereign grace of God can save you.

Furthermore, I am sure that there will be no reception and acceptance of grace by any man, till there is a full confession of sin and a burdensome sense of its weight. Why should you receive grace when you do not want it? What is the use of it to you? Why should you bow your knee to God, and receive, as the free gift of his charity, that which you feel you deserve? Have you not already earned eternal life? Are you not as good as other people? Have you not some considerable claim upon God? Do I startle you with these plain questions? Have I not heard you say much the same? The other day when we preached the electing love of God, you grumbled and muttered that God was unjust to choose one rather than another. What did this mean? Did it not mean that you felt you had some claim upon God? O sir, if this is your spirit, I must deal plainly with you! If you have any claim upon your Maker, plead it, and be you sure that he will not deny you your just rights. But I would advise you to change your method of dealing with your Judge: you will never prevail in this fashion. In truth, you have no claim upon him; but must appeal to his pure mercy. You are not in a position for him to display free grace to you till your mouth is shut, and you sit down in dust and ashes, silently owning that you deserve nothing at his hands but infinite displeasure. Confess that whatever he gives you that is good and gracious must be given freely to one who deserves nothing. Hell gapes at your feet: cease from pride, and humbly sue out a pardon.

You see, then, the use of the law: it is to bring you where grace can be fitly shown you. It shuts you up that you may cry to Jesus to set you free. It is a storm which wrecks your hopes of self-salvation, but washes you upon the Rock of Ages. The condemning sentence of the law is meant to prepare you for the absolution of the gospel. If you condemn yourself and plead guilty before God, the royal pardon can then be extended towards you. The self-condemned shall be forgiven through the precious blood of Jesus, and the sovereign grace of God. Oh, my hearer, you must sit down there in the dust, or else God will not look at you! You must yield yourself to him, owning his justice, honouring his law: this is the first condition of his mercy, and to this his grace brings all who feel its power. The Lord will have you bow before him in self-abhorrence, and confess his right to punish you. Remember, "He will have mercy on whom he will have mercy, and he will have compassion on whom he will have compassion," and he will have you know this, and agree to it. His grace must reign triumphantly, and you must kiss its silver sceptre.

Thus has the first sentence served us for a preface: God bless it to us!

I. The doctrine of the text itself is this, that "where sin abounded, grace did much more abound"; and I shall try to bring out that truth, first, by saying that THIS IS SEEN IN THE WHOLE WORK OF GRACE, from beginning to end.

I would direct your attention to the context. The safest way to preach upon a text, is to follow out the idea which the inspired writer was endeavouring to convey. Paul has, in this place, been speaking of the abounding result for evil of one sin in the case of Adam, the federal head of the race. That one sin of Adam's abounded terribly. Look at the multitudinous generations of our race which have gone down to death. Who slew all these? Sin is the wolf which has devoured the flocks of men. Sin has poisoned the streams of manhood at their fountain-head, and everywhere they run with poisoned waters. Concerning this, Paul says, "Where sin abounded, grace did much more abound."

First, then, *sin abounded in its effect upon the whole human race:* one sin overthrew all humanity; one fatal fault, the breach of a plain, and easy law, made sinners of us all. "By one man's disobedience many were made sinners." Simple as was the command which Adam broke, it involved obedience or disobedience to the sovereignty of God. All the trees of the garden were generously given to happy Adam in Paradise: "Of every tree of the garden thou mayest freely eat." There was but one tree reserved for God by the prohibition, "Thou shalt not eat of it: for in the day that thou eatest thereof thou shalt surely die." Adam had no need to touch that fruit, there were all the other trees for him. Nothing was denied him which was really for his good; he was only forbidden that which would ruin him. We all look back to that Paradisaical state and wish we could have been put in some such a position as he: yet he dared to trespass on God's reserves, and thus to set himself up above his Maker. He judged it wise to do what God forbade: he ran the risk of death in the foolish hope of rising into a still higher state.

See the consequences of that sin on all sides, the world is full of them. Yet, saith Paul, "Where sin abounded, grace did much more abound," and he gives us this as a proof of it: "And not as it was by one that sinned, so is the gift: for the judgment was by one to condemnation, but the free gift is of many offences unto justification" (Rom. 5:16). The Lord Jesus came into the world, not alone to put away Adam's sin, but all the sins which have followed upon it. The second Adam has repaired the desperate ruin of the first, and much more. By his death upon the cross, our Divine Substitute has put away those myriads of sins, which have been committed by men since the first offence in Eden. Think of this! Take the whole aggregate of believers, and let each one disburden his conscience of its load of sin. What a mountain! Pile it up! Pile it up! It rises huge as high Olympus! Age after age believers come and lay their enormous loads in this place. "The Lord hath made to meet on him the iniquities of us all." What Alps! What Himalayas of sin! If there were only mine and yours, my brother, what mountains of division would our sins make! But the great Christ, the free gift of God to us, when he bare our sins in his own body on the tree, took all those countless sins away. "Behold the Lamb of God, which taketh away the sin of the world"! Here is infinite grace to pardon immeasurable sin! Truly the "one man's offence" abounded horribly; but the "one man's obedience," the obedience of the Son of God, hath superabounded. As the arch of heaven far exceedeth in its span the whole round globe of the earth, so doth grace much more abound over human sin.

Follow me further, when I notice, secondly, that *sin abounded in its ruinous effects*. It utterly destroyed humanity. In the third chapter of the Romans you see how, in every part of his nature, man is depraved by sin. Think of the havoc which the tyrant, sin, has made of our natural estate and heritage. Eden is withered—its very site is forgotten. Our restfulness among the trees of the field, freely yielding their fruit, is gone, and God hath said, "In the sweat of thy face shalt thou eat bread." The field we till has lost its spontaneous yield of corn: "Thorns also and thistles shall it bring forth to thee." Our life has lost its glory and immortality; for "Dust thou art, and unto dust shalt thou return." Every woman in her pangs of travail, every man in his weariness of labour, and all of us together in the griefs of death, see what sin has done for us as to our mortal bodies. Alas, it has gone deeper: it has ruined our souls. Sin has unmanned man. The crown and glory of his manhood it has thrown to the ground. All our faculties are out of gear; all our tendencies are perverted. Beloved, let us rejoice that the Lord Jesus Christ has come to redeem us from the curse of sin, and he will undo the evil of evil. Even this poor world he will deliver from the bondage of corruption; and he will create new heavens and a new earth, wherein dwelleth righteousness. The groans and painful travail of the whole creation shall result in a full deliverance, through the grace of our Lord Jesus Christ, and somewhat more. As for ourselves, we are lifted up to a position far higher than that which we should have occupied had the race continued in its innocence. The Lord Jesus Christ found us in a horrible pit and in the miry clay, and he not only lifted us up out of it, but he set our feet upon a rock, and established our goings. Raised from hell, we are lifted not to the bowers of Eden, but to the throne of God. Redeemed human nature has greater capacities than unfallen human nature. To Adam the Lord did not say, "Thou art a son of God, joint heir with the Only-Begotten"; but he has said that to each believer redeemed by the precious blood of Jesus. Beloved, such a thing as fellowship with Christ in his sufferings could not have been known to Adam in Paradise. He could not have known what it is to be dead, and to have his life hid with Christ in God. Blessed be his name, our Lord Jesus Christ can say, "I restored that which I took not away"! He restored more than ever was taken away from us; for he hath made us to be partakers of the divine nature, and in his own person he hath placed us at God's right hand in the heavenly places. Inasmuch as the dominion of the Lord Jesus is more glorious than that of unfallen Adam, manhood is now more great and glorious than before the Fall. Grace has so much more abounded, that in Jesus we have gained more than in Adam we lost. Our Paradise Regained is far more glorious than our Paradise Lost.

Again, *sin abounded to the dishonour of God*. I was trying the other day to put myself into the position of Satan at the gates of Eden, that I might understand his diabolical policy. He had become the archenemy of God, and when he saw this newly-made world, and perceived two perfectly pure and happy creatures placed in it, he looked on with envy, and plotted mischief. He heard the Creator say, "In the day that thou eatest thereof thou shalt surely die," and he hoped here to find an opportunity for an assault upon God. If he could induce those new-made creatures to eat of the forbidden fruit, he would place their Maker upon the horns of a dilemma: either he must destroy the creatures which he had made, or else he must be untrue. The Lord had said, "Ye shall surely die," and he must thus undo his own work, and destroy a creature which he had made in his own image, after his own likeness. Satan, probably, perceived that man was an extraordinary being, with a wonderful mystery of glory hanging about his destiny; and, if he could make him sin, he would cause God to destroy him, and so far defeat the eternal purpose. On the other hand, if the Lord did not execute the sentence, then he would not be truthful, and throughout all his great universe it would be reported that the Lord's word had been broken. Either he had changed his mind, or he had spoken in jest, or he had been proven to have threatened too severe a penalty. In either case, the evil spirit hoped to triumph. It was a deep, far-reaching scheme to dim the splendour of the King of kings.

Beloved, did it not seem as if sin had abounded beyond measure, when first the woman and then the man had been deceived, and had done despite to God? Behold how grace, through our Lord Jesus Christ, did much more abound! God is more honoured in the redemption of man than if there had never been a Fall. The Lord has displayed the majesty of his justice, and the glory of his grace, in the great sacrifice of his dear Son, in such a manner that angels, and principalities, and powers will wonder throughout all ages. More of God is to be seen in the great work of redeeming love than could have been reflected in the creation of myriads of worlds, had each one of them been replete with marvels of divine skill, and goodness, and power. In Jesus crucified Jehovah is glorified as never before. Where sin abounded to the apparent dishonour of God, grace doth much more abound to the infinite glory of his ever-blessed name.

Again, *sin abounded by degrading human character.* What a wretched being man is, as a sinner against God! Unchecked by law, and allowed to do as he pleases, what will not man become? See how Paul describes men in these progressive times—in these enlightened centuries: "This know also, that in the last days perilous times shall come. For men shall be lovers of their own selves, covetous, boasters, proud, blasphemers, disobedient to parents, unthankful, unholy, without natural affection, trucebreakers, false accusers, incontinent, fierce, despisers of those that are good, traitors, heady, highminded, lovers of pleasures more than lovers of God; having a form of godliness, but denying the power thereof." Human nature was not at all slandered by Whitefield when he said that, "left to himself, man is half beast and half devil." I do not mean merely men in savage countries, I am thinking of men in London. Only the other day a certain newspaper gave us plenty of proof of the sin of this city: I will say no more—could brutes or demons be worse? Read human history, Assyrian, Roman, Greek, Saracenic, Spanish, English; and if you are a lover of holiness, you will be sick of man. Has any other creature, except the fallen angels, ever become so cruel, so mean, so false? Behold what villains, what tyrants, what monsters sin has made!

But now look on the other side, and see what the grace of God has done. Under the moulding hand of the Holy Spirit a gracious man becomes the noblest work of God. Man, born again and rescued from the Fall, is now capable of virtues, to which he never could have reached before he sinned. An unfallen being could not hate sin with the intensity of abhorrence which is found in the renewed heart. We now know by personal experience the horror of sin, and there is now within us an instinctive shuddering at it. An unfallen being could not exhibit patience, for it could not suffer, and patience has its perfect work to do. When I have read the stories of the martyrs in the first ages of the Christian church, and during the Marian persecution in England, I have adored the Lord, who could enable poor feeble men and women thus to prove their love to their God and Saviour. What great things they suffered out of love to God; and how grandly did they thus honour him! O God, what a noble being thy grace has made man to be! I have felt great reverence for sanctified humanity, when I have seen how men could sing God's praises in the fires. What noble deeds men have been capable of, when the love of God has been shed abroad in their hearts! I do not think angels, or archangels, have ever been able to exhibit so admirable an all-round character as the grace of God hath wrought in once fallen men whom he has, by his grace, inspired with the divine life. In human character, "where sin abounded, grace did much more abound." I believe God looks out of heaven to-day, and sees in many of his poor, hidden people such beauties of virtue, such charms of holiness, that he himself is delighted with them. "The Lord taketh pleasure in them that fear him." These are such true jewels that the Lord has a high estimate of them, and sets them apart for himself:

"They shall be mine, saith the Lord of hosts, in that day when I make up my jewels."

Again, dear friends, *sin abounded to the causing of great sorrow*. It brought with it a long train of woes. The children of sin are many, and each one causeth lamentation. We cannot attempt to fathom the dark abysses of sorrow which have opened in this world since the advent of sin. Is it not a place of tears—yea, a field of blood? Yet by a wonderful alchemy, through the existence of sin, grace has produced a new joy, yea, more than one new joy. The calm, deep joy of repentance must have been unknown to perfect innocence. This right orient pearl is not found in the rivers of Eden. Yea, and that joy which is in heaven in the presence of the angels of God over sinners that repent is a new thing, whose birth is since the Fall. God himself knows a joy which he could not have known had there been no sin. Behold, with tearful wonder, the great Father as he receives his returning prodigal, and cries to all about him, "Let us eat, and be merry: for this my son was dead, and is alive again; he was lost, and is found." O brethren, how could almighty love have been victorious in grace had there been no sin to battle with? Heaven is the more heaven for us, since there we shall sing of robes washed white in the blood of the Lamb. God hath greater joy in man, and man hath greater joy in God, because grace abounded over sin. We are getting into deep waters now! How true our text is!

Once more, *sin abounded to hinder the reign of Christ*. I believe that Satan's design in leading men into sin at the first, was to prevent the supremacy of the Lord Jesus Christ as man and God in one person. I do not lay it down as a doctrine, specifically taught in Scripture, but still it seems to me a probable truth, that Satan foresaw that the gap which was made in heaven by the fall of the angels was to be filled up by human beings, whom God would place near his throne. Satan thought that he saw before him the beings who would take the places of the fallen spirits, and he envied them. He knew that they were made in the image of the Only-Begotten, the Christ of God, and he hated him because he saw united in his person God whom he abhorred, and man whom he envied. Satan shot at the second Adam through the breast of the first Adam. He meant to overthrow the Coming One; but, fool that he was, the Lord Jesus Christ, by the grace of God, is now exalted higher than ever we could conceive him to have been, had there been no sin to bear, no redemption to work out. Jesus, wounded and slain, has about him higher splendour than before. O King of kings and Lord of lords, Man of Sorrows, we sing hallelujahs unto thee! All our hearts beat true to thee! We love thee beyond all else! Thou art he whom we will praise for ever and ever! Jesus sits on no precarious throne in the empire of love. We would each one maintain his right with the last pulse of our hearts. King of kings and Lord of lords! Hallelujah! Where sin abounded, grace hath much more abounded to the glory of the Only-Begotten Son of God.

II. I find time always flies fastest when our subject is most precious. I have a second head, which deserves a lengthened consideration; but we must be content with mere hints. This great fact, that where sin abounded, grace did much more abound, crops up everywhere. THIS IS TO BE SEEN IN SPECIAL CASES.

The first special case is *the introduction of the law*. When the law of Ten Commands was given, through man's sin, it ministered to the abounding of the offence; but it also ministered to the aboundings of grace. It is true there were ten commands; but there was more than tenfold grace. With the law there came forward a High Priest. The world had never seen a High Priest before, arrayed in jewelled breastplate, and garments of glory and beauty. There was the law; but at the same time there was the holy place of the Tabernacle of the Most High with its altar, its laver, its candlestick, and its table of shew-bread. There was, also, the secret shrine where the majesty of God dwelt. God had, by those symbols and types, come to dwell among men. It is true, sin abounded through the law; but, then, sacrifices for sin also abounded. Heretofore, there had been no morning and evening lambs; there had been no day of atonement; no sprinkling of blood; no benediction from the Lord's High Priest For every sin that the law revealed, a sacrifice was provided. Sins of ignorance, sins of their holy things, sins of all sorts were met by special sacrifices; so that the sins uncovered to the conscience, were also covered by the sacrifice.

The story of Israel is another case in point. How often the nation rebelled; but how often did mercy rejoice over judgment! Truly the history of the chosen people shows how sin abounded, and grace did much more abound.

Run your eye down history and pause at *the crucifixion of our Lord Jesus*. This is the highest peak of the mountains of sin. They crucified the Lord of glory. Here sin abounded. But do I need to tell you that grace did here much more abound? You can look at the death of Christ till Pilate vanishes, and Caiaphas fades away, and all the clamour of the priests and Jews is hushed, and you see nothing and hear nothing but free grace and dying love.

There followed upon the crucifixion of our Lord, *the casting away of the Jewish people for a while*. Sin abounded when the Lord thus came to his own and his own received him not. Yes; but the casting away of them was the saving of the nations. "We turn to the Gentiles," said the apostle; and that was a blessed turning for you and for me. Was it not? They that were bidden to the feast were not worthy, and the master of the house, being angry, invited other guests. Mark, "being angry"! What did he do when he was angry? Why, he did the most gracious thing of all; he said, "Go ye out into the highways and hedges, and as many as ye shall find bid to the supper." Sin abounded, for Israel would not enter the feast of love; but grace did much more abound, for the heathen entered the kingdom.

The heathen world at that time was sunk in the blackest darkness, and sin abounded. You have only to study ancient history and you will fetch a heavy sigh to think that men could be so vile. A poor and unlettered people were chosen of God to receive the gospel of Jesus, and they went about telling of an atoning Saviour, in their own simple way, until the Roman empire was entirely changed. Light and peace and truth came into the world, and drove away slavery and tyranny and bestial lust. Where sin abounded, grace did much more abound. What wonderful characters were produced in the terrible reign of Diocletian! What consecration to God was seen in the confessors! What fearlessness in common Christians! What invincible loyalty to Christ in the martyrs! Out of barbarians the Lord made saints, and the degraded rose to holiness sublime.

If I were to ask you, now, to give the best illustrations of grace abounding in individuals, I think your impulse would be to choose *men in whom sin once abounded.* What characters do we preach of most, when we would magnify the grace of God? We talk of David, and Manasseh, and swearing Peter, and the dying thief, and Saul of Tarsus, and the woman that was a sinner. If we want to show where grace abounded, we naturally turn our eyes to the place where sin abounded. Is it not so? Therefore, I need not give you any more cases—it is proven that where sin abounded, grace did much more abound.

III. Lastly; and this is what I want to hold you to, dear friends, at this time: THIS HOLDS TRUE TO EACH ONE OF US.

Let me take the case of the *open sinner*. What have you been? Have you grossly sinned? Have you defiled your body with unhallowed passions? Have you been dishonest to your fellow-men? Does some scarlet sin stain your conscience, even as you sit in the pew? Have you grown hardened in sin by long perseverance in it? Are you conscious that you have frequently, wilfully, and resolutely sinned? Are you getting old, and have you been soaking these seventy years in the crimson dye of sin till you are saturated through and through with its colour? Have you even been an implacable opponent of the gospel? Have you persecuted the saints of God? Have you tried by argument to batter down the gospel, or by ridicule to put it to reproach? Then hear this text: "Where sin abounded, grace did much more abound"; and as it was in the beginning, it is now and ever shall be, till this world shall end. The grace of God, if thou believest in the Lord Jesus Christ, will triumph over the greatness of thy wickedness. "All manner of sin and blasphemy shall be forgiven unto men." Throw down your weapons of rebellion; surrender at discretion; kiss the pierced hand of Jesus which is now held out to you, and this very moment you shall be forgiven, and you shall go your way a pardoned man, to begin a new life, and to bear witness that "where sin abounded, grace did much more abound."

Perhaps this does not touch you, my friend. Listen to my next word which is addressed to *the instructed sinner*. You are a person whose religious education has made you aware of the guilt of sin; you have read your Bible, and you have heard truthful preaching; and although you have never been a gross open sinner, yet you know that your life teems with sins of omission and commission. You know that you have sinned against light and knowledge. You have done despite to a tender conscience very often; and therefore you rightly judge that you are even a greater sinner than the more openly profane. Be it so; I take you at that. Do not run back from it. Let it be so; for "where sin abounded, grace did much more abound." Oh, that you may be as much instructed in the remedy, as you are instructed in the disease! Oh, that you may have as clear a view of the righteousness of Christ, as you have of your own unrighteousness! Christ's work is a divine work, broad enough to cover all your iniquity, and to conquer all your sin. Believe this! Give glory to God by believing it; and according to your faith, so be it unto you.

I address another, who does not answer either of these two descriptions exactly; but he has lately begun to seek mercy, and the more he prays the more he is *tempted*. Horrible suggestions rush into his mind; damnable thoughts beset and bewilder him. Ah, my friend, I know what this means: the nearer you are to mercy, the nearer you seem to get to hell-gate! When you most solemnly mean to do good you feel another law in your members bringing you into captivity. You grow worse where you hoped you would have grown better. Very well, then; grip my text firmly as for your life: "Where sin abounded, grace did much more abound." If a whole legion of devils should be let loose upon you, Christ will glorify himself by mastering them all. If now you cannot repent, nor pray, nor do anything, remember that text, "When we were yet without strength, in due time Christ died for the ungodly." Look over the heads of all these doubts, and devils, and inabilities, and see Jesus lifted on the cross, like the brazen serpent upon the pole; and look thou to him, and the fiery serpents shall flee away from thee, and thou shalt live. Believe this text to be true, for true it is: "Where sin abounded, grace did much more abound."

"Ah!" saith another, "my case is still worse, sir; I am of a *despondent* turn of mind; I always look upon the black side of everything, and now if I read a promise I am sure it is not for me. If I see a threatening in God's Word, I am sure it is for me. I have no hope. I do not seem as if I should ever have any. I am in a dungeon into which no light can enter: it is dark, dark, dark, and worse darkness is coming. While you are trying to comfort me, I put the comfort away." I know you. You are like the poor creature in the Psalm, of whom we read—"His soul abhorreth all manner of meat." Even the gospel itself he cannot relish. Yes; I know you; you are writing bitter things against yourself: this morning you have been newly dipping your pen in gall; but your writing is that of a poor bewildered creature; it is not to be taken notice of. I see you writing, in text hand, great black words of condemnation; but there is nothing in them all. Verily, verily I say unto thee, thine handwriting shall be blotted out, and the curse, causeless, shall not come. Thus saith the Lord, "Your covenant with death shall be disannulled, and your agreement with hell shall not stand, for the Lord Jesus Christ has redeemed you, and where sin abounded, grace shall much more abound." Broken in pieces, all asunder, ground between the millstones, reduced to nothing, yet believe this revelation of God, that where sin abounded, grace did much more abound." Notice that *"much more"*— "much more abound." If thou canst grip it, and know it to be of a certainty the great principle upon which God acts, that grace shall outstrip sin, then there is hope of thee; nay, more than hope, there is salvation for thee on the spot. If thou believest in Jesus, whom God has set forth to be a propitiation for sin, thou art forgiven.

Oh, my hearers, do not despise this grace! Come, and partake of it. Does any one say, as Paul foresaw that some would say, "Let us sin, that grace may abound"? Ah, then, such an infamous inference is the mark of the reprobate, and your damnation is just He that turns God's mercy into a reason for sin, has within him something worse than a heart of stone: surely his conscience is seared with a hot iron. Beloved, I hope better things of you, for I trust that on the contrary, the sound of the silver bells of infinite love, free pardon, abounding grace, will make you hasten to the hospital of mercy, that you may receive healing for your sinfulness, strength for you feebleness, and joy for your sorrow. Lord, grant that in this house, in every case wherein sin has abounded, grace may yet more abound, for Jesus' sake! Amen.

PORTION OF SCRIPTURE READ BEFORE SERMON—Romans 5.

HYMNS FROM "OUR OWN HYMN-BOOK"—174, 233, 231.[14]

---

[14] Spurgeon, C. H. (1888). Grace Abounding over Abounding Sin. In *The Metropolitan Tabernacle Pulpit Sermons* (Vol. 34, pp. 133–144). London: Passmore & Alabaster.

GROWTH IN GRACE

A Sermon

INTENDED FOR READING ON LORD'S-DAY, NOVEMBER 11TH, 1900, DELIVERED BY

C. H. SPURGEON,

AT NEW PARK STREET CHAPEL, SOUTHWARK,

On a Lord's-day Evening, in the autumn of 1858.

"But grow in grace, and in the knowledge of our Lord and Saviour Jesus Christ."—2 Peter 3:18.

IT is worth while to remark that this passage immediately follows the seventeenth verse, where the apostle says, "Beloved, seeing ye know these things before, beware lest ye also, being led away with the error of the wicked, fall from your own stedfastness. But grow in grace, and in the knowledge of our Lord and Saviour Jesus Christ." He puts the one after the other, as if the one must be the means of the other. There had been some, in the apostle's day, who had wrested, to their own destruction, certain expressions in the Epistles of Paul which Peter said were "hard to be understood;" and, therefore, he warned Christian men and women to take heed lest they, "being led away with the error of the wicked," should "fall from" their "own stedfastness." In order that they might know how to stand, and to be preserved from falling, he gave them this direction: "grow in grace;" for the way to stand is to grow; the way to be steadfast is to go forward. There is no standing except by progression. If you see even such a simple thing as a child's toy rolling along your floor at home, you will observe that it will always stand upright as long as it keeps on rolling; but when it stops, down it goes. So is it with the Christian; as long as he is in motion, so long he stands; but if it were possible for the motion to cease, then the Christian would fall from his steadfastness. Glory be to God, he will be kept from falling, and he shall be presented faultless before the throne of God! The way to stand, then, is to go forward; the way to be steadfast is to progress; the way to be alive, according to the apostle, is to "grow in grace, and in the knowledge of our Lord and Saviour Jesus Christ."

We will offer, first of all, two or three remarks upon *growth "in grace" in general;* and, secondly, a few remarks upon *growth in grace being intimately connected with growth "in the knowledge of our Lord and Saviour Jesus Christ."*

I. First, then, we shall offer some remarks upon GROWTH "IN GRACE" IN GENERAL. What shall we say about it?

The first remark we make is, that *there is a sense in which there is no such thing at all as growth in grace.* If you understand the word grace as signifying free favour, and the love of God towards his people, there is not, and there cannot be, any growth in that at all.

> "The moment a sinner believes,
> And trusts in his crucified God,"—

he is, by the grace of God, there and then justified, and complete in Christ Jesus. And if he lives till his hair is grey, he will never be more justified, and never be more beloved, than he is the very first moment in which he believes in Christ. As soon as ever I have a vital connection with the Lamb of God, I am "in grace." Let me live on, let my grace grow, let my faith increase, let my zeal become warmer, let my love be more ardent, yet I shall not be more "in grace" than I was before. God will not love me more, he will not have a deeper and a purer affection in his heart to me then than he has the very first moment when I turn to him; nor will his grace the less justify me, or less accept me, the first moment when I come to him with all my sins about me, than it shall do when I stand before the throne. We never grow in the grace of election. We are always, as Peter says in his first Epistle, "elect according to the foreknowledge of God the Father;" and in that sense of being "in grace" there is neither growth nor any retrograde movement. So also is it in the matter of justification.

> "In union with the Lamb,
> From condemnation free,

> The saints for ever were,
> And shall for ever be."

And they are at any one time as much justified as they are at any other time. Give me to be justified to-day, then I was justified yesterday, and I shall be justified to-morrow. As soon as I put my trust in the Saviour, I became complete in grace; so far as that was concerned, I was made perfect in Christ Jesus. I cannot be more than perfect; and, therefore, I cannot in that respect grow in grace; I cannot receive more justifying mercy; I cannot receive more pardoning grace; for I have had it all at once, and have so become perfect in Christ.

But you will remark that our text does not say anything about grace growing; it does not say that grace grows. It tells us to "grow in grace." There is a vast difference between grace growing and our growing in grace. God's grace never increases; it is always infinite, so it cannot be more; it is always everlasting; it is always bottomless; it is always shoreless. It cannot be more; and, in the nature of God, it could not be less. The text tells us to "grow in grace." We are in the sea of God's grace; we cannot be in a deeper sea, but let us grow now we are in it. We cannot be more in it than we are, or than we always have been. We are in God's grace; we are in the covenant; we are in the scheme of redemption; we are in union with Jesus; we cannot be more or less so, for we are eternally secure through the blood of our Saviour. But while it cannot grow more, we can grow more in it, and so we shall "grow in grace."

I must make another remark. *It is certain that, while the grace of God toward us does not grow, yet there is such a thing as the development of grace.* There are some persons who strongly object to the doctrine of progressive sanctification, and to our mentioning anything like growth in grace. My brethren are welcome to object if they like, but I am sure, if they read the Scriptures (they will surely not object to Scriptural terms), they will find growth in grace very frequently mentioned; if that does not mean progressive sanctification, then I do not understand the term "growth in grace" at all. It is quite certain that there are degrees in the development of grace. You will surely not say that the young man, who has been converted only for the last few months, knows as much of grace, understands as much about it, and has as much faith, and as much love, as the man who has for the last twenty or thirty years been earnestly engaged in his Master's service. You will not tell me that one man, who is scarcely ever seen coming up to the house of God, and who is daily in a state of religious starvation, stands on a par in grace with a man who is labouring for his Master, whose love is evident to all, and whose faith is testified before the whole congregation. You will not tell me there is a dead level in Christianity, which all alike reach. If you do say so, I shall tell you that you have no eyes, or that you do not look about you. For it is certain that there are some who are further advanced than others are, some with greater faith than others have. There are "great faiths" as well as "little faiths", great loves as well as little loves; there are men of ardent spirits who have grace more fully developed in them than it is in others. It is true, they are not more loved of God than others are, and not more justified, nor more accepted, for in that respect we all stand on a level, and there is no difference; but as to the development of grace in our souls, and the display of grace in our lives, everyone must admit that there is a difference between different saints. I cannot understand the difference existing between various ministers of Christ, if it is not because of the difference in the degrees of grace which they possess. Some have just started in the Christian ministry, and have preached a little about redemption, but they have not gone far enough to preach about election; or, at least, not about the vital union of every blood-bought child of God with the person of Emmanuel; or if they should now and then preach upon that blessed truth, they cannot talk about the eternal security of the saints, and declare how, against wind and tide, they shall all sail safely into the heavenly harbour. They have not grown enough in grace to preach on such themes as these; so will not everyone admit that there are degrees of development in grace, while it is also true that there are none of us more justified, more elect, more chosen of God and loved of him than any other believers are?

Now for a third remark, which is, *that growth in grace is not to be measured by weeks, and months, and years.* There are persons who think that the age of a man will tell how much he knows about divine things. "Oh!" say some, "So-and-so is such a young man, what should he know about divine grace? There is a hoary-headed father there; he must know a great deal more." If you talk like that, you will soon find out your mistake. God often delights to show how he scorns and scoffs at all the distinctions of man. He makes the young men prudent, and he gives even to children knowledge and discretion. Out of the mouth of babes and sucklings he ordains strength because of his enemies. It is true, we do believe, and we should believe, that there is more knowledge beneath the grey hairs than under the youth's curly locks; generally speaking, it is so. Yet God, in order to display his sovereignty, has so arranged that he sometimes puts his treasures into an earthen vessel that has not been fashioned more than a few years.

Do not suppose that persons grow in grace according to their years. Some grow faster in grace in five minutes than others do in fifty years. I believe that some saints progress further in grace in one single month than others do in twelve months or twelve years. I am sure I may speak concerning myself. I have sometimes grown more in grace, in one hour, than I have at other seasons in a week, a month, or a year, when God, in his infinite wisdom, has been pleased to give me a vision of the Saviour, or to break up the fountains of wickedness that lay hidden in my soul. I have learnt more in one hour, when the Holy Spirit's hand has been upon me, than I have in weeks and months simply with my own study. God's people grow like trees grow. Sometimes they take a start, and grow upward; at another time, they are growing downward. Sometimes, apparently, the sap sleeps within the branch;—a winter time comes over it, and it is asleep.

Do not imagine, my dear friends, that because you are getting old, you are growing in grace. People are continually warning young men of their danger. No doubt we are in danger; but let me remind you that there is not an instance in Sacred Scripture of a young man disgracing his profession; but there are instances in Scripture of men of middle age and of grey hairs doing so. It is thus: we, who are young, are in the greatest danger; and, therefore, God upholds us to show the power of his grace; but some of you older folk conceive that you are not in peril; and, therefore, God suffers you to fall, that he may stain the pride of your self-glorying, and let you see that it is not anything in flesh, neither age, nor standing, nor rank, nor condition, which ensures our safety; but that he holdeth up the humble, and casteth down the proud. David did not fall into his great sin until he had come certainly to maturity, and into the very prime of life, and then he sinned with Bathsheba. Lot did not transgress so grossly before he became an old man. If you turn to the pages of Scripture, you will notice that, wherever there has been a lamentable fall,—as in the case of Peter,—it has been a man who has grown up, and become strong in years. God thus shows us that it is not mere years that can teach us grace,—in fact, that years, and age, and learning, and talent, have nothing to do with grace; and he could, if he pleased, take a child six years old, and pour wisdom and knowledge into the lips of that child that could puzzle the seers of this world. He often takes the most unlikely instruments, and uses them for the accomplishment of his purposes; and because men have said that experimental preachers must have grey heads, he says, "Nay; it shall be a youth who shall lead the multitude; it shall be a child, out of whose mouth I will pour words of wisdom, for I will overthrow all human glory, and show mankind that it is not the preacher who is to be praised, but God." Salvation is not of him that willeth, nor of him that runneth; but it is God that showeth mercy. It is not the man who preaches, who accomplishes the work; but God working through the man. He could dispense with the man altogether if he pleased; at any rate, he will have the man he pleases, and at what age he pleases, and qualify him as he pleases.

Once more, *growth in grace is not to be estimated by our feelings.* There are some of you, beloved, who think you are not growing in grace because you do not feel so lively as you used to do. "Ah!" say you, "when I was young, everything was bright then. What peaceful hours I then enjoyed! I would go over hedge and ditch to hear the gospel preached; I had such an intense desire to hear about God and Jesus Christ, such love to the gospel that, when I once got to hear a minister preach, it mattered not whoever he might be, it all seemed sweet. But now I am so depressed that I cannot enjoy the truth as I used to do." Do not think, because your wild heat is gone, that you have not grown. When we light a fire, we always put the straw and kindling at the bottom; and when we first light it, there is a deal of flame, and a great deal of smoke. But, afterwards, when the flame gets hold of the coals, there is not so much blaze, but there is really more heat. You may have lost some of your flame and smoke, but then you have more solid fire; we would rather warm our hands by the coals than by the straw, for that must soon go. So is it with grace; it begins with a flame which catches the lighter substances, and lays hold on the imagination and the passions; but, in after life, it appeals to the judgment, and makes the man one solid lump of burning fire. He is not a little flame, rising towards heaven, that the wind might blow out with a puff; but he becomes so strong a fire that the wind shall but increase the flame, and shall make the heat the greater. So it may be with you. Perhaps you have become more solid though you are less fiery.

Do not suppose, when you are depressed, that, therefore, you are not growing. Many of God's plants grow best in the dark, and he often puts them in the dark to make them grow. When you are growing upwards, recollect that there is such a thing as growing downward. You may have had, yesterday, a divine manifestation that took you up to the top of the Delectable Mountains. You must not think you are big because you are up on high, for pigmies perched on Alps are pigmies still; and if you were ever so little, it would not make you any bigger if you were taken to the top of St. Paul's. If, on the other hand, you are deep down in a mine, do not imagine that you are any the smaller for that reason. I can tell you that you will often grow faster in the dungeon than on the top of a mountain; but it is not a pleasant place to be in. When our depravity is revealed to us, when our desolation of spirit, and our utter hopelessness and powerlessness are uncovered and made manifest by God's Holy Spirit, we grow, I believe, even faster than we do when, on the wings of seraphs, we are privileged to mount on high. So, do not measure your growth in grace by your feelings. Some of you make a kind of barometer of your feelings. Do not do so. If we are in Christ, we are in Christ by faith, and not by feelings; and recollect that, whether your feelings are good or bad, you are no more or less a child of God. Your faith, sinner, unites you with the Lamb,— not your feelings. Trust him in darkness, trust him in distress, lean on him when you cannot see him; and when there seems nothing to walk on, still tread, for the ground is firm beneath the foot of faith.

Just by way of warning, let me urge you not to think that you are growing in grace *because you happen to be doing a little more for the church externally*. "Oh!" we often say, "now I am progressing, am I not? I am busy in the Sunday-school, labouring hard there; I am preaching; I am doing this, or that, or the other; now I am growing in grace." Ah! it is a proper thing to be diligent in good works, and to be abounding in acts of righteousness; but if you begin to say, "Now I am growing," because of this or because of that, you have made a great mistake. It often happens that, when we are very full of public labours, we are very short in private devotions. I must myself confess that it has been so with me;—and that is a very lamentable thing,—for then I was not really growing. A man may have his hands ever so full before the world, and think he is doing much; but he may not be really growing in grace after all. Do not think that this is an excuse for anybody who is not doing much, you Issachar-like people, like "a strong ass between two burdens," too lazy to lift either. I am not giving you a word of comfort. You are not growing, for you are doing nothing; and those who are doing something must not boast of their growth. It hath more to do with private devotion than with public exercise; it hath more to do with meditation than with explanation; it hath more to do with contemplation and adoration than with public service. We must look more to the state of the internal matters, keeping up private prayer, and attending to the reading of the Scriptures. If we do not, however much we may seem to progress outwardly, we are not any richer; we are only beating out the little gold we had into a thinner plate, and spreading it over a wider surface. The more we do for Christ, the more he will do for us; but let us take heed that, whilst we water other people's vineyards, our own is not neglected, and that the stones of the hedges thereof are not cast down. May God grant you, brethren, to grow in grace!

II. Now we come to the second thought, THAT GROWTH IN GRACE IS INTIMATELY CONNECTED WITH GROWTH "IN THE KNOWLEDGE OF OUR LORD AND SAVIOUR JESUS CHRIST." In fact, there cannot be any grace at all except as we know Christ, and there can be no growth in grace except as we grow in our knowledge of Christ. We may always test whether we are growing by this question,—Do I know more of Christ to-day than I did yesterday? Do I live nearer to Christ to-day than I did a little while ago? For increase in the knowledge of Christ is the evidence as well as the cause of true growth in grace. In order to prove this, I will mention one or two Christian virtues, and you will see that they must increase as we know more of Christ.

With regard to love, some of us say, "How little we love Christ!" Many of you sing,—

> "'Tis a point I long to know,
>   Oft it causes anxious thought,—
> Do I love the Lord, or no?
>   Am I his, or am I not?"

That is a very good hymn,—I find no fault with it;—but please do not sing it too often. Now and then, you are welcome to it, but get through it as quickly as you can. I would far rather hear you sing that grand hymn of Toplady's,—

> "A debtor to mercy alone,
>   Of covenant mercy I sing;
> Nor fear, with thy righteousness on,
>   My person and offering to bring."

"Oh!" say you, "I long to grow in love. I want to know that I love Jesus. I want to feel my heart going out after him, and my soul knit to him." Well, the way to grow in love is to know more of Christ. The more you know of the Saviour, the better you must love him; the more you discover of his beauties, of his excellences, of his virtues, of his perfections, and of his glories, the more your soul will be drawn towards him. I tell you, who do not love Christ at all, that it is because you do not know him; for if you knew anything of him, you would love him in proportion to your knowledge. The more you know of my Master, the more you will love him. You have only lifted one corner of the veil that shrouds his forehead, you have seen but one portion of his visage, so you love him; but if you had faith to lift the veil entirely, to see all of his blessed countenance, to mark the majestic sweetness which sits enthroned upon his lofty brow; if you could descant on his eyes, which are "like the fishpools in Heshbon, by the gate of Bath-rabbim,"—if you could describe him as being "altogether lovely," ah! you would love him more. Blessed are the men that improve upon acquaintance! Jesus Christ is one of those blessed ones; the more you know of him, the more you love him. Sweet Jesus! when I first saw thee, I loved thee! When first thy wounded hand and bleeding side were uncovered to me, then I loved thee. Ah! but that love is nothing compared with what I have now. And, oh! when I shall see thee as thou art,—when my soul becomes changed into love,—the love I have now shall seem to have been nought but a spark compared with that vehement flame of love which I shall have to thee then. Know more of Christ; read more of him; think more of him; ask about him more; because you will be sure to grow in the grace of love, in proportion as you know more of Christ.

So is it with regard to *faith*. What is the reason why so many of us groan because our faith is so feeble? It is because we do not know enough of Christ. There are many people who need to know a great deal more about Jesus than they know at present; and if they knew more about Jesus, they would have more faith. "Oh!" says one, "when I look at myself, I think, 'Oh, what is to become of me?' Then I search to see if there are not some evidences of grace." That is all wrong! You have no business to look there; you will not grow in faith by looking at yourself. One look at Jesus is worth fifty at yourself. If you would have more faith, keep your eye on Jesus. The wounds of Christ on Calvary are the mothers of faith; these are the breast from which faith must draw its nourishment. If you would grow in faith, you must live near to the cross. The sweet flower of faith was first sown in Christ's precious blood, and it must be watered by it every day. Know more of Christ; think more of him; and your faith will increase. Your little faith would soon get strong if you lived more on Jesus. If you would become Great-hearts by-and-by, and knock those giants about as terribly as Mr. Great-heart did of old, live near to Jesus; live with Jesus; feast at his banqueting table; for there is no food so strengthening to the spirit as the flesh of your Lord, and no wine can so invigorate your soul as the blood of Jesus Christ your Saviour.

So is it with regard to our *courage*; for that is a Christian grace, and one in which many are terribly deficient. Our Christian courage will always increase in proportion as we know Christ. We have far too many timid Christians who have not courage enough, I was about to say, to speak to a cheese-mite; they would not be able to profess the name of Christ before the smallest creature in the world; they would be almost ashamed to declare that they loved the Saviour even within bare walls, for fear some bird of the air should hear them, and go and tell the tale. They are so ashamed of their own faith (and yet it is real faith) that they scarcely dare to speak. The smallest stone in the road would make them stumble; a straw would be almost as great to them as a range of mountains like the Himalayas would be to others; they would be entirely cast out of the road if they had the least prospect that there could be a shadow in it for them to pass by. It is because we do not know enough of Christ that we are afraid of anything. I believe that, when we come truly to know Christ, we shall be afraid of nothing at all. Shall we be afraid of man? Nay; we shall say, "Whether it is right to obey God rather than man, judge ye." Shall we be afraid of the devil when we know Christ? Nay; we shall say, "Christ hath the devil chained, and he can always pull the dog of hell in when he attempts to bite us. Christ hath hold of the dragon, and he cannot inflict deeper wounds than Christ willeth." We shall not be afraid of the messenger of death, for we shall regard him as an angel of the covenant sent to fetch God's people up to heaven. Courage will always be increased in proportion as we know more of Jesus; and if we could have Christ for our daily and hourly Companion, I believe all the hosts of hell, marshalled in battle, would no more affright us than would a flock of small birds that might settle upon our path, but we should say, "In the name of the Lord, we will destroy them." If you would have more true Christian courage, get more of "the knowledge of our Lord and Saviour Jesus Christ."

So is it with regard to our *zeal*, which is a grace sadly lacking in these times. If we would be more zealous, we must live nearer to Christ. If the Son of man were to come now, would he find zeal upon the earth? His own question was, "Shall he find faith?" But would he find zeal? It would be difficult even for him to discover much of it amongst Christians. There is sound orthodoxy, but no zeal; there is heterodoxy, but still no zeal. Where do you find it? Just here and there. There is a remnant, according to the election of grace, who are zealous for God; but, in these times, we are sorry to say it, religion has degenerated into a kind of formality. It is a fashionable thing to be pious. We have been going on in the same track as other people; there was an old cartrut, and we all drive along it. We have kept on at the same pace as our fathers; but, oh! if we knew more of Christ, we should have more zeal.

I cannot think it possible for men to lack zeal when they know Christ. They would then say, "Did my Saviour shed his blood for me, and shall I fear even to die for him? Did he come all the way from heaven to earth to save souls, and shall not I also seek to win them for him?" Should we have so many lazy preachers if they had more of Christ in their hearts? If they understood more of Jesus, should we have so many slothful, sluggish members in our churches, with so many who can make any excuse rather than labour for Christ, patching up any empty apology for idleness? No; brethren, if we knew more of the Saviour, if we had more frequent visions of him, if we saw him oftener on his cross, and viewed him more frequently sitting with the crown upon his head, we should say, "I vow revenge against my sloth; all I can do will be too little for so good a Lord.

> " 'All that I am, and all I have,
>   Shall be for ever thine;
> Whate'er my duty bids me give,
>   My cheerful hands resign.
>
> " 'Yet if I might make some reserve,
>   And duty did not call,
> I love my God with zeal so great,
>   That I should give him all.' "

It is no use to try to get more zeal except in the right way, knowing more of Christ; and if we seek to grow in zeal as certain people we might mention have done, we shall have a zeal like a house on fire; it will do more mischief than it will do good. There may be some heat, and a deal of illumination; but it will die away, by-and-by, into black ashes, poisoning the churches everywhere. I have seen a certain kind of revival in England, and I can always tell where such "revivals" have been by the scarred state of the places after them. These so-called "revivals" have been wrought by excitable meetings, held by sundry preachers, who have invented strange doctrines, but have said nothing about the grace of God. They have for a time stirred up the people to a kind of religious *furor*, and they have left behind them a very desert. Before them it was like a garden of the Lord, but behind them barrenness and desolation. The church has been divided; there has been a reaction, and the people have sunk into the most lamentable condition. If we would have true zeal, it must be by the preaching of the good old doctrine, proclaiming Jesus Christ and him crucified; for anything else comes of the devil, and to hell it shall tend; its issue shall be destruction, and not salvation. But if we keep to the truth of God, there will be "revival" enough. We want nothing but the good old-fashioned gospel to stir the world again. Though men have tried new schemes, God will not own them. All these heresies must be swept away, and the true gospel—distinguishing grace of God in all the sovereignty of election—must yet again be preached; and when it is preached in all its fulness, then shall the church be zealous, and then shall Zion arise, and shake herself from the dust, and put on her beautiful garments.

Further, if we would grow also in *the grace of brotherly kindness*, we must know more of Christ. O beloved, we must lament that there is too little brotherly kindness in the world! There is a great deal of that mawkish, mistaken kindness which says, "We must never say anything contrary to anybody else's opinion. If we know of a doctrinal error, we must not expose it, because love of our brethren implies that, even if they are wrong, we would not tell them of it." But I think true brotherly kindness is always to preach the truth, and tell our brethren where they are wrong, and give them the opportunity of getting set right; to preach whatever we believe to be true, and to maintain what God has taught us; and then, after all, to say, "Well, brother, you differ from me. I am not infallible; I still love you." But that is no love which makes us hide the truth. True love will make us honest, zealous, and affectionate.

Why don't we love one another as much as we ought? It is because we do not love the Saviour enough, and we have not seen enough of him. If we had known more of the Saviour, I am sure we should love him better. I met with a strange idea when reading a book by old Burroughs, the other day. He says, "If Jesus Christ were to come down to his church now, he would see some of his children with black eyes; some others would be seen scratched in the face, and some bruised all over. He would say to them, 'What have you been doing?' If one should answer, 'Lord, I have been fighting with my brother, and he did this;' the Lord would say, 'Children of one family fight! the birds of one nest disagree! how sad it is!'" It is a queer thought, but it may be a profitable one; for if our Lord Jesus Christ finds his people quarrelling, what will he say? You may remember a story I have told you before. An old Scotch elder had been disputing with his minister at an elders' meeting. He said some hard things, and almost broke the minister's heart. Afterwards, he went home, and the minister went home too. The next morning, when the elder came down, his wife said to him, "Eh, Jan! ye look very sad this morning; what's the matter wi' ye?" "Ah!" said he, "you would be sad too if you had had such a dream as I've had." "Weel, and what did ye dream about?" "Oh! I dreamed I had been at an elders' meeting, and I said some hard things, and grieved the minister; and as he went hame, I thought he died, and went to heaven. A fortnight after, I thought I died, and that I went to heaven, too; and when I got to the gates of heaven, out came the minister, and put out his hand to welcome me, saying, 'Come alang, Jan, there's nae strife up here, and I'm happy to see ye.'" The elder went to the minister to beg his pardon, but he found that he was dead; and he laid it so to heart that, within a fortnight, the elder himself departed; and I should not wonder if he did meet the minister at heaven's gate, and hear him say, "Come alang, Jan, there's nae strife up here." It will be well for us to recollect that there is no strife up there. Glorified saints have no strife among themselves; and we should love one another more in brotherly kindness if we thought more of heaven, and more of our blessed Jesus.

Lastly, there is another grace in which we need to grow; that is, *the grace of humility*. I am sure we should increase in that grace if we lived nearer to Christ. O humility, most precious thing, thou art most rare!

He who talks most of it hath least of it. He who preaches of it best full often is least the subject of its power. O humility! I have sometimes thought that thou wert a phantom, and that pride was the reality. Humility, where art thou? The depths of poverty say, "Thou art not in me," for the poor are often proud. The heights of riches say, "Thou art not here," for the rich are often proud, too. O humility! Thou art not to be found in science, for philosophy puffeth up. Thou art not to be found in ignorance, for that is the mother of pride. O humility, where can I find thee? Where art thou? Nowhere can I see thee, or know what thou art, except I sit at the feet of Jesus, and behold myself a lost, ruined sinner purchased by divine love. If you, dear friend, would be truly humble, you must look at your Saviour, for then you will say,—

> "Alas! and did my Saviour bleed?
> And did my Sovereign die?
> Would he devote that sacred head
> For such a worm as I?"

You will never feel yourself such a worm as when, by faith, you see your Saviour dying for you; you will never know your own nothingness so well as when you see your Saviour's greatness. When you grow in the grace and knowledge of our Lord and Saviour Jesus Christ, you will be sure to grow in humility. Growing Christians think themselves nothing, but full-grown Christians think themselves less than nothing; and the nearer we get to Jesus, the smaller self will appear to be. Self and Christ can never come close together. When I stand near self, Christ is small; when I stand near Christ, self is small. May God grant to you, dear friends, to grow in the knowledge of Christ! Read the Scriptures more. Seek more the influences of the Holy Spirit upon them; spend more time in devotion; ask God the Holy Spirit to give you a fresh sight of Calvary; be oftener on the mount of transfiguration, in the garden of suffering, in the hall of agony, under the cross of crucifixion; live with Jesus, and near to him; and so, changed from glory to glory as by the Spirit of the Lord, you shall each one of you grow unto the stature of a perfect man in Christ Jesus.[15]

---

[15] Spurgeon, C. H. (1900). Growth in Grace. In *The Metropolitan Tabernacle Pulpit Sermons* (Vol. 46, pp. 529–540). London: Passmore & Alabaster.

GRACE EXALTED—BOASTING EXCLUDED

A Sermon

Delivered on Sunday Morning, January 19th, 1862, by

REV. C. H. SPURGEON,

At the Metropolitan Tabernacle, Newington

"Where is boasting then? It is excluded. By what law? of works? Nay: but by the law of faith."—Romans 3:27.

Pride is most obnoxious to God. As a sin, his holiness hates it; as a treason, his sovereignty detests it; as a rebellion, the whole of his attributes stand leagued to put it down. God has touched other sins with his finger, but against this vice he has made bare his arm. There have been, I know, terrible judgments against lust, but there have been ten times as many against that swelling lust of the deceitful heart. Remember, the first transgression had in its essence pride. The ambitious heart of Eve desired to be as God, knowing good and evil, and Adam imagined that he should be lifted up to divine rank if he dared to pluck and eat. The blasting of Paradise, the sterility of the world, the travail of human birth, the sweat of the brow, and the certainty of death, may all be traced to this fruitful mother of mischief, pride. Remember Babel, and how God has scattered us and confounded our tongues. It was man's pride which led him to seek for an undivided monarchy that so he might be great. The tower was to be the rallying-point of all the tribes, and would have been the central throne of all human grandeur, but God has scattered us, that pride might not climb to so high a pitch. Pride, thou hast indeed suffered severe strokes from God. Against thee has he furbished his sword, and prepared his weapons of war. The Lord, even the Lord of hosts hath sworn it, and he will surely stain the pride of all human glory, and tread all boasting as straw is trodden for the dunghill. Talk no more so exceeding proudly; let no arrogancy come out of your mouth, for the bows of the mighty have been broken, and the haughtiness of man has been bowed down. Remember Pharaoh and the plagues which God brought on Egypt, and the wonders which he wrought in the field of Zoan. Remember the Red Sea, and Rahab cut, and the dragon broken. Think of Nebuchadnezzar, the mighty architect of Babylon, driven out to eat grass like the oxen till his nails grew like birds' claws, and his hair like eagles' feathers. Remember Herod, eaten of worms, because he gave not God the glory; and Sennacherib, with the Lord's hook in his jaws, turned by the way he came to the place where his sons became his slayers. Time would fail to tell of the innumerable conquerors and emperors and mighty men of earth who have all perished beneath the blast of thy rebuke, O God, because they lifted up themselves and said, "I am, and there is none beside me." He hath turned wise men backward, and made their knowledge foolishness, and no flesh may glory in his presence. Yea, when pride has sought to shelter itself in the hearts of God's chosen people, still the arrows of God have sought it out and have drunk its blood. God loves his servants still, but pride even in them he abhors. David may be a man after God's own heart, but if his pride shall lift him up to number the people, then he shall have a choice between three chastisements, and he shall be fain to choose the pestilence as being the least of the plagues. Or if Hezekiah shall show to the ambassadors of Babylon his riches and his treasures, there shall come to him the rebuke—"What have they seen in thy house?" and the threatening—"Behold they shall take thy sons to make them eunuchs in the palace of the king of Babylon." Oh, brethren, forget not that God has uttered the most solemn words as well as issued the most awful judgments against pride. "Pride goeth before destruction, and a haughty spirit before a fall." "Him that hath a high look and a proud heart will I not suffer." "Pride and arrogancy do I hate." "The Lord will destroy the house of the proud." "The day of the Lord shall be upon every one that is proud and lofty, and upon every one that is lifted up, and he shall be brought low." "I am against thee, O thou most proud, saith the Lord God of Hosts." There are hundreds of terrible texts like these, but we cannot now recount them all. Now mark, to put an everlasting stigma upon human vanity, and to hurl once for all mire and filth upon all human glorying, God has ordained that the only way in which he will save men shall be a way which utterly excludes the possibility of man's having a single word to say by way of vaunting. He has declared that the only foundation which he will ever lay shall be one by which man's strength shall be broken in pieces, and by which man's pride shall be humbled in the dust. To this subject I ask your attention this morning. It is to enlarge and amplify the sentiment of the text that I seek. "Where is boasting, then? It is excluded. By what law? of works? Nay: but by the law of faith."

We shall notice first of all, *the rejected plan or law;* then we shall note *the excluded vice;* having so done, we shall notice in the third place, *that the very fact that boasting is excluded permits of the reception of the worst of sinners;* and we shall close by observing *that the same system which excludes boasting includes humble and devout gratitude to God for his grace and mercy.*

I. First, then, THE REJECTED PLAN.

There are two ways by which man might have been for ever blessed. The one was by works:—"This do and thou shalt live; be obedient and receive the reward; keep the commandment and the blessing shall be thine, well earned and surely paid." The only other plan was—"Receive grace and blessedness as the free gift of God; stand as a guilty sinner having no merit, and as a rebellious sinner deserving the very reverse of goodness, but stand there and receive all thy good things, simply, wholly, and alone of the free love and sovereign mercy of God." Now, the Lord has not chosen the system of works. The word *law* as used twice in the text is employed, it is believed by many commentators, out of compliment to the Jews, who were so fond of the word, that their antagonism might not be aroused; but it means here, as elsewhere in Scripture, plan, system, method. There were two plans, two systems, two methods, two spirits,—the plan of works and the plan of grace. God has once for all utterly refused the plan of merit and of works, and has chosen to bless men only, and entirely through the plan, or method, or law of faith. Now, brethren, we have put the two before you, and we beg you to mark that there is a distinction between the two, which must never be forgotten. Martin Luther says:—"If thou canst rightly distinguish between works and grace, thank God for thy skill, and consider thyself to be an able divine." This indeed is the bottom of theology, and he who can understand this clearly, it seems to me, can never be very heterodox; orthodoxy must surely follow, and the right teaching of God must be understood when we once for all are able to discriminate with accuracy between that which is of man—works, and that which is of God—faith, and grace received by faith. Now, the plan of salvation by works is impossible for us. Even if God had ordained it to be the way by which men should labour to be saved, yet it is certain that none would have been saved by it, and therefore all must have perished. For if thou wouldst be saved by works, remember O man, that the law requires of thee perfection. One single flaw, one offence, and the law condemns thee without mercy. It requires that thou shouldst keep it in every point, and in every sense, and to its uttermost degree, for its demands are rigorous in the extreme. It knows nothing of freely forgiving because thou canst not pay, but like a severe creditor, it takes thee by thy throat, and says, "Pay me all;" and if thou canst not pay even to the uttermost farthing, it shuts thee up in the prison of condemnation, out of which thou canst not come. But if it were possible for you to keep the law in its perfection outwardly, yet, remember, that you would be required to keep it in your heart as well as in your external life. One single motion of the heart from the right, one reception of even the shadow of a passing temptation, so as to become a partaker of sin, would ruin you. "Thou shalt love the Lord thy God with all thy heart, and with all thy mind, and with all thy soul, and with all thy strength, and thy neighbour as thyself." Fail here, and oh! who among us can be such a hypocrite as to think he has not failed ten thousand times!—fail here, and though your life were virtuous, though your exterior were such as even criticism itself must commend, yet you perish because you have not kept the law and yielded its full demands. Remember, too, that it is clear you can never be saved by the law, because if up to this moment your heart and life have been altogether without offence, yet it is required that it should be so even to your dying day. And do you hope that as temptations come upon you thick as your moments, as your trials invade you numerous as the swarms which once thronged from the gates of Thebes, you will be able to stand against all these? Will there not be found some joint in your harness? Will there not be some moment in which you may be tripped up—some instant when either the eye may wander after lust, or the heart be set on vanity, or the hand stretched out to touch that which is not good? Oh! man, remember, we are not sure that even this life would end that probation, for as long as thou shouldst live and be God's creature, duty would still be due, and the law still thine insatiable creditor. For ever would thy happiness tremble in the scales; even in heaven itself the law would follow thee; even there, as thy righteousness would be thine own, it would never be finished; and even from yonder shining battlements thou mightest fall, and amid those harps, wearing that white robe, if thou wert to be saved by thine own works, there might be a possibility of perishing. The obedience of a creature can never be finished; the duty of a servant of the law is never over. So long as thou wast the creature of God, thy Creator would have demands upon thee. How much better to be accepted in the Beloved, and to wear his finished righteousness as our glory and security. Now in the face of all this, will any of you prefer to be saved by your works? or, rather, will you prefer to be damned by your works? for that will certainly be the issue, let you hope what you may.

Now I suppose that in this congregation we have but very few—there may be some—who would indulge a hope of being saved by the law in itself; but there is a delusion abroad that perhaps God will modify the law, or that at least he will accept a sincere obedience even if it be imperfect; that he will say, "Well, this man has done what he could, and, therefore, I will take what he has given as though it were perfect." Now, remember against this the Apostle Paul declares peremptorily, "By the works of the law shall no flesh living be justified," so that that is answered at once. But more than this, God's law cannot alter, it can never be content to take less from thee than it demands. What said Christ? "It is easier for heaven and earth to pass, than one tittle of the law to fail," and again he expressly said, "Think not that I am come to destroy the law, or the prophets, I am not come to destroy, but to fulfil." The law's demands were met and fulfilled for believers by Christ; but as far as those demands are concerned to those who are under it, they are as great, as heavy, and as rigorous as ever they were. Unless his law could be altered, and that is impossible, God cannot accept anything but a perfect obedience; and if you are hoping to be saved by your sincere endeavours to do your best, your hopes are rotten things, delusions, falsehoods, and you will perish wrapped up in the shrouds of your pride. "Yes," some say, "but could it not be partly by grace and partly by works?" No. The apostle says that boasting is excluded, and excluded by the law of faith; but if we let in the law of works in any degree, we cannot shut out boasting, for to that degree you give man an opportunity to congratulate himself as having saved himself. Let me say broadly—to hope to be saved by works is a delusion; to hope to be saved by a method in which grace and works are co-acting, is not merely a delusion, but an absurd delusion, since it is contrary to the very nature of things, that grace and merit should ever mingle and co-work. Our apostle has declared times without number, that if it be of grace it is not of works, otherwise grace is no more grace; and if it be of works, then it is not of grace, otherwise work is no more work. It must be either one or the other. These two cannot be married, for God forbids the banns. He will have it all grace or all works, all of Christ or all of man; but for Christ to be a make-weight, for Christ to supplement your narrow robes by patching on a piece of his own, for Christ to tread a part of the winepress, and for you to tread the rest; oh! this can never be. God will never be yoked with the creature. You might link an angel with a worm and bid them fly together, but God with the creature—the precious blood of Jesus with the foul ditch-water of our human merits—never, never. Our paste gems, our varnished falsehoods, our righteousnesses which are but filthy rags, put with the real, true, precious, everlasting, divine things of Christ! Never! Unless heaven should blend in alliance with hell, and holiness hold dalliance with impurity! It must be one or the other, either man's merit absolutely and alone, or unmixed, unmerited favour from the Lord. Now, I suppose if I were to labour never so arduously to hunt out this evil spirit from the sons of men, I should miss it still, for it hides in so many shapes, and therefore let me say, that in no shape, in no sense, in no single case, and in no degree whatsoever, are we saved by our works or by the law. I say in no sense, because men make such shifts to save alive their own righteousness. I will show you one man who says, "Well, I don't expect to be saved by my honesty; I don't expect to be saved by my generosity, nor by my morality; but then, I have been baptized; I receive the Lord's Supper; I have been confirmed; I go to church, or I have a sitting in a meeting-house; I am, as touching the ceremonies, blameless." Well, friend, in that sense you cannot be saved by works, for all these things have no avail whatever upon the matter of salvation, if you have not faith. If you are saved, God's ordinances will be blessed things to you, but if you are not a believer you have no right to them; and with regard to Baptism and the Supper, every time you touch them you increase your guilt. Whether it be Baptism or the Lord's Supper, you have no right to either, except you be saved already, for they are both ordinances for believers, and for believers only. These ordinances are blessed means of grace to living, quickened, saved souls; but to unsaved souls, to souls dead in trespasses and sins, these outward ordinances can have no avail for good, but may increase their sin, because they touch unworthily the holy things of God. Oh! repose not in these; oh! dream not that a priestly hand and sacred drops, or a God-ordained baptism in the pool, can in any way redeem you from sin, or land you in heaven: for by this way salvation is impossible. But if I drive the lover of self-righteousness out of this haunt, he runs to another. You will find others who suppose that at least *their feelings*, which are only their works in another shape, may help to save them. There are thousands who think, "If I could weep so much, and groan so deeply, and experience so much humiliation, and a certain quantity of repentance, and so much of the terrors of the law, and of the thunders of conscience, then I might come before God." Souls, souls, this is work-mongering in its most damnable shape, for it has deluded far more than that bolder sort of work-trusting, which says, "I will rely upon what I do." If you rely upon what you feel, you shall as certainly perish as if you trust to what you do. Repentance is a blessed grace, and to be convinced of sin by God the Holy Ghost is a holy privilege, but to think that these in any way win salvation, is to run clean counter to all the teachings of the Word, for salvation is of the free grace of God alone. There are some, moreover, who believe that if their feelings cannot do it, still *their knowledge can*. They have a very sound creed; they have struck out this doctrine and that; they believe in justification by faith, and their sound creed is to them a confidence. They think that because they hold the theory of justification by faith, therefore they shall be saved. And oh! how they plume their feathers; how they set up their peacock tail because they happen to be orthodox! With what awful pride do they exult over their fellow professors because they hold *the truth*, and all the rest of the Church they think is deluded with a lie. Now this is nothing but salvation by works, only they are works performed by the head instead of by the hand, and oh! sirs, I will tell you—if you rest in creeds, if you hope to be saved because you can put your hand to the thirty-nine articles of an Episcopalian prayer-book, or to the solemn league and covenant of the Presbyterian, or to the confession of faith of the Calvinist—if you fancy that because you happen to receive truth in the head you shall be saved, you know not the truth, but still do lie, because you cling to Satan's falsehood—that salvation is of man and not of God. I know that self-righteousness was born in our bone and that it will come out in our flesh, and even that man in whom its reigning power is kept down will still feel it sometimes rising up. When he has preached a sermon and has got on pretty well, the devil will come up the pulpit stairs and say "Well done.' When he has prayed in public and has had unusual fluency, he will have to be careful lest there should be a whisper behind—"What a good and gifted man you are." Ay, and even in his hallowed moments, when he is on the top of the mountain with his Lord, he will have to watch even there, lest self-congratulation should suggest—"Oh, man, greatly-beloved, there must surely be something in thee, or else God would not have done thus unto thee." Brethren, when you are thinking of your sanctification, if you are tempted to look away from Christ— away with it; and if when you are repenting of sin you cannot still have one eye on Christ, recollect it will be a repentance that will need to be repented of, for there is nothing in ourselves that can be offered to God. There is a stench and putridity in everything that is done of the creature, and we can never come before God save through Christ Jesus, who is made of God unto us, wisdom, and righteousness, and sanctification, and redemption. I have thus tried to denounce the plan which God has rejected.

II. I shall now, in the second head, SHOW THAT BOASTING IS EXCLUDED, for in a blessed sense God has accepted the second plan, namely, the way of salvation by faith through grace.

The first man that entered heaven, entered heaven by faith. "By faith Abel offered a more acceptable sacrifice than Cain." Over the tombs of all the goodly who were accepted of God, you may read the epitaph—"These all died in faith." By faith they received the promise; and among all yonder bright and shining throng, there is not one who does not confess, "We have washed our robes and made them white in the blood of the Lamb." The plan, then, which God has chosen, is one of grace alone. I will try and picture that plan before our mind's eye. We will imagine Boasting to be exceedingly desirous to enter into the kingdom of heaven. He marches to the door and knocks. The porter looks out and demands, "Who stands there?" "I am Boasting," saith he, "and I claim to have the highest seat; I claim that I should cry aloud and say, Glory be unto man, for though he has fallen, he has lifted himself up, and wrought out his own redemption." And the angel said, "But hast thou not heard that the salvation of souls is not of man, nor by man, but that God will have mercy on whom he will have mercy, and will have compassion on whom he will have compassion? Get thee gone, Boasting, for the highest seat can never be thine, when God in direct opposition to human merit, has rejected the Pharisee, and chosen the publican and the harlot, that they may enter into the kingdom of heaven." So Boasting said, "Let me take my place, then, if not in the highest seat, yet somewhere amid the glittering throng; for instance, let me take my place in the seat of *election;* let it be said and taught, that albeit God did choose his people, yet it was because of their works which he foresaw, and their faith which he foreknew, and that, therefore, foreseeing and foreknowing, he did choose them because of an excellence which his prescient eye discovered in them; let me take my seat here." But the porter said, "Nay, but thou canst not take thy place there, for election is according to the eternal purpose of God, which he purposed in Christ Jesus before the world was. This election is not of works, but of grace, and the reason for God's choice of man is in himself, and not in man; and as for those virtues which thou sayest God did foreknow, God is the author of all of them if they exist, and that which is an effect cannot be a first cause; God foreordained these men to faith and to good works, and their faith and good works could not have been the cause of their foreordination." Then straight from heaven's gate the trumpet sounded—("For the children being not yet born, neither having done any good or evil, that the purpose of God according to election might stand, not of works, but of him that calleth;) it was said unto her, The elder shall serve the younger," Then Boasting found that as works had no place in election, so there was no room for him to take his seat there, and he bethought himself where next he could be. So after a while Boasting said to the porter, "If I cannot mount the chair of election, I will be content to sit in the place of conversion, for surely it is man that repents and believes." The porter did not deny the truth of that, and then this evil spirit said, "If one man believes and not another, surely that must be the act of the man's will, and his will being free and unbiassed, it must be very much to that man's credit that he believes and repents and is therefore saved, for others, having like opportunities with himself, and having the same grace no doubt, reject the proferred mercy and perish, while this man accepts it, and therefore let me at least take my seat there." But the angel said in anger, "Take thy seat there! Why, that were to take the highest place of all, for this is the hinge and turning-point, and if thou leavest that with man then thou givest him the brightest jewel in the crown. Does the Ethiopian change his skin and the leopard his spots? Is it not God that worketh in us to will and to do of his own good pleasure? Of his own will begat he us with the word of truth, and it is not of the will of man, nor of blood, nor of birth. Oh, Boaster, thy free-will is a lie; it is not man that chooses God, but God that chooses man; for what said Christ, "Ye have not chosen me but I have chosen you;" and what said he to the ungodly multitude, "Ye will not come unto me that ye might have life;" in which he gave the death-blow to all ideas of free-will, when he declared that man *will not* come to him that he might have life; and when he said again in another place, as if that were not enough, "No man can come unto me except the Father which hath sent me draw him." So Boasting, though he were fain not to admit it, was shut out, and could not take his place in heaven upon the stool of conversion; and while he stood there but little abashed, for bashfulness he knows not, he heard a song floating over the battlements of heaven from all the multitude who were there, in accents like these, "Not unto us, not unto us, but unto thy name, O Lord, be all the praise."

> "'Twas the same love that spread the feast
>   That gently forced us in;
> Else we had still refused to taste,
>   And perished in our sin."

"But then," said Boasting, "if I may not have so high a place, let me at least sit on the lowly stool of perseverance, and let it at least be said that while God saved the man and is therefore to have the glory, still the man was faithful to grace received; he did not turn back unto perdition, but watched and was very careful, and kept himself in the love of God, and therefore there is considerable credit due to him; for while many drew back and perished, and he might have done the same, he struggled against sin, and thus by his using his grace he kept himself safely; let me sit, then, on the chair of perseverance." But the angel replied, "Nay, nay, what hast thou to do with it? I know it is written, 'Keep yourselves in the love of God,' but the same apostle forbids all fleshly trust in human effort by that blessed doxology,—'Now unto him that is able to keep you from falling, and to present you faultless before the presence of his glory with exceeding joy, to the only wise God our Saviour, be glory and majesty, dominion and power, both now and ever. Amen.' That which is a command in one Scripture is a covenant promise in another, where it is written, 'I will put my fear in their hearts that they shall not depart from me.'" Oh! brethren, well do you and I know that our standing does not depend upon ourselves. If that Arminian doctrine, that our perseverance rests somewhere in our own hands, were true, then damnation must be the lot of us all. I cannot keep myself a minute, much less year after year.

> "If ever it should come to pass,
> That sheep of Christ should fall away;
> My fickle, feeble soul, alas!
> Would fall a thousand times a day."

But what saith the Scripture?—"I give unto my sheep eternal life, and they shall never perish, neither shall any one pluck them out of my hand; my Father who gave them me is greater than all, and none is able to pluck them out of my Father's hand." And what says the apostle—"I am persuaded, that neither death, nor life, nor angels, nor principalities, nor powers, nor things present, nor things to come, nor height, nor depth, nor any other creature, shall be able to separate us from the love of God, which is in Christ Jesus our Lord." I have not time to quote all the innumerable passages, but it is absolutely certain that if there be one doctrine in Scripture more clearly revealed than another, it is the doctrine of the perseverance of the saints by the power of the Holy Ghost, and the man who doubts that precious truth, has quite as much reason to doubt the Trinity, to doubt the divinity of Christ, or the fact of the atonement; for nothing can be more clear in the plain, common-sense meaning of the words than this, that they who are in Christ have, even to-day, eternal life and shall never perish. Now since this perseverance is not dependant upon our works, but like all the rest of salvation is an efflux from the bottomless love of God, boasting is manifestly excluded. But once again, and lastly, Boasting sometimes asks to be admitted a little into glorification. I fear sometimes that a doctrine which is popular in the Church, about degrees of glory, is not altogether unassociated with that old self-righteousness of ours which is very loath to die. "One star differeth from another star in glory" is a great truth—but this the stars may do without differing in degrees. One star may shine with one radiance, and another with another; indeed, astronomers tell us that there are many varieties of colour among stars of the same magnitude. One man may differ from another, without supposing a difference in rank, honour, or degree. For my part, I do not see anything about degrees in glory in Scripture, and I do not believe in the doctrine; at least if there be degrees, mark this, they cannot be according to works, but must be of grace alone. I cannot consider that because one Christian has been more devoted to Christ than another, therefore there will be an eternal difference, for this is to introduce works; this is to bring in again the old Hagar marriage, and to bring back the child of the bond-woman, whereof God has said, "The son of the bond-woman shall not be heir with my son, even with Isaac." Oh! brethren, I think we can serve God from some other motive than that base one of trying to be greater than our brethren in heaven. If I should get to heaven at all, I do not care who is greater than I am, for if any one shall have more happiness in heaven than I shall, then I shall have more happiness too; for the sympathy between one soul and another will there be so intense and so great, that all the heavens of the righteous will be my heaven, and therefore, what you have I shall have, because we shall all be one in fellowship far more perfectly than on earth. The private member will there be swallowed up in the common body. Surely, brethren, if any of you can have brighter places in heaven, and more happiness and more joy than I, I will be glad to know it. The prospect does not excite any envy in my soul now, or if it did *now*, it certainly would not *then*, for I should feel that the more *you* had the more *I* should have. Perfect communion in all good things is not compatible with the private enrichment of one above another. It is all joint-stock in heaven. Even on earth the saints had all things common when they were in a heavenly state, and I am persuaded they will have all things common in glory. I do not believe in gentlemen in heaven, and the poor Christians behind the door; I do believe that our union with each other will be so great, that distinctions will be utterly lost, and that we shall all have such a joint communion, and interest, and fellowship, that there will be no such thing as private possession, private ranks, and private honours—for we shall there, to the fullest extent, be one in Christ. I do believe that Boasting is shut out there, but I think that if there were these degrees in glory, I mean if they are dependant on works done on earth, Boasting would at least get his tail in; if it did not insinuate its whole body, it would at least get some of its unhallowed members over the wall, whereas, the text says it is excluded. Let me enlarge this one word, and then proceed. It does not say, "Boasting, you are to be allowed to come in and sit down on the floor." No, shut the door and do not let him in at all. "But let me in," says he, "and I will be quiet." No, shut him out altogether. "But at least let me put my foot in." No, exclude him; shut him out altogether. "But at least let me sometimes go in and out." No, shut him out altogether; exclude him; bolt the door; put double padlocks on it. Say once for all, "Boasting, get thee gone; thou art hurled down and broken in pieces, and if thou canst refit thyself, and come once more to the gate to ask admittance, thou shalt be driven away with shame." It is *excluded;* it cannot be let in, in any sense, in any term, nor in any degree. As Calvin says, "Not a particle of boasting can be admitted, because not a particle of work is admitted into the covenant of grace;" it is of grace from top to bottom, from Alpha to Omega; it is not of man nor by man, not of him that willeth, nor of him that runneth, but of God that showeth mercy, and therefore, boasting is excluded by the law of faith.

III. And now, thirdly, and very briefly. Beloved in Christ Jesus, what a precious truth I have now to hold up to the eyes of poor lost sinners, who to-day are aware that they have no merits of their own. Soul, THE VERY GATE WHICH SHUTS OUT BOASTING, SHUTS IN HOPE AND JOY FOR YOU.

Let me state this truth broadly, that the ignorant may catch it. You say to-day, "Sir, I never attend the house of God, and up to this time I have been a thief and a drunkard." Well, you stand to-day on the same level as the most moral sinner, and the most honest unbeliever, in the matter of salvation. They are lost, since they believe not, and so are you. If the most honest be saved, it will not be by their honesty, but by the free grace of God; and if the most roguish would be saved, it must be by the same plan. There is one gate to heaven for the most chaste and the most debauched. When we come to God, the best of us can bring nothing, and the worst of us can bring no less. I know when I state it thus, some will say, "Then what is the good of morality?" I will tell you. Two men are overboard there; one man has a dirty face, and the other a clean one. There is a rope thrown over from the stern of the vessel, and only that rope will save the sinking men, whether their faces be fair or foul. Is not this the truth? Do I therefore underrate cleanliness. Certainly not; but it will not save a drowning man; nor will morality save a dying man. The clean man may sink with all his cleanliness, and the dirty man may be drawn up with all his filth, if the rope do but get its hold of him. Or take this case. Here we have two persons, each with a deadly cancer. One of them is rich and clothed in purple, the other is poor and wrapped about with a few rags; and I say to them—"You are both on a par now, here comes the physician himself—Jesus, the king of disease; his touch can heal you both; there is no difference between you whatever." Do I therefore say that the one man's robes are not better than the other's rags? Of course they are better in some respects, but they have nothing to do with the matter of curing disease. So morality is a neat cover for foul venom, but it does not alter the fact that the heart is vile and the man himself under condemnation. Suppose I were an army-surgeon, and there had been a battle. There is one man there—he is a captain and a brave man; he led his rank into the thick of the battle, and he is bleeding out his life from a terrible gash. By his side there lies a man of the rank and file, and a great coward too, wounded in the same way. I come up to both of them, and I say, "You are both in the same condition; you have both the same sort of wound, and I can heal you both." But if either of you should say, "Get you gone; I'll have nothing to do with you," your wound will be your death. If the captain should say, "I do not want you; I am a captain, go and see to that poor dog yonder." Would his courage and rank save his life? No, they are good things, but not saving things. So is it with good works, men can be damned with them as well as without them if they make them their trust. Oh! what a gospel is this to preach in our theatres; to tell those hedge-birds, those who are full of all manner of loathsomeness, that there is the same way of salvation open to them as to a peer of the realm, or a bishop on the bench; that there is no difference between us in the way of mercy, that we are all condemned; that there may be degrees as to our guilt, but that the fact of our condemnation is quite as certain to the best as to the worst! "Oh" you say, "this is a levelling doctrine!" Ah! bless God if you are levelled. "Oh," you say, "but this cuts at everything that is good in man!" Ah! thank God, if it kills everything in which man glories, for that which man thinks to be good is often an abomination in the sight of God. And oh! if all of us together, moral or immoral, chaste or debauched, honest or unholy, can come with the rope about our neck, and with the weeds of penitence upon our loins, and say, "Great God, forgive us; we are all guilty; give us grace; we do not deserve it; bestow upon us thy favour, we have no right to it, but give it to us because Jesus died." Oh! he will never cast out one that way, for that is the way of salvation. And if we can put our hand this morning—no matter though it was black last night with lust, or red up to the elbow with murder—yet if we can put our hand on Jesu's head, and believe on him—the blood of Jesus Christ, God's dear Son, cleanseth us from all sin. Where is boasting now? You who have done so much for humanity—you cannot boast, for you have nothing to boast of. You fine gentlemen and noble ladies, what say you to this. O be wise, and join in the prayer, "But thou, O Lord, have mercy upon us, miserable sinners!" And may the Lord then pronounce over us his sentence, "Ye are clean, go and sin no more; your iniquities are all forgiven you."

IV. I close by just observing, that THE SAME PLAN WHICH SHUTS OUT BOASTING LEADS US TO A GRACIOUS GRATITUDE TO CHRIST.

We are sometimes asked by people, "Do you think that such a thing is necessary to salvation?" or, perhaps, the question is put in another way, "How long do you think a man must be Godly in order to be saved?" I reply, dear friend, you cannot understand us, for we hold that these things do not save in any sense, "Why, then," they say, "are you baptized?" or, "Why do you walk in holiness?" Well, not to save myself, but because I am saved. When I know that every sin of mine is forgiven, that I cannot be lost, that Christ has sworn to bring me to the place where he is; then I say, Lord what is there that I can do for thee? Tell me. Can I burn for thee? Blessed were the stake if I might kiss it. If thou hast done so much for me, what can I do for thee? Is there an ordinance that involves self-denial? Is there a duty which will compel me to self-sacrifice? So much the better.

> "Now for the love I bear his name,
> What was my gain I count my loss;
> My former pride I call my shame,
> And nail my glory to his cross."

This is the way to do good works; and good works are impossible until we come here Anything that you do by which to save yourself is a selfish act, and therefore cannot be good. Only that which is done for God's glory is good in a Scriptural sense. A man must be saved before he can do a good work; but when saved, having nothing to get and nothing to lose; standing now in Christ, blessed and accepted—he begins to serve God out of pure gratitude and love. Then, virtue is possible, and he may climb to its highest steeps, and stand safely there without fear of the boasting which would cast him down, though he will feel even then that his standing is not in what he has done, nor in what he is, nor in what he hopes to be, but in what Christ did, and in the "It is finished," which made his eternal salvation secure.

O for grace, that we may live to the praise of the glory of his grace, wherein he hath made us accepted in the beloved, bringing forth the fruits of righteousness, which are by Jesus Christ unto the glory and praise of God. Of Him, and through Him, and to Him are all things; to Him be glory for ever. Amen.[16]

---

[16] Spurgeon, C. H. (1862). Grace Exalted—Boasting Excluded. In *The Metropolitan Tabernacle Pulpit Sermons* (Vol. 8, pp. 25–36). London: Passmore & Alabaster.

EARLY AND LATE, OR HORÆ GRATIÆ

A Sermon

Delivered On Sunday Morning, December 10th, 1865, by

C. H. SPURGEON,

At the Metropolitan Tabernacle, Newington

"For the kingdom of heaven is like unto a man that is an householder, which went out early in the morning to hire labourers into his vineyard.... And he went out about the third hour, and saw others standing idle in the market-place.... Again he went out, about the sixth and ninth hour, and did likewise. And about the eleventh hour he went out, and found others standing idle, and saith unto them, Why stand ye here all the day idle?"—Matthew 20:1, 3, 5, 6.

We have frequently observed that we do not think it right to neglect the connection of Scripture. We have no right to tear passages of Scripture from their context and make them to mean what they were not intended to teach; and therefore I have in the reading given you, according to my ability, what I think to be the immediate design of the present parable. It is a rebuke to those who fall into a legal spirit and begin calculating as to what their reward ought to be in a kingdom where the legal spirit is entirely out of place, since its reward is not of debt but of grace. I think I may now, without any violation of propriety, dwell upon one very distinct fact in connection with the parable. It is not right to violate the drift of the parable, but having already observed it and made it as clear as we can, we believe that we are now authorized to make use of one of the main circumstances mentioned in it.

This morning I intend to call your attention to the fact that the labourers were hired at different periods of the day, by which doubtless we are taught, that God sends his servants into his vineyard at different times and seasons; that some are called in early youth, and others are not led to enter into the service of the Master until declining years have brought them almost to the eventide of life.

I must, however, ask you to remember that *they were all called*: by the mention of which the Saviour would teach us that no man comes into the kingdom of heaven of himself. Without exception, every labourer for Jesus has been called in one sense or another, and he would not have come without being so called. They are all called. Were a man what he should be he would need no pressing and invitation to come to the gospel of Christ; but since human nature is perverted, and men put bitter for sweet and sweet for bitter, darkness for light and light for darkness, man needs to be called by the outward word; he needs to be invited, persuaded, and entreated; he needs, to use the strong expression of the apostle Paul, that as though God did beseech him by us we should pray him in Christ's stead to be reconciled to God. Nay, further than this, although some men come to work in a legal spirit in the vineyard through this common call of the gospel, yet no man in spirit and in truth comes to Christ without a further call, namely, the effectual call of God's Holy Spirit. The general call is given by the minister, it is all that he can give. If the preacher attempts to give the particular call as some of my hyper-calvinistic brethren do, confining the gospel command to a certain character and trying to be themselves the discoverers of God's elect, and to make that particular which is always universal; if the preacher acts thus, and virtually endeavours to give the particular call, he makes a sorry mess of it, and usually fails altogether to preach the gospel of glad tidings to the sons of men. But when man is content to do what he can do, namely, preach the commandment "that we believe on the Lord Jesus Christ," and that "God commandeth all men everywhere to repent," then there comes with the general call to the chosen of God a particular and special call which none but the Holy Ghost can give, but which he gives so effectually that all who hear it become willing in the day of God's power, and turn with full purpose of heart unto the Lord. In what sense is it true that many are called but few chosen, if none are to be called by the preaching of the Word but those who are chosen? There are two callings, the one is general to all who hear of Jesus, and many who are thus called are not chosen; the other is personal and peculiar to the elect, "for whom he did predestinate them he also called." To return to our point; all in the vineyard are in some sense called. There is not a solitary exception to this rule in the entire Christian Church. The doctrine of free-will has not a single specimen to show to prove itself. There is not a sheep in all the flock that came back to the shepherd unsought; there is not a single piece of money which leaped again into the woman's purse, she swept the house to find it: nay, I will go further, and say there is not even a single prodigal son in the entire family who did ever say, "I will arise, and go unto my Father," till first the Father's grace, veiling itself in the afflicting providence of a mighty famine, had taught the prodigal the miserable results of sin, as he fed the swine, and fain would have filled his belly with the husks that the swine did eat, but could not do so.

I want you to notice another fact before I come to the subject now in hand, and that is, that *all those who are called, are said to have been hired*. Of course in a parable no word is to be construed harshly; we are to give the meaning according to the drift; but still I think we may say that there is this likeness between hiring a servant and the engagement of a soul to Christ, that henceforth a man hired has no right to serve another, he serves the master who has hired him. When a soul is called by grace into the service of the Lord Jesus Christ, he cries, "O Lord, other lords have had dominion over me, but now thee only will I serve." He plucks off the yoke of sin, its pleasure, its custom, and he puts upon him that yoke of which the Master says it is easy, and he bears that burden which Jesus tells us is light. A hired servant must not work for another, he works for his master; and so a man who is called by grace lives not for any sinister object or motive, but to his Master only. A hired servant, again, does not work on his own account, he is not his own master; and "ye are not your own, ye are bought with a price." Henceforth, though he calls no man "Master" on earth, yet he remembers that one is his Master in heaven, to whom all his service is due. There is a compact between the hired man and his master, and there is a solemn compact of spirit between the true believer and his Lord. We have devoted ourselves to his service, we have given up all liberty of self-will, and henceforth our will is at the government, of our Lord, and all our powers and passions are to be, we hope will be, through God's grace, obedient to him who has hired us into the vineyard. Now the word "hired" was used in order to bring in the idea of reward. It was used to suit Peter's view of the case; it was used in order that his legal question of "What shall we have therefore?" might be clearly brought out, and its folly shown in the light of that sovereign grace which does as it wills with his own. Yet for all that believers are hired in an evangelical sense, they do not serve God for nought, they shall not work without a reward. "The wages of sin is death, but the gift of God is eternal life." We shall have our reward for what we do for the Master, and though it be not wages in the sense of debt, yet verily I say unto you, there shall not be a single true-hearted worker for God who shall not receive of his Master most blessed wages of grace in the day when he comes to take account of his servants.

Now to the point, *the master calls these hired servants of his at different hours of the day*; and, in the second place, *distinguishing grace shines forth in each case*, and is illustrated and made more manifest in its varieties of glorious compassion and lovingkindness by the different hours at which the chosen ones are called.

I. ALL ARE NOT CALLED BY GRACE AT THE SAME TIME. Some, according to the parable, are called *early in the morning*. Thrice happy are these! The earliest period at which a child may be called by grace it would be difficult for us positively to define, because children are not all of the same age mentally when they are of the same age physically, and even in the matter of menial development we dare not limit the Holy One of Israel as to the chosen period of operation. As far as our observation goes, grace works upon some little ones at the very dawn of moral consciousness. There are, no doubt, precocious children, whose intellect and affections are very much developed, and very deeply sanctified even so early as two or three years of age. Such children usually are intended by the Master to be taken home at once. There are interesting biographies extant, which prove that holiness may bloom and ripen in the youngest heart, and many anecdotes are treasured up in such collections as "Janeway's Token for Children," of children whom I might call infants with strict propriety, out of whose mouth God ordained praise, and did, through them, still the enemy and the avenger. Little prattlers, whose tongues it would have been supposed could only have talked of toys, have been able to speak with an apparent profundity of knowledge of spiritual, and especially of heavenly things. It is certain that some have wrought their day's work for the Master in their mother's arms; they have spoken of the Saviour in tones which have melted a mother's heart and gone to a father's conscience, and then they have been taken home. "Whom the gods love die young," said the heathen, and doubtless it is no small privilege to be so soon admitted into glory. Only shown on earth, and then snatched away to heaven, too precious to be left below. Precious child, how dear wert thou to the good God who sent thee here and then took thee home! Fair rose bud! yet in the perfection of thy young beauty taken to be worn by the Saviour on his bosom, how can we mourn thy translation to the skies?

> "No bitter tears for thee be shed,
>   Blossom of being seen and gone!
> With flowers alone we strew thy bed,
>   O blest departed one!
> Whose all of life, a rosy ray,
> Blush'd into dawn and pass'd away."

"Early in the morning," would also include those who have passed the first hour of the day, but who have not yet wasted the second opening hour. I mean those hopeful lads and girls who perhaps would rather I should call them youths;—those who have reached their teens, have overleaped infancy and childhood, and are growing up in the heyday and vigour of youth. Youngsters still more at home in the playground than in the work-field, fitter, as Satan tells them, to be sporting in the market-place than busy in the vineyard; such as these, to the praise of divine love, are often hired by the householder. It is worth while to warn some of our brethren who seem to be exceedingly dubious of boyish and girlish piety,—to warn them against indulging harsh and suspicious doubts. We have remarked, and I think those who have watched our membership carefully will have remarked it too, that among all the slips and falls which have caused us sorrow, we have had but little sorrow from those who were added to us as boys or girls. There are those preaching the gospel this day with acceptance and power whom these hands baptized into Jesus Christ very early in their boyhood, and there are among us honoured servants of God who have served this Church well, who, while they were yet at school were joyful followers of the Lord Jesus Christ. With our earliest gettings some of us got an understanding of the things of the kingdom; our Bible was our child's primer, our spelling-book, the guide of our youth and the joy of our earliest years. We thank God that there are Timothys still among us, and those not few and far between; and young Samuels, who, being brought as infants to the Lord's house, have from that day forth worn the linen ephod and served after their fashion as priests unto God, serving him with all their hearts. Happy those who are called early in the morning! they have peculiar reasons for blessing and praising God.

> "Grace is a plant, where'er it grows,
> Of pure and heavenly root;
> But fairest in the youngest shows,
> And yields the sweetest fruit."

Let us spend a minute in thinking of their happy case who are saved in boyhood. Early in the morning the dew still twinkles on the leaves, the maiden blush of dawn remains and reveals an opening beauty, which is lost to those who rise not to see the birth of day. There is a beauty about early piety which is indescribably charming, and unutterably lovely in freshness and radiance. We remark in childhood an artless simplicity, a child-like confidence, which is seen nowhere else. There may be less of knowing but there is more of loving; there may be less of reasoning, but there is more of simply believing upon the authority of revelation; there may be less of deep-rootedness, but there is certainly more of perfume, beauty, and emerald verdure. If I must choose that part of the Christian life in which there is the most joy, next to the land Beulah, which I must set first and foremost by reason of its lying so near to Canaan, I think I would prefer that tract of Christian experience which lieth toward the sun-rising, which is sown with orient pearls of love, and cheered with the delicious music of the birds of hope.

Early in the morning, when we have just risen from slumber, work is easy; our occupation in the vineyard is a cheerful exercise rather than a toil such as those find it who bear the burden and heat of the day. The young Christian is not oppressed with the cares and troubles of the world as others are; he has nothing else to do but to serve his God. He is free from the embarrassments which surround so many of us, and prevent our doing good when we would consecrate ourselves wholly to it. The lad has nought to think of but his Lord. There are his books and his lessons, but he can be fervent of spirit in the midst of them. There are the companions of his childhood, but in guilelessness and simplicity he may be of service to them and to God through them. Give me, I say, if I would have an auspicious time to work for Jesus, give me the blessed morning hours, when my heart is bounding lightest and joy's pure sunbeams tremble on my path; when my glowing breast lacks no ardour, and my happy spirit wears no chain of care.

One would prefer early conversion because such persons have not learned to stand idle in the market-place. A fellow, you know, who has been for hours standing with his hands in his pocket, talking with drunken men and so on, is not worth much at the eleventh hour, nay even by the middle of the day it has become so natural to him to prop the walls, that he is not likely to take to work very readily. Begin early with your souls, break in the colts while they are young, and they are likely to take well to the collar. There are no workers like those who commenced work while they were yet children. What a promise of a long day there is for young believers; the sun has just risen, and he has to travel to his zenith and to descend again. There is ample room and verge enough though none to spare. If God in his providence permit it so to happen, that youngster yonder has twelve hours' work before him—what may he not accomplish? For a grand and glorious life early piety if not essential, is certainly a very great advantage. To give those first days to Jesus will spare us many sad regrets, prevent us acquiring many evil habits, and enable us to achieve good success through the Holy Spirit's blessing. It is well to begin to fly while yet the wings are strong, for if we live long in sin the wing may be broken and then they will flap wearily through the rest of our days, even when grace shall call us. Let it be the desire of parents here to have their children converted as children! And oh! may God cast that desire into the hearts of some of you young people that are here this morning that before you reach one-and-twenty, before you are called men, you may be perfect men in Christ Jesus, that while you are yet children you may be children of God. May you as "newborn babes receive the sincere milk of the Word," and the Lord grant that you may "grow thereby." Happy, happy, happy souls, whom the Master thus by distinguishing grace brings "early in the morning!"

The householder went out again *at the third hour*. This may represent the period in which we have mounted above being children and youths and are entitled to be called men. Suppose we settle the first hour as extending over the earliest seven or eight years of age; then the second hour runs on from that to twenty-one or thereabouts; and then we have a good length of time between twenty and thirty and onwards to reckon as the third, and fourth, and fifth hours. There are some whom divine grace renews at the third hour. This is late! one-and-twenty is grievously late, when you consider how much of early joy is now impossible, how much of sinful habit has now been acquired, how many opportunities for usefulness are now gone past recall. A quarter of the day has flown away for ever when we reach the third hour. It is the best quarter of the day, too, that has gone past recall. The first meal of the day is over,—that blessed breaking of the fast with Christ is no more possible. A very precious meal is that, when the Saviour gives us the morning portion, the manna which melteth when the sun is up. Blessed is the child's feeding upon Jesus: truly I remember when I was awakened like Elias from under the juniper tree, and fed on such dainty fare that to this day the flavour abideth with me. The man of one-and-twenty has lost that first meal, breakfast is all over; Christ will say to him as he will to some others, "Come and dine," and that is precious; but the daintiest meal is over, the first early enjoyment, the first early rapture can never be known.

I have no doubt there are many here who think that to be converted at one-and-twenty is very soon; but why one-and-twenty years given to Satan? Why a fourth of man's existence devoted to evil? Besides, it may not be a fourth, it may be one half, nay, in how many cases it is the whole of life. The sun goes down ere it is yet noon, and the idler in the market-place has no hope of ever being a worker in the vineyard. Death who comes when God wills, and gives us no notice, may cut down the flower before it has fully opened. "In the morning it is like grass that groweth up, in the evening it is cut down and withereth." It is late, it is sadly late! It is a sad thing to have lost those bright days in which the mind was least engaged, in which it was the most susceptible of forming godly habits. It is a sad thing to have learned so much of sin as one may have learned by one-and-twenty, a sad thing to have seen so much of iniquity, to have treasured up in one's memory so much of defilement. Twenty years with God; one might have been in such a time a good scholar in the kingdom; but twenty years in the world one begins to be like scarlet that has been lying in the dye till it is stained through and through. *It is late, but we thank God that it is not too late.* Nay, it is not too late even for the grandest of purposes. Not only is this period of life not too late for salvation, but it is not too late to do much for Jesus Christ. Some of us when we were one-and-twenty, had finished five years of Christian ministry, and had been the means of bringing many souls to the cross of Christ; but if others are led by grace to begin then, why there is a good period still remaining if God in providence spares our lives. The young man is now in all his strength and vigour, his bones are full of marrow, and his heart is full of fire. He ought to have acquired a good degree of education, and be prepared to acquire more.

Now he is just in the time when he should work. His plans of life are not settled as yet; he is not married yet, probably; as yet there are no children about him to have been injured by his ill example; he has an opportunity of rearing up a household in the fear of God. He is commencing business, he has an opportunity of so conducting that business that there may never need to be a time when he shall have to tack about and steer another course. He may, if called by God's grace at one-and-twenty, begin an honourable career, in which there need not be an angle or a curve, but straight to the harbour's mouth he may steer and mark upon the sea of life one shining furrow which shall reach in a direct line from the present moment straight to the lights of heaven, which he shall reach with his sail full and a priceless cargo on board to the praise of the glory of divine grace. It is late, it is very late in some respects, but oh! it is not too late to serve the Master well, and to win a crown of great reward, the gift of love divine.

There is abundance of work to do for us who are in this third, fourth, and fifth hour of the day. In fact, I suppose the Church must look to us for its most active work. After this period and the next, a man frequently becomes rather a recipient from the Church than a donor to it in the matter of activity. Its fresh blood, its energy, its warmth of heart, its ready action, must to a great extent come from the young men who are converted. Oh, you of one-and-twenty, I would to God that you were all born from heaven! You maidens, in your early beauty may the Master in his infinite mercy bring you in! Oh, could you know the sweetness of his love, you would not need persuading! Could you understand the joy of true religion, you would not want entreating! There is more hallowed mirth enjoyed in secret with the Lord Jesus Christ, than in all the merriment the world can yield. One ounce of Christ's love is better than a ton of the world's flatteries. The world offers bubbles with fair hues, bright to look upon, but vanishing at a breath; but Christ gives real treasure, enduring as eternity. The world's gold is all base money; it glitters, but it is not precious. There may be less glitter about the things of God, but there is a "solid joy and lasting pleasure," which "none but Zion's children know." May the Master come this morning to your hearts, and by my simple words may he call you at the third hour of the day into the vineyard.

The Master's grace was not exhausted, and therefore *he went out at the sixth hour*. We find him going into the market at high noon. Half the day was over. Who is going to employ a man, and give him a whole day's wages when twelve o'clock has come? He will not do too much if you hire him at six, what will he do if you engage him at twelve? Half a day's work! that is a poor thing to seek or to offer. The Master, however, seeks and accepts it. He promises, "Whatsoever is right, I will give you;" and there are some found who at the sixth hour enter into the vineyard and, being saved by grace, begin their work for Jesus. This may represent the period of life in which man is supposed to be in his prime—when he is past forty and onward. *This is sadly late, very sadly late*. Sadly late in a great many respects, not only because there is so little time left, but because so very much of energy, and zeal, and force, which should have been given to God, has been wasted; and has to some extent been used to fight against God. Forty years of hardness of heart! That is a long time for divine patience. Forty years of sin! That is a long season for conscience to mourn over. "Forty years long was I grieved with this generation," said God. In the wilderness they hardened their hearts all that time; and he sware in his wrath that they should not enter into his rest. What a blessing for you of forty and unconverted, that he has not sworn so terrible an oath concerning you, that still his longsuffering lingers, still his patience bears with you, still does he say to you, "Go, work, my son—go work this day in my vineyard." It is sadly late, because it has become so more than natural to you to walk in the way of sin. You will have so much to contend with in future, as the result of the past. Putting the ship of the soul about is not such easy work as turning a vessel by her helm; only a divine hand can steer a soul upon the tack of grace. You will need much grace to conquer those corruptions which have had forty years to take root in. You have a tenant in your house who is in possession, and you will find that possession to be nine points of the law; it will be a hard ejectment for you to effect, so hard indeed, that only a "stronger than he" can cast him out. To your dying day the recollection of evil things which you heard during these forty years of unregeneracy will stick by you; you will hear the echoes of an old song just when you are trying to pray, and some deed which you regret and mourn over, will come to check you just when you are about to say, "Abba Father," with an unstammering tongue. It is late, it is very, very late, this sixth hour, *but it is not too late.* It is not too late for some of the richest enjoyments; you can yet dine with Jesus; he can yet manifest himself unto you, as he doth not unto the world; you can have yet much time to serve him in. It is not too late yet to be distinguished among his servants. Take John Newton's life; he was called in the middle of the day, but John Newton left his mark in God's vineyard, a mark that will never be forgotten. I suppose Paul could not have been much less than of that age when he was called by sovereign grace; nay, the most of the apostles were probably very little short of this age when mercy met with them; still they did a glorious day's work. If saved by grace in middle life, my brother, you must work harder, you must let the time past suffice you to have wrought the will of the flesh, and now you must redeem the time, because the days are evil. Why, a man converted at forty should go double quick march to heaven, there should not be a moment lost now. Work the engine at high pressure, and give two strokes for every one that might be given by younger men and younger minds. Seek in the divine strength to do twice as much in the time, since you have only half the time to do a life's work in. Crowns for Christ, I know you wish to win them; then be up and doing, beloved. You are saved by grace, and by grace alone. You pant to honour Christ, because of his free love to you; cannot you endeavour to honour him as much in the remnant which remains as others do in the whole length of their life? You may by zeal, and prudence, and discretion, and perfect consecration, yet serve the Master well.

The householder *went out at the ninth hour*, at three o'clock in the afternoon. Nobody thinks of engaging day-labourers at three o'clock in the afternoon. A day's work to be done from three till six! It shows you that this gospel hiring is nothing like a legal hiring; it must be all of grace, or a man would not think of doing such a thing. Well now, three o'clock in the afternoon, that is from sixty to seventy. The prime of life has gone. *It is late, it is sadly late, very sadly late*. It is late because all the powers of the man are weak now. His memory begins to fail; he thinks his judgment better than ever it was, but probably that is only his own opinion. Most of the faculties lose their edge in old age. He has acquired experience, but still there is no fool like an old fool; and a man who has not been taught by divine grace learns very little of any value in the school of providence. Sixty thousand years would not make a man wise if grace did not teach him. Now think of it, is it not late? Here is the man: if he be converted now, what is there left of him? He is just a candle end. He may give a little light, but it is almost like a snuff burning in the socket. All those sixty years, seventy years, have been spent, where? Cover it all up. Let us go backward as Noah's sons did, and cover it all up; and oh, may almighty grace cover it too! The fact is terribly appalling—sixty, seventy years spent in the service of Satan! Oh what good the man might have done! Had he but served his God as he served the world, what good he might have done! He has made a fortune, has he! How rich he might have been in faith by this time. He has built a house! Yes, but how he might have helped to build the Church. The man has been playing at card-houses; he has been like boys by the sea-shore building castles of sand, which must all come down, and must come down very soon too, for I hear the surges of the dread tide of death, it is rolling in even now. Those teeth which have fallen out, those pains and rheumatics, and so on, all show that this is not his rest. The tabernacle is beginning to crumble about the man, and the warning is loud which reminds him that he must soon be gone, and leave his wealth and his house; and so if this be all, in the end it will turn out that he has done nothing; he has piled up shadows, heaped together thick clay, and that is all he has done; when he might, if he had believed in Jesus, have done so much for God and for the souls of men. What evil habits he has acquired! What can you ever make of this man? If he be saved, it will be so as by fire. He is called, and he shall enter heaven, but oh! how little can he do for the Master, and what strong corruptions will he have to wrestle with, and what an inward conflict even till he gets to heaven! It is late, it is very late, but oh! blessed be God! *it is not too late*. We have had within these walls persons who have long passed the prime of their days, who have come forward and said, "We will cast in our lot with you because the Lord is with you." We have heard their joyous story of how the old man has become a babe, and how he that was hoary with years has been born again into the kingdom of Christ. It is not too late. Did the devil say so? The gate is shutting; I can hear it grating on the hinges, but it is not shut! The sun is going down, but he is not lost beneath the horizon yet; and if the Master calls thee, only run thou the faster because it is so; and when thou art saved, serve him with all thy might and main, because thou hast so little time to glorify him here on earth, and short space in which to show thy sense of deep indebtedness to his surpassing love.

 The day is nearly over, *it has come to the eleventh hour*, five o'clock! The men have been looking at their watches to see whether it will not soon be six; they are longing to hear the clock strike; they hope the day's work will soon close. See; the Master goes out into the marketplace among those hulking fellows who are still loitering there, and he pitches upon some and asks them, "Why stand ye here all the day idle? Go and work! and whatsoever is right I will give you." At the eleventh hour they come in—half-ashamed to come I will be bound,— hardly liking the others to see them; ashamed to begin work so late. Still they did steal in somewhere; and there were generous labourers who looked over the tops of the vines, and said to them, "Glad to see you, friends! glad to see yon, however late." There were a few, I dare say, among the labourers, at least there are if this be the vineyard, who would even stop their work and begin to sing and praise God to think that their fellows had been brought in at the eleventh hour. Now the eleventh hour must be looked upon as any period of life which is past threescore years and ten; how late it may extend I cannot tell. There is an authentic instance of a man converted to God at the age of a hundred and four, during the last Irish revival, who walked some distance to make a confession of his faith in Jesus Christ; and I recollect a case of one converted in America by a sermon which he had heard, I think, eighty-one years previously. He was fifteen when he heard Mr. Flavell at the end of a discourse, instead of pronouncing the blessing, say, "I cannot bless you. How can I bless those who do not love the Lord Jesus Christ? 'If any man love not the Lord Jesus Christ let him be Anathema Maranatha;' " and eighty-one years or more afterwards that solemn sentence came to the man's recollection when he was living in America, and God blessed it to his conversion. There have been some to whom the eleventh hour has been the very hour of death; some, I say, how many or how few is not for me to know. There is one instance we know in Scripture, it was the dying thief. There is but one; God however, in his abundant mercy can do as he wills to the praise of the glory of his grace, and at the eleventh hour he can call his chosen. It is very late, it is very very, very late, it is sorrowfully late, *it is dolefully late, but it is not too late*, and if the Master call thee, come—though an hundred years of sin should make thy feet heavy to thee, so that thy steps are painfully limping. If he call thee it is late but not too late, and therefore come. Have you ever thought of how the thief worked for his Lord? It was not a fine place for working, hanging on a cross dying, just at the eleventh hour; but he did a deal of work in the few minutes. Observe what he did. First he confessed Christ—he acknowledged him to be Lord, confessed him before men. In the second place he justified Christ—"This man has done nothing amiss." In the next place he worshipped the Lord Jesus, calling him "Lord." He even began to preach, for he rebuked his fellow sinner; he told him that he should not revile one who was so unrighteously condemned. He offered a petition which has become a very model of prayer—"Lord, remember me when thou comest into thy kingdom." At any rate I wish I could say of myself what I can say of the thief, *he did all he could*; I cannot say that of myself, I am afraid I cannot say it of any of you. I do not know anything the thief could have done on the cross which he did not do. As soon as ever he was called, he seems to have worked in the vineyard to the utmost extent of his ability; and so let me say to you, if you should be called at the eleventh hour, my dear hearer, though thou be well stricken in years and aged, yet for Jesus Christ's sake out of great love for all the great things which he hath done for thee, go thy way and praise him with all thy might.

II. My time has gone, and I wanted to have shown that DISTINGUISHING GRACE SHONE RESPLENDENTLY IN EVERY INSTANCE. Those called in the early morning have delightful reason for admiring sovereign grace, for they are spared the ills and sins of life. I must content myself, however, by repeating concerning them the lines of Ralph Erskine.

> "In heavenly choirs a question rose,
> That stirred up strife will never close;
> What rank of all the ransomed race,
> Owes highest praise to sovereign grace.
>
> Babes thither caught from womb and breast,
> Claimed right to sing above the rest;
> Because they found the happy shore,
> They never saw nor sought before."

What distinguishing grace is that which called us when we were young! Herein is electing love. "When Ephraim was a child then I loved him, and called my son out of Egypt." Some of us in time and in eternity will have to utter a special song of thankfulness to the love which took us in our days of folly and simplicity, and conducted us into the family of God. It was not because we were better disposed children than others, or because there was naturally anything good about us; we were wilful, heady, and high-minded, proud, wayward, and disobedient as other children are, and yet mercy separated us from the rest, and we shall never cease to adore its sovereignty.

Look at the grace which calls the man at the age of twenty, when the passions are hot, when there is strong temptation to plunge into the vices and the so-called pleasures of life. To be delivered from the charms of sin, when the world's cheek is ruddy, when it wears its best attire, and to be taught to prefer the reproach of Christ to all the riches of Egypt, this is mighty grace for which God shall have our sweetest song.

To be called of the Lord at forty, in the prime of life. This is a wonderful instance of divine power, for worldliness is hard to overcome, and worldliness is the sin of middle age. With a family about you, with much business, with the world eating into you as doth a canker, it is a wonder that God should in his mercy have visited you then, and made you a regenerate soul. You are a miracle of grace, and you will have to feel it and to praise God for it in time and eternity.

Sixty again. "Can the Ethiopian change his skin, or the leopard his spots? If so, then ye who are accustomed to do evil may learn to do well." And yet you have learned, you have had a blessed schoolmaster who sweetly taught you, and you have learned to do well. Though your vessel had begun to rot in the waters of the Black Sea of sin, you have got a new owner, and you will run up a new flag, and you will sail round the Cape of Good Hope to the Islands of the Blessed, in the Land of the Hereafter.

But what shall I say of you that are called when you are aged? Ah you will have to love much, for you have had much forgiven. I do not know that you may be in thankfulness a whit behind those of us who are called in our early youth; we have much to bless God for, and so have you. We are at one extreme and you are at the other; we would love much because we have been spared much sinning, and you must love much because you have been delivered from much sinning. Not to go through the fire is a theme for song; but to traverse the flame and not be burned, to walk the furnace and to be delivered from its vehement fire, oh! how should you find words with which to express your gratitude! Called early or called late, called at midday or called at early noon, let us together, since we have been called by grace alone, ascribe it all to the Lord Jesus, and moved by the mighty constraints of his love, let us work with body, soul, and spirit—work for him till we can work no longer, and then praise him in the rest of glory.

I pray you, brethren, suffer no idleness to creep over you. If you have sought to extend the Redeemer's kingdom, do it more. Give more, talk more of Christ, pray more, labour more! I often receive the kind advice, "Do less." I cannot do less. Do less! Why, better rot altogether than live the inglorious life of doing less than our utmost for God. We shall none of us, I am afraid, kill ourselves with working too hard for Jesus. It were such a blessed act of suicide that if there be a sin that is venial, it would certainly be that. I am not afraid that you are likely to perpetrate such an enormity. Work for the Master! Labour for the Master! We must spend and be spent, and wear ourselves out for him! Make no reserve for the flesh to fulfil the lusts of it! And oh, how happy shall we be, if we may be privileged to finish the work, and hear him say, "Well done, good and faithful servant, enter thou into the joy of thy Lord." May the Lord bless you for Christ's sake. Amen.

PORTION OF SCRIPTURE READ BEFORE SERMON—Matthew 19:27 to end of chapter; 20 to end of verse 29.[17]

---

[17] Spurgeon, C. H. (1865). Early and Late, or Horæ Gratiæ. In *The Metropolitan Tabernacle Pulpit Sermons* (Vol. 11, pp. 685–696). London: Passmore & Alabaster.

Printed in Poland
by Amazon Fulfillment
Poland Sp. z o.o., Wrocław